One for All

Complete services for
the whole church family

Claire Benton-Evans

kevin
mayhew

To the many talented people with whom I have worked
on the following all-age, all-sorts services:

Open Door at St Margaret's, Northam
Second Sunday at St John's, Ivybridge
'It's church, Jim, but not as we know it' at St Thomas', Camelford
Tea at Tetha's at St Tetha's, St Teath

With special thanks to John, Chris and Jim; also to the Methodist children's leaders in Cornwall who gave me such warm encouragement at their conference.

For Phoebe,
who dares me to
do church differently.

kevin mayhew

First published in Great Britain in 2010 by Kevin Mayhew Ltd
Buxhall, Stowmarket, Suffolk IP14 3BW
Tel: +44 (0) 1449 737978 Fax: +44 (0) 1449 737834
E-mail: info@kevinmayhewltd.com

www.kevinmayhew.com

9 8 7 6 5 4 3 2 1

ISBN 978 1 84867 292 5
Catalogue No. 1501239

Cover design by Rob Mortonson

Edited by Alison Evans
Typeset by Richard Weaver
Illustrations by Melody-Anne Lee

Printed and bound in Great Britain

Contents

About the Author

Claire Benton-Evans wrote her first prayers at the age of eight and read English at Oxford before teaching in London and North Devon. She is currently working with church groups to devise fresh, dynamic worship for all ages; this has developed her interest in creative approaches to prayer and praise. She lives with her husband – a Church of England minister – and three children in North Cornwall.

Details of Claire's other titles can be found at the end of this book.

Introduction

What do we mean when we talk about all-age worship? This question can stir up some strong opinions, as these comments on a Christian website[1] have shown:

> You don't make a normal Eucharist into an all-age worship service by throwing in a children's sermon and an action song.

This kind of service is familiar to all those of us who have struggled to contain bored and fidgety children in a pew during a long Old Testament reading or full-length intercessions. Neither is it all-age worship when the regular service runs parallel to a separate 'children's church' service or Sunday school, traditionally the home of craft, worksheets and Bible-story colouring. This mother of boys aged four and two has this to say:

> My children get enough craft-quizzes-colouring at home and kindergarten. It does very much seem that children are 'tidied away'; I would prefer them to grow up experiencing the full range of what goes on at a service, accepted as they are but given a chance to learn to be quiet when called for, a real part of the congregation.

There is such longing here for real, shared worship and a sense of belonging; her feeling that children are 'tidied away' in church is one that many of us may recognise. When we send our children out of the service at the beginning and invite them back in at the end, we marginalise their role in our church; we reduce their spiritual journey to a five-minute 'show and tell' spot after the notices, in which they present what they have learnt. (How many of us could do this at the end of a Sunday service?) This state of affairs is noted by the Church of England's National Children's Adviser, the Revd Mary Hawes, who has said that children in church are often treated as 'Christians in waiting rather than disciples in training. We still tend to see

1. www.ship-of-fools.com, 'The magazine of Christian unrest', 11.11.09.

them as needing to be taught and kept out of the way until they have learnt how to behave.'[2]

This view of children as 'Christians in waiting' reflects the fact that until recently, children's spirituality was assumed to be an immature, incomplete version of adult spirituality. Research which has sought to examine it on children's own terms has found that it has its own rich and complex character. Rebecca Nye has summarised the key features of children's spirituality.[3] First of all, it is rooted in ordinary, everyday experience; it is an integrated part of their lives, so that an experience of God may be discussed as freely and excitedly as an encounter in the playground or a discovery in the garden. From this comes the seemingly erratic nature of children's spirituality: Nye says, 'One minute they are having profound, sacred experiences, and the next they are thinking about custard.'[4]

There are two further aspects of children's spirituality which are particularly significant for those of us seeking to involve them in worship. Children's spirituality is both verbal and non-verbal: like so much of their play and learning, their spiritual life is experienced and expressed not only through words but also through actions, through all their senses, their emotions, imagination and intuition. When we recognise this, we may realise that our own spirituality is not so different, and that we also need opportunities to explore it non-verbally. Finally, Nye says that all these features of children's spirituality combine to surprise and challenge adults. Our own experience gives us plenty of examples of this. Every parent is familiar with children's God-related questions which ask, 'Why?' about everything from cancer to headlice; my young daughter asked me, crossly, 'What's the point of church?' and I heard recently about a teenager who came upon a group of youth leaders in prayer before the start of a holiday club: 'What are you doing?' he asked. 'Why are you all looking at the floor? Have you lost something?' Nye describes this as children's ability 'to speak out, to be prophetic, to articulate (not necessarily

2. *Church Times*, 1.5.09.
3. Rebecca Nye, 'Spirituality' chapter in *Through the eyes of a child*, ed. Anne Richards and Peter Privett, Church House Publishing 2009.
4. *Church Times*, 1.5.09.

through words alone) the need for a change or to offer a new way of seeing things.'[5] Children are unafraid to wonder aloud and they challenge us directly with their questions about the fundamentals of faith, worship and church practice.

If we agree that children's spirituality is both a force to be reckoned with and a challenge to all of us to do church differently, then what we need is a bold re-imagining of what all-age worship can and should be. We need to create a way of joining people of all ages together in *worship*, not just tolerant co-existence. Since becoming involved with all-age worship almost as soon as I became a parent, I have been privileged to work with teams of talented and creative people in different churches; we have been blessed with open-minded clergy and congregations who allowed us to experiment and offered us generous feedback. My thinking about all-age worship has also been inspired, in recent years, by the hands-on practicality of Messy Church and by the child-centred spirituality and reflective storytelling of Godly Play.[6] Through these years of shared debate, experiment and exploration, and as I began regularly to devise and lead my own all-age worship services, I have found myself returning again and again to my daughter's question: 'What is church *for*? What's the point of it?'

This question goes to the heart of why we do what we do on a Sunday morning – and on the other six days of the week. Archbishop Rowan Williams describes the Church like this:

> . . . the Church is first of all a kind of space cleared by God through Jesus in which people may become what God made them to be (God's sons and daughters), and that what we have to do about the Church is not first to organise it as a society but to inhabit it as a climate or landscape. It is a place where we can see properly – God, God's creation, ourselves.[7]

5. *Through the eyes of a child*, p.72.
6. See Jerome Berryman, *Godly Play*, Augsburg Books, 1995 and Lucy Moore, *Messy Church*, BRF, 2006 or www.godlyplay.org.uk and www.messychurch.org.uk. See also *The Spirit of the Child* by David Hay with Rebecca Nye, Jessica Kingsley Publishers, 2006.
7. Rowan Williams, 'The Christian Priest Today', quoted by Justin Lewis-Anthony, *If You Meet George Herbert on the Road . . . Kill Him!*, Mowbray, 2009, p.81.

This description transcends denominational differences and begs a more fundamental question: how many of us would describe our own church as a space in which to live and grow and see more clearly? Yet at the centre of this wonderful vision is a practical direction: '. . . what we have to do about the Church is not first to organise it as a society but to inhabit it as a climate or landscape.' Like tracing the source of the Nile, we need to move through our contemporary landscape of committees and Sunday schools, fêtes and flower rotas, and find our way back to the Church's origin: Jesus, a small band of followers and some heady days which we now celebrate as the Ascension and Pentecost. This is where the Church was born, when Christ entrusted his disciples with his mission:

> 'You will receive power when the Holy Spirit has come upon you; and you will be my witnesses in Jerusalem, in all Judea and Samaria, and to the ends of the earth.' *(Acts 1:8)*

After all their questions about when Christ would accomplish the work he came to do, they are told, 'It's up to you, now.' This was their mission and our mission in the Church today: to do Christ's work in the world. And what is the first act of the embryonic Church? On the day of Pentecost, when the disciples are filled with the Holy Spirit, they tell all sorts of people about Jesus in a language which each can understand. This is a Church which embraces variety ('from every nation under heaven' – Acts 2:5), which responds to different needs ('We hear, each of us, in our own native language' – Acts 2:8) and which, above all, communicates the truth about Jesus: 'Therefore let the entire house of Israel know with certainty that God has made him both Lord and Messiah' (Acts 2:36). This is not so far, after all, from Dr Williams' vision of a Church in which we may see God and ourselves properly, and have the space to become what God made each of us to be.

The Church was not created as a fixed, inward-looking, self-serving institution which focuses on its own ways of doing things. It is a living body of believers, a Church made of 'living stones' which is both upward-looking – to Christ, its head – and outward-looking, to the world which it was made to serve. This Church springs up between Ascension and Pentecost: it stands with one foot on the holy mountain and the other in the crowded marketplace.

In our worship we express what we believe the Church is for. Firstly, our worship should be *welcoming* to people of all sorts, not just those who are used to our way of doing things. Secondly, if we wish to engage a wide variety of people in worship, then it needs to be as *varied* as possible; we also need to use as many channels of communication as we have available to us, which means using not just words but all the senses. Like the disciples speaking in many different languages, we need to communicate in *multi-sensory* ways, through actions, visual stimuli, music, tactile objects and food. Finally, we should aspire to be a church which is 'a place where we can see properly – God, God's creation, ourselves.' In our worship we need *clear* teaching, but also opportunities to *explore* our own responses to God and our own place in the church and in the world. The services in this book are shaped by these principles: they are designed to be *welcoming, varied, multi-sensory, clear* and *exploratory*.

Welcoming

These 'one for all' services must welcome and include not only people of all ages, but children at all educational stages, grown-ups of any age, people who are single, part of a childless couple or part of a family – all together in church. These services should engage people who are new to church and those who are returning to church after many years' absence. They should also involve those who have different physical and mental abilities, like the profoundly disabled teenagers who regularly attend a church I know well. They come in their electric wheelchairs with their carers and they, too, are part of the church family. That family should be characterised by its variety, inclusivity and unity, as described by Paul in his letter to the church at Corinth:

> For just as the body is one and has many members, and all the members of the body, though many, are one body, so it is with Christ. For in the one Spirit we were all baptised into one body – Jews or Greeks, slaves or free – and we were all made to drink of one Spirit.

> Indeed, the body does not consist of one member but of many. If the foot were to say, 'Because I am not a hand, I do not belong to the body', that would not make it any less a part of the body . . . As it is, there are many members, yet one body. The eye cannot say to the hand, 'I have no need of you', nor again the head to the feet, 'I have no need of you'. *(1 Corinthians 12:12–15, 20, 21)*

If we truly believe our Church to be one body, then all of us – all ages and all sorts – need to be welcome to worship together as one. Everything about the way one of these services is designed, planned and conducted should shout, 'Welcome!' from beginning to end:

- Before the service, posters in local schools, toddler groups and shops should invite everyone in the community, not just the church. For those leaders who are online, social networking sites such as Facebook are increasingly useful for publicising services.
- On the day, leaders should greet people at the door, and outside on the church steps, to welcome them in and help with access if necessary. Heavy church doors are not very welcoming – especially for people with prams, buggies or wheelchairs!
- In the church, seating should be arranged in a way that encourages people to feel relaxed and unconfined, because the activities are mostly designed to get them moving around. (This can be the single thing which makes parents of young children feel most welcome, given the impossibility of keeping a toddler still for any length of time.)
- These services have been designed to be easy for newcomers to follow, without the need for service sheets or for more than one hymn book.
- 'Feed my lambs . . . feed my sheep', Jesus commanded Peter. Taken literally, his words remind us that there should *always* be food at these services. Hospitality welcomes people to our churches, and the promise of food will invariably keep my own children in church. I have called the post-service refreshments 'a feast', and so they should be. It is as easy to provide several kinds of shop-bought cake as it is to open packets of mixed biscuits; better still,

invite your church's best bakers to contribute cakes. At our Sunday tea-time service we have even provided hot buttered toast, crumpets and cocktail sausages. It is important to allow time for the feast: we usually plan on 90 minutes for an all-age service, of which one half is worship and the other half is hospitality. There is absolute continuity between the service which talks about loving your neighbour and the opportunity, afterwards, to drink tea, eat cake together and ask each other, 'How are you?'

Clear

Each service is based on passages from Scripture which have inspired a single clear theme: this integrates every detail of the service from the title to the concluding prayer. I would suggest that this theme is expressed visually on your church's publicity posters. In following this single, clear idea, I have kept three questions in mind for each service:

- *'What is the story?'* This reminds us simply to tell and retell the stories of our faith through the Church year. Just as Jewish families at Passover recount the story of the Exodus in answer to a child's question, 'Why is this night different?', so we should imagine a child at every service asking us, 'Why is this day different?' We answer them by telling the story.
- *'What does it mean?'* This question is asked of all of us. It provides opportunities for teaching as well as individual reflection and shared discussion. It gives us a chance to explore our faith together.
- *'What does it tell us to do?'* This question turns our attention outwards: it encourages us to keep our faith active and real in our lives outside church.

Maintaining a clear focus in our worship also requires a certain economy. The services in this book are designed to last approximately 45–50 minutes. No single component lasts longer than about 15 minutes; there is usually a change of activity every five or ten minutes, in order to encourage concentration and engagement. These services have been tried and tested in my local parish church and subjected to the critical judgements and various attention spans of my own children, their friends and families. This process has encouraged me to keep our worship clear, concise and to the point.

Varied

Within each element of these services, I have created as much variety as possible from week to week. For example, the storytelling might involve puppets one week, a dramatised dialogue the next and a reading accompanied by audio-visual aids the week after. In each case I have chosen the medium to suit the message. The range of prayers which I explored in *All-sorts Prayer* [8] has informed the wide variety of prayer actions offered here. They give people the opportunity to confess, to wonder, to give thanks, offer intercessions and be contemplative; they may involve writing, a creative act, movement, stillness, words, sound or silence. Finally, even the structure of the service itself might be varied to suit a particular purpose. In general, our worshippers should come to expect the unexpected!

Multi-sensory

It is in this respect that children can best help us transform what we do in church. I recently invited children to design their ideal church. The many and varied responses to this challenge were a revelation: they depicted worship in hot air balloons, in tents lined with cushions and rugs, in hi-tech spaces with plasma screen TVs and disco lights, in tree houses and on beaches. These churches featured tasty snacks, drinks and other home comforts such as pews which convert into beds. The detailed design by Phoebe, aged ten, epitomises many children's desire for a multi-sensory worship space in which they might relax, explore and discover. The addition of an 'escape pod' also speaks volumes about her own response to traditional church services!

Children remind us that our spiritual selves are intertwined with our hearing, seeing, smelling, tasting, feeling bodies, and that our worship might be more wholehearted if we adopted a more holistic approach. In our prayer and worship, we seek to tune in to God, and so these services appeal to the senses in an attempt to open up more channels of communication.

Exploratory

In these services, I have moved away from the traditional 'educational' model of children's church, which presupposes that the (spiritually mature and well-versed)

8. Kevin Mayhew, 2010.

'Design for a brilliant church' by Phoebe (10)

teacher instructs the (spiritually less knowledgeable and less developed) children. The services in this book embrace the new understanding of children's spirituality and acknowledge that all of us – leaders and congregation, adults and children – are fellow travellers on our spiritual journey. Consequently, the 'Teaching' element is now part of 'Exploring', which is more creative, interactive and shared. This exploratory approach is more in sympathy with Godly Play's 'wondering' and with the freely chosen responses to Bible stories which it encourages.

When knowledge and information are shared in these services, there is no testing or assessment. God is not an educational Attainment Target, and we can't presume to know whether those we have led in worship have 'achieved' a certain level of spiritual development. What the exploratory approach recognises is that any such development is – wonderfully – out of our control and in the hands of the Holy Spirit, who is active in the space between the worship which is offered and the people of all ages and abilities who engage in that worship. It is a space for spiritual adventure and wondering exploration – a space which I hope may help us 'to see properly – God, God's creation, ourselves'.

What about Holy Communion?

These are services of the Word; however, there is certainly scope to adapt them to incorporate a service of Holy Communion. Our church has tried this on occasions and the experiment has proved interesting and worthwhile, since it takes everyone involved a little way outside their comfort zone. The service is inevitably longer and wordier than our all-age congregation is used to, while being more informal and interactive than the regular Sunday worshippers expect. Such experiments may point the way towards an all-age Communion which is a service in its own right, but that is a subject for a different book.

The Cover Sheets

Photocopiable Cover Sheet

This contains the essential information for everyone involved in the service, from the person designing the poster to the wonderful lady who – in one of our local churches – decorates themed cakes for the end of the service. The running order is vital for leaders, especially when several are involved: everyone needs to see at a glance where their 'bit' fits in.

Resources

A long list of resources is usually a feature of any all-age worship service, since visually rich storytelling and multi-sensory prayers inevitably involve a certain amount of kit. Please don't be put off by the length of some of these lists: firstly, they are there as comprehensive checklists for use at every stage of service, from the first planning meeting to the last-minute checks, early on Sunday morning. Secondly, the resources themselves are not usually expensive or hard to find. If these lists were recipes (and there are some similarities), they would call for carrots and onions rather than quails' eggs and caviar. Most of the items listed can be borrowed from schools and Sunday schools or bought from local shops relatively cheaply.[9] I would only add that you should try to provide the best resources you can afford, as a box of feeble felt-tip pens with missing lids suggests that our all-age congregations deserve no better. Good-quality resources show that we value the people who will use them in their prayers and worship.

These resources lists do not include 'human resources' such as the Sunday school, the Brownies or the youth group. It is wonderful if such groups can be involved in these services, but I have never made it a requirement. Ministers and leaders have enough to do in preparation for a service, without fitting in weeks of rehearsal for a specific group's contribution.

The last thing to say about the resources lists is that they are not set in stone. They list the optimum amount of resources, and may be adapted with ingenuity and imagination to take account of particular constraints, such as the absence of a screen and projector.

Leaders

These services have been written so that any designated person, lay or ordained, might lead them. A new

9. Many craft materials are available in newsagents, toy shops and pound shops as well as art shops. An excellent resource is your local scrapstore: this is a centre for craft and textile bits and bobs which are donated by industry; for a small annual fee, you can go as often as you like and stock up for free on everything from gold paper to sequinned scraps to giant cardboard tubes (see national directory on www.childrensscrapstore.co.uk). The internet is your best source of audio-visual resources: for photographs, there are websites such as www.shutterstock.com which allow you to purchase copyright-free images.

leader can use the script straight off the page, exactly as written, but it is not at all prescriptive – experienced leaders may well wish to use their own words. The minimum leadership requirement reflects a reality of church life: often too many jobs are done by too few people. However, the optimum number should point us in a more hopeful direction. We can encourage more people to take on a leadership role, however small, and in the spirit of these services we should be welcoming and inclusive. This means inviting those who do not usually do 'this sort of thing' to play a part; in particular, it means encouraging children and teenagers to get involved. Ideally, your leadership team should be as varied as the people in your all-age congregation.

Music

Primary school children today will often sing in assembly, even if theirs is not a Church school; at secondary level, singing in school tends to be occasional rather than the norm. Hymn practice – once a regular feature of the school week – has given way to staffing pressures and the increasing demands of the curriculum. When children do sing in school, they are likely to sing secular songs, not traditional hymns. So unless children are regular church-goers, they do not have the opportunity to become familiar with the wealth of church music, old and new, which should be theirs to enjoy. All-age worship can offer them just such an opportunity. If many in your all-age congregation are new to church, you might like to introduce some informal music teaching of your own, perhaps with a five-minute practice of that Sunday's hymns just before the service (this also works well as a way of 'warming up' a congregation!). Alternatively, you may like to invite your musicians to play through each hymn as people are coming into church, as a way of subliminally familiarising them with the tunes.

As any church which has ever tried to woo a new organist knows, we need to cherish our musicians. There are many opportunities to celebrate musical skill and enthusiasm in all-age worship: in my own church, we established The Really Brilliant Music Group, featuring a skilled accordion player, junior recorders and a variety of keen percussionists. There is undoubtedly a place for musical excellence – young pianists can flourish if given the chance to play in public – but there should also be opportunities for babies and toddlers to get their hands on a tambourine and join with the rest of us in making 'a joyful noise unto the Lord'. Every resources list for these services contains the catch-all item, 'Music and words': this will depend on your own church's musical resources, and could mean anything from a piano and hymn books to the youth group's rock band and words projected from a laptop onto an overhead screen.[10]

Get stuck in!

This book contains enough services for every Sunday of the year, with extra services for festivals and special occasions. These services were originally published as *All-Sorts Worship* Year A and followed the Church of England's Common Worship Lectionary, Year A: this cycle of readings include, passages from the Old and New Testaments, the Psalms and Matthew's Gospel, with some passages from John's Gospel (see the Scriptural index for further details). Years B and C follow a similar pattern, focusing on Mark's and Luke's Gospels respectively.

You may choose to use these services straight off the page, exactly as written: complete scripts and instructions lay everything out clearly from the Welcome to the Conclusion. Alternatively, you and your worship team may prefer to use a particular service as a springboard for your own ideas, adapting the various components within the outline I have provided in order to suit your own purposes and available resources. Equally, you may simply want to dip into this book as a source of bright ideas, creative prayers and interactive storytelling to engage all ages. A Scriptural index is provided to make this 'pick-and-mix' approach easier. Whatever you do, feel free to engage with these services with energy and imagination. I hope that they help us all join together as one in joyful, whole-hearted worship.

10. In deciding the minimum leadership requirements for a service, I have assumed that the congregation will either sing unaccompanied, or will have technological help with the music, for example a CD such as *No Organist? No Problem?* (see CDs for hymns and worship songs at www.kevinmayhew.com).

Christian Seasons

Advent

Newborn

Theme	Jesus' birth and a fresh start for all
Scripture	Matthew 1:18–25

Running order	Total: 50 minutes
Welcome	Lighting a votive candle each and then the Advent Candle(s) *(5 minutes)*
Introduction	Opening the theme
Activity	Filling in possibilities for a new life *(10 minutes)*
Storytelling	Reading of Matthew 1:18–25 – interactive dialogue *(10 minutes)*
Music	Infant holy *(5 minutes)*
Exploring	What does the baby Jesus mean for us? *(10 minutes)*
Prayer action	Newborn baby – written intercessions *(5 minutes)*
Music	Away in a manger *(5 minutes)*
Conclusion	Closing prayer and invitation

Resources

- Advent wreath, votive candles and matches
- Three 'stations' around the church or café-style seating
- On a whiteboard or OHP: a large outline of a new baby *(see appendix)*
- Drywipe markers
- At each station or on each table: A4 pieces of paper with the outline of a new baby *(see appendix)*; pens or pencils
- Music and words
- Small pieces of paper with the outline of a new baby *(see appendix)*
- Pens or pencils

Leaders

Minimum: 2

- Leader
- Additional Storyteller

Optimum: 7

- Leader *(Introduction and Conclusion)*
- Activity Leader
- Storytellers x 2
- Music Leader
- Explorer
- Prayer Leader

Suggestions for additional music

- The Virgin Mary had a baby boy
- The angel Gabriel from heaven came
- For Mary, mother of our Lord

Service

Welcome

Light a votive candle each and then the Advent Candle(s).

Introduction

At the centre of our Advent story is Mary. We remember her, waiting patiently and faithfully, for the birth of her son who would change the world for ever. Her particular experience was unique, but all of us who have become parents know how the birth of a child changes lives: a new life begins, and our lives will never be the same again. Today we will be thinking about the new life that Mary brought into the world.

Activity

Introduce the big outline of a baby on the whiteboard or OHP.

This is a new baby. This child could grow up to be or do anything – but at the moment of birth, everything is an unexplored possibility, like a blank sheet of paper. Imagine this is a new baby, born today. What could he/she be when he/she grows up? What things could he/she do?

Ask for and give suggestions to start the ball rolling: a good friend, a footballer, funny, a dentist, artistic, a daredevil, a parent . . .

Gather round one of these blank outlines and fill it in with as many ideas as you can think of. What might this baby be or do when he or she grows up?

Allow plenty of time for people to fill the outlines with their ideas, then come together again.

In this Christmas season, we are thinking about one special baby in particular. Mary and Joseph knew more than most parents about what their baby would be when he grew up. Listen carefully to this bit of the Christmas story, and pay attention to what the angel tells Joseph about Mary's baby. If you hear something that Mary and Joseph could fill in on a blank outline like this, wave your hand in the air. So listen carefully . . .

Storytelling

Read Matthew 1:18–25 with two voices: the narrator and the angel. Encourage the waving!

Who heard something that Mary and Joseph could fill in on a blank outline like this? Even before he was born, Mary and Joseph knew their baby would be . . . what?

Elicit these points and write them inside the baby outline on the whiteboard or OHP.

- a boy
- called Jesus
- Son of God the Holy Spirit
- Saviour – he would save people from their sins

During the following hymn, wipe these points and use a different colour to fill the baby outline with messy, scribbled words – taken from the opening activity – and some negative words such as 'angry', 'impatient', 'disappointed', some of which are crossed out.

Music

Infant holy

Exploring

Let's look again at these baby outlines which we filled in earlier. *(Show one of the filled-in A4 outlines.)* Here is a brand-new life, full of possibilities: the problem is, as we get older, we can start to feel a bit like this:

Show your whiteboard/OHP baby outline full of scribbled words and crossings-out.

There are lots of things we are and still lots that we can be – but there are also quite a lot of things we wish we weren't, and things we have failed to be. This person wishes she wasn't quite so angry – but she is. This person is never going to be the completely perfect, ever-patient parent he planned on being.

Indicate the baby outlines from the opening activity.

Gather round one of these outlines again and this time, add things which a person might not want to grow up to be or do – things they might regret or feel sorry for.

Fill it in with as many ideas as you can think of and cross each one out as you write it, as if you are trying to make it go away. What might this baby not want to be or do when he or she grows up?

Allow plenty of time for people to fill the outlines with their ideas, then come together again. Return to your whiteboard/ OHP baby outline full of messy, scribbled words.

God understands that we are not perfect, and that our lives can become like this – rather messy and full of mistakes as well as possibilities. That is why he gave us his son, Jesus. What Jesus offers us is the chance to start again – to say sorry, to be forgiven and to have a fresh start *(rub out all the words and scribble)* just like a newborn baby.

Prayer action

Hand out small baby outlines and pens.

Take a fresh outline of a new baby and as you look at it, think about fresh starts and new beginnings. Perhaps you know a new baby; perhaps you know someone older who is trying to make a fresh start. Perhaps you are beginning something new, or perhaps there are things in your life that you'd like to put behind you, so that you can start afresh. Whoever or whatever it is, write or draw it on this picture of a newborn baby, then offer it to God as your prayer for a new beginning.

Allow enough time for people to think and complete their prayers. Then invite people to come and lay their prayers on the altar, or perhaps at the foot of the crib if your church has a large Nativity scene. When all the prayers have been offered, call for a moment of quiet in which to bring them before God.

Lord Jesus,
you came here as a new baby and grew up among us.
We offer you our own prayers for new beginnings
in your name,
Amen.

Music Away in a manger

Conclusion Living Lord,
may we, like Mary,
give ourselves body and soul
to the service of your life-giving love.
Amen.

Give notices, announce the next all-age service and invite everyone to the feast.

Christmas Day

A child is born

Theme	The angels' good news
Scripture	Luke 2:1–20

Running order	Total: 50 minutes
Welcome	Lighting all the candles on the Advent wreath *(5 minutes)*
Introduction	Opening the theme
Music	O little town of Bethlehem *(5 minutes)*
Activity	Hunt the picture – a vision of angels *(5 minutes)*
Storytelling	Imagining Luke 2:8–20 *(5 minutes)*
Music	While shepherds watched *(5 minutes)*
Exploring	What message do the angels bring? *(10 minutes)*
Music	It came upon the midnight clear *(5 minutes)*
Prayer action	Holy light – lighting votive candles *(5 minutes)*
Music	O come, all ye faithful *(5 minutes)*
Conclusion	Closing prayer and invitation

Resources

- Advent wreath and matches
- Postcard-sized pieces of a large picture of an angel *(see appendix)*
- Board and Blu-tack
- Basic angel costume (white sheet/tunic, tinsel halo)
- Two large cardboard speech bubbles: *Do not be afraid* and *This is Love*
- Music and words
- A large candle *(already lit)* and as many candlesticks and candelabra as your altar will hold. Next to the altar, place stands for votive candles and on the floor in front of it, lie a piece of board on which tea-lights may safely stand
- Lots of *(unlit)* candles and tea-lights, plus matches and tapers

Leaders

Minimum: 2

- Leader
- ***Oriel***

Optimum: 7

- Leader
- Activity Leader
- Storyteller
- Music Leader
- Explorer
- *Oriel*, in a suit and carrying a briefcase
- Prayer Leader

Suggestions for additional music

- Mary had a baby
- Little Jesus, sweetly sleep
- Angels from the realms of glory

Service

Welcome

Light all the candles on the Advent wreath.

Introduction

Happy Christmas! Let's begin this joyful day by singing.

Music

O little town of Bethlehem

Activity

Now I want to get you out of your seats and moving around. Hidden all around the church are pieces of a picture. Here is one of them *(show a piece):* can you find the rest? I wonder whether you can help me fit them together like a jigsaw, so we can see what picture they make?

Invite all volunteers to hunt around the church for the pieces and bring them to the front, where you can assemble them on the board. Encourage general participation in fitting together the jigsaw, perhaps accompanied by the odd Rolf Harris-style comment: 'Can you tell what it is yet?' When it is finished, invite comments:

What is this a picture of? Do you think this is what angels look like?

Storytelling

Today's story is full of angels. Why don't you close your eyes and imagine yourself in the story as I tell it to you? Imagine you are a shepherd, sitting on the rocky hills with your sheep. You are wearing long, rough robes and sheepskins to keep out the cold. It is dark and you are sleepily trying to keep an eye on your flock. The sheep are munching loudly. There are other shepherds around you, and you can hear some of them chatting quietly. Some of the younger boys have dozed off, even though the ground is hard and frosty. It is a cold, still night; the sky is vast and inky-black and the stars twinkle brightly.

Suddenly – whoosh! – an enormous explosion of bright, white light tears open the sky. It looks like the end of the world – as if the sun has exploded. You have never seen anything like it, and the hillside around you erupts in noise and panic: the sheep scatter in every direction, bleating madly at the sky; the other shepherds yell and the boys run, screaming, to hide in the caves. The explosion becomes a column of fierce brilliance, and rays of light fan out like wings, spanning the sky.

As you stay rooted to the spot in terror, an unearthly voice rings out above all the racket: 'Do not be afraid! I bring good news! Today a Saviour, the Messiah, has been born! You will find him in the city of David: a child wrapped in bands of cloth, lying in a manger.'

Your ears are ringing with the voice when the whole sky becomes filled with light, as if it were the middle of a summer's day. But instead of sun and blue sky, there is a shimmering whiteness from east to west; beams of light spread and dazzle, pulsing like the beating of wings. You stand with your mouth open as the angel-song fills the air: 'Glory to God in the highest! Peace on earth and goodwill to all!'

Music While shepherds watched

Exploring Today we will be thinking about the angels in our story and the message that they bring. Now, no Nativity play is complete without angels. Who can tell me what angels wear? *(As people say 'A white sheet!', 'A tinsel halo!' and so on, invite a volunteer to dress up in these items.)* So this is the kind of angel we all recognise – the kind of angel who decorates our Christmas cards. But think about the angels in our story. How did those shepherds feel, surrounded by angels on that cold hillside? How did you feel as I was telling the story? *(Invite responses.)* Who can remember the very first thing the angel said? *(Invite responses.)* It was the first thing that angels in the Bible always say to people: 'DO NOT BE AFRAID!' Our angel here is very beautiful, but I don't think we are frightened of her, do you? Angels are out of this world: they are God's servants and messengers and they give us a glimpse of his almighty power. No wonder they are awe-inspiring!

Angel holds up a speech bubble saying, 'Do not be afraid'.

Here is another kind of angel. He is the Archangel Oriel and he and his diary were imagined by the writer, Robert Harrison. Oriel is an important manager in heaven: he organises things for God, and in particular makes the arrangements for Jesus' birth. In his diary, Oriel confesses that he cannot understand why almighty God should want to become a human being at all. This is what he says:

Oriel — And now, the One who held every atom in his grasp is no more than a clutch of watery cells in the midst of a teenage girl, in an obscure village, in a defeated nation, on one of the smaller planets that orbit an ordinary star, in an uneventful galaxy that turns on its little axis in that gassy cloud that is the Universe, which the Son himself made.

Such smallness I can barely begin to imagine. This is Love.[1]

Oriel holds up a speech bubble saying, 'This is Love'.

Explorer — Instead of remaining in power and glory with all his angels, God made himself human in the form of his Son, Jesus, and he came to live among us. This is the message of the angels: the baby lying in the manger is Love – God's love for each and every one of us.

Music — It came upon the midnight clear

Prayer action — *Arrange for two volunteers to light all the candles on the altar and turn off the lights in church as you introduce this prayer.*

In the beginning, God said, 'Let there be light'; and there was light. On that first Christmas Day, there was the light of a new star and the promise that Jesus had come to be a light for all people – a light which would shine in the world's darkness and never be extinguished. Today we will each light a candle as a prayer in the darkness and a sign of our faith.

1. Robert Harrison, *Oriel's Diary*, Scripture Union, 2002, p.11.

Pause until all the altar candles are lit.

Each person comes up and lights a candle to add to the lights around the altar.

You are invited to join in the words of a very ancient song of praise by saying simply, 'Holy, holy, holy Lord'. Let us pray together with the words of the angels:

Holy, holy, holy Lord,
The whole earth is full of your glory,[2]
the world blazes with your light.
Holy, holy, holy Lord.
Amen.

Music O come, all ye faithful

Conclusion Living Lord,
may the good news which the angels brought
be shared by us today,
and may your love live in our hearts and homes
this Christmas.
Amen.

Give notices, announce the next all-age service and invite everyone to the feast.

2. From Isaiah 6:3.

God is with us

Theme	God is with us (wherever we are)
Scripture	Matthew 2:13–23

Running order	Total: 50 minutes
Welcome	Lighting the Advent wreath *(5 minutes)*
Introduction	Opening the theme
Activity	Audio-visual meditation – 'Hallelujah' *(7 minutes)*
Music	Unto us a boy is born *(5 minutes)*
Storytelling	Telling the story of Matthew 2:13–23 *(3 minutes)*
Exploring	Where is God when bad things happen? *(15 minutes)*
Music	Abba, Father *(5 minutes)*
Prayer action	Patchwork of prayer and praise *(5 minutes)*
Music	Joy to the world! *(5 minutes)*
Conclusion	Closing prayer and invitation

Resources

- Advent wreath and matches
- Audio-visual equipment: a laptop connected to a projector, a screen and a speaker system. If your church does not have these things in place, it can be done with a borrowed projector and screen, (talk to local schools) domestic stereo speakers and lots of extension leads
- A volunteer who is confident in using computers. This is an ideal job for a teenager or two. Their brief is to create the following:
  – A 'meditation montage' of images on a computer to accompany Leonard Cohen's 'Hallelujah', introduced to a new audience by *The X Factor (see appendix)*
- Several tables around which people can gather, set with one each of the following:
  – Blue paper and cut-out shapes *(see appendix)*
- Music and words
- Lots of small squares of paper in different colours. The blocks of paper sold as telephone memo pads are good for this
- Felt-tip pens in a variety of colours
- Some reels of Sellotape and several pairs of scissors

Leaders

Minimum: 2

- Leader
- Technical person/helper

Optimum: 7

- Leader
- Activity Leader
- Technical person
- Storyteller
- Music Leader
- Explorer
- Prayer Leader
- Helpers to make the patchwork *(may be any of the above leaders)*

Suggestions for additional music

- Praise, my soul, the King of heaven
- Let us praise God together
- Alleluia! We sing your praises

Service

Welcome

Light all the candles on the Advent wreath.

Introduction

Praise the Lord! The Christmas story is full of angels who sing God's praise – that is their job. But one of today's Bible readings reminds us that praise is not just the business of angels in heaven. Everything on earth should praise him, too:

> Praise the Lord from the earth,
> you sea monsters and all deeps,
> mountains and all hills,
> fruit trees and all cedars!
> Wild animals and all cattle,
> creeping things and flying birds!

That's right – sea monsters, sycamores, worms and parrots should all praise God! Last but by no means least, all of us should praise him, too:

> Young men and women alike,
> old and young together!
> Let them praise the name of the Lord.

It couldn't be clearer: all things everywhere are called to praise God. There is a single word which sums up this praise: 'Alleluia' – it means 'Praise God'. We are going to listen to a song today called 'Hallelujah' which many of you may know. The words remind us that if we are called to praise God always and everywhere, then that means we praise him whether we are happy or sad. In good times and bad, we say 'Hallelujah'. The pictures which accompany this song invite you to reflect on what this might mean.

Activity

Turn off the lights, then play the music and watch the meditation montage. Pause for a moment once it has finished.

Music

Unto us a boy is born

Storytelling

Retelling Matthew 2:13–23

After the Christmas story, some terrible things happened while Jesus was still a new baby. In the middle of the night, an angel appeared to Joseph with an urgent warning: 'Run away, now! King Herod wants to kill Jesus!' So Mary and Joseph bundled up their belongings and carried their precious son through the night. They kept travelling, day and night, until they reached Egypt, where they would be safe. Meanwhile, Herod discovered that Jesus had got away and he was so angry that he ordered his soldiers to kill all the babies and toddlers in and around Bethlehem.

After Herod died, the angel returned to Joseph: 'It's safe to go home to Israel now'. But when they went back, they found that Herod's son was king of Judea, and Joseph had a dream which warned him that Jesus' life might still be in danger. So they moved to a safe little country town called Nazareth, near the lake of Galilee, and Jesus grew up there.

Exploring

Today's story has some terrible things in it, and it makes me wonder: where is God when bad things happen? It might help us to think about this if we think in simple pictures. If you would like to gather round these tables, you will find that on each one there is a collection of shapes. Let's fit them together. First, there is heaven *(place blue rectangle first)* then came the world which God made *(place green hill).* Then there is each one of us *(place the string of figures).* But our lives aren't always the same: sometimes, good things happen to us and we are happy *(place the yellow 'sunburst' shape, with the single figure on it);* sometimes, bad things happen to us and we are sad. It can feel as if we are in a dark place, like this *(place the cave shape and move the single figure into it).* There is someone missing from this picture: God. Where should we put God? *(Hand round the 'God' sign and allow time for discussion and decisions.)*

Now, remember today's story, in which Herod ordered his soldiers to kill the babies? If this were a picture of that story, a lot of people would be here *(put the string of figures in the cave).* Where is God then? Where would you put God in this picture? *(Allow time for discussion and decisions.)*

Here's a clue: think where Jesus is in the story. *(Allow further time for discussion and decisions.)*

(Place God in the cave with the people) God is here – in the thick of it – because that is where Jesus is. Jesus is the baby who is hunted down by a king's soldiers. He is the child who grows up in hiding, with his parents terrified of powerful people who want to kill him. From the moment he was born, he was in the middle of fear and suffering. So we know that whenever we are afraid, or sad, God knows how we feel because he became one of us and lived through those same feelings himself. So when we ask ourselves the question, 'Where is God when bad things happen?' the answer is, 'He is with us'. This is what one of Jesus' names means: he is sometimes called 'Emmanuel', which means 'God with us'. God is always with us, wherever we are and whatever we are going through. He is with us and he loves us.

Music Abba, Father

Prayer action At the beginning of today's service, we heard that we should praise God in good times and bad – and now we know why. Because he is always with us, whatever we are going through. Our prayers today will reflect the way our lives are chequered with happiness and sorrow: we will make a patchwork of prayer and praise. Take a small square and fill it with whatever you would like to bring before God in prayer. You might be full of thankfulness and praise for something wonderful that has happened to you; you might be sad or afraid, or worried about someone you love. Whatever it is, write or draw it on one or more squares of paper, then bring your prayers to the front and lay them face down with all the others to create our patchwork.

Allow enough time for everyone to fill their square and bring it to the front. Keeping the squares face down, the leader and/or the helpers should assemble them into a rectangle. Tape the squares to each other as they arrive, with no spaces in between. When the last prayers have been attached, invite everyone to return to their seats and lift the sheet of prayers to show it the right way round. It should look like a small patchwork quilt, each square densely covered with coloured words or pictures.

Loving Lord, Emmanuel,
we offer you this patchwork of prayer and praise
and leave it in your hands.
Whatever our prayers and wherever we are,
may we trust that you are with us,
always and forever.
Amen.

Music

Joy to the world!

Conclusion

Invite everyone to join in with the opening and closing 'Hallelujah'.

Hallelujah.
In our happiness and sadness,
in our work and our play,
in our busyness and our loneliness,
in conflict and peace,
in disaster and joy,
you are always with us, Lord.
We praise you:
Hallelujah.

Give notices, announce the next all-age service and invite everyone to the feast.

The Light of the world

Theme	The Incarnation
Scripture	John 1:1–9, 14

Running order	Total: 50 minutes
Welcome	Lighting the Advent wreath *(5 minutes)*
Music	As with gladness men of old *(3 minutes)*
Introduction	Opening the theme
Activity	Newspaper collage: picturing 'the world' *(15 minutes)*
Storytelling	Reading John 1:1–9, 14 *(2 minutes)*
Music	Like a candle flame *(5 minutes)*
Exploring	Why did the Word become flesh and live among us? *(10 minutes)*
Prayer action	Light of the world – lighting candles *(5 minutes)*
Music	Lord, the light of your love is shining *(5 minutes)*
Conclusion	Closing prayer and invitation

Resources

- Advent wreath and matches
- A large circle of paper (three or four lengths of lining paper joined together and cut to shape)
- Lots of newspapers and magazines with a focus on ecological and global issues: e.g. *National Geographic* and colour supplements on climate change
- Scissors and glue sticks
- Music and words
- A string of white fairy lights, arranged in the shape of a heart and plugged into a double socket
- A child's illuminated globe
- A two-socket electrical extension lead, hidden somewhere under the church seats
- A large sign suspended from the lead, reading *Jesus: the Word*
- Paschal candle or other large candle
- Thin votive candles
- Cardboard 'globes' *(see appendix)*

Leaders

Minimum: 1

- Leader

Optimum: 6

- Leader
- Activity Leader
- Storyteller
- Music Leader
- Explorer
- Prayer Leader

Suggestions for additional music

- What child is this?
- Angel-voices, ever singing

Service

Welcome Light the Advent wreath.

Music As with gladness men of old

Introduction Our service today is all about Jesus being the Light of the world. We'll be thinking about how he is 'the light' later on, but first we need to think about 'the world'. We often pray for the world, but what are we thinking about when we do? What pictures come into your head when we talk about 'the world'?

Invite some comments.

Activity Today we will make a collage which uses lots of these ideas. Here is a big, empty globe *(hold up the large circle of paper)* and here are lots of newspapers, magazines and pictures which may help us fill in our picture of the world. Come and choose something to cut out and stick on to this collage to make our collective view of the world.

Spend some time creating the collage by simple patchworking or by using the pictures to form the shapes of continents. Hold up the finished piece for all to see.

This is our world. In today's Bible story, we will be hearing about the world, and also about the Word – which is another name for Jesus.

Storytelling Read John 1:1–9, 14

Music Like a candle flame

Exploring Today's Bible reading may make us ask some big questions. It calls Jesus 'the Word' – what does that mean? And why did the Word become a human being and live among us? Let's think big – with some big props to help us.

Turn off the church lights and turn on the fairy-light heart.

This represents God – bright, light and full of love.

Show the unlit globe.

This represents the world. It doesn't shine with a light of its own, and sometimes it can be a dark place. What we need is a way of bringing this bright, lovely light *(indicate the fairy-light heart)* from God to the world – but how? Can anyone find something under their seat which might help us to make a connection between these two?

Someone brings forward the connecting lead with the sign attached to it. Plug it in at both ends so that the globe is illuminated. Then ask these or similar questions:

What is happening here? What job is this lead doing? If this represents Jesus, what difference does he make?

Invite comments and try to value whatever is offered – all responses are valid.

When we call Jesus the Word, we might compare him to the verb in a sentence – the 'doing word' that connects the parts of a sentence together and gives it life. This idea, and our image of an electric wire, help us see Jesus as the vital connection: he connects us all, forever, to God. Because of Jesus, we can trust that God will never leave us alone – he will never break that connection. Through Jesus, his love flows like light into our world and into our lives. And that light will never go out.

Prayer action

Place the large, lighted candle in the centre of the world collage.

Through Jesus, the light of God's love lights up the world. One way in which that light can spread is through the love we share with one another. In our prayers today, we are going to pass the light of this candle from one to another, and pray that love might shine its light in all the dark places of the world and of our lives. Take a moment to call to mind those in particular need at this time, and light your candle with the words, 'Lord, let there be light.'

Allow enough time for all the candles to be lit and for prayers to be offered. Then keep them alight as you sing.

Music Lord, the light of your love is shining

Conclusion *Blow out the candles.*

Lord of light and life,
though these little lights go out,
your light still shines in the darkness
and the darkness will never overcome it.
May it shine in our hearts,
now and always.
Amen.

Give notices, announce the next all-age service and invite everyone to the feast.

One for All

Epiphany

Gold, frankincense and myrrh

Theme	God revealed to the world
Scripture	Matthew 2:1–12

Running order	Total: 50 minutes
Welcome	Making footprints or handprints *(5 minutes)*
Introduction	Opening the theme
Activity	Dressing up and tableau of the three wise men *(5 minutes)*
Storytelling	Visual retelling of Matthew 2:1–12 *(10 minutes)*
Music	We three kings *(5 minutes)*
Exploring	What is Epiphany? *(10 minutes)*
Music	What child is this? *(5 minutes)*
Prayer action	Gold, frankincense and myrrh *(5 minutes)*
Music	The first Nowell *(5 minutes)*
Conclusion	Closing prayer and invitation

Resources

- A sheet of lining paper and felt-tip pens, in front of the altar
- Basic Nativity costumes:
  - Brown fabric for Joseph
  - Blue fabric for Mary
  - A manger / wooden crate with hay
  - A baby Jesus doll
  - Shiny or velvety cloaks for kings
  - Three cardboard crowns
- Large piece of brown felt in the shape of a cross
- The gifts: *(see appendix)*
  - 'Gold' (a small box covered in gold foil), wrapped in a stiff rectangular piece of gold paper
  - A box of frankincense granules, wrapped in white crepe paper cut in a cross shape, smaller than the brown cross
  - A bottle of myrrh oil, wrapped in three red ribbons
- Music and words
- Four 'prayer stations' around the church, with the following:
  - A frameless mirror or mirror tile (to reflect and intensify the glitter of the gold)
  - A small thurible or charcoal burner for the frankincense
  - A small dish for the myrrh oil
  - A space for the media pieces which will be produced during the Exploring
- A sign for each station:
  - *GOLD for the King*
  - *FRANKINCENSE for God*
  - *MYRRH for the body*
  - *JESUS for us*
- Several copies of each of the four media sheets, spread out on some tables *(see appendix)*
- Pens and pencils

Leaders

Minimum: 2

- Leader / Storyteller
- Storyteller

Optimum: 7

- Leader
- Activity Leader
- Storytellers x 2
- Music Leader
- Explorer
- Prayer Leader

Suggestions for additional music

- He's got the whole world in his hands
- Lord Jesus Christ
- Glorious light

Service

Welcome

Invite people to come up to the altar and draw round their feet or hands on the sheet of lining paper as a way of saying, 'Here I am, Lord'.

Introduction

Today is called Epiphany. It is the day when we remember the wise men who visited Jesus. I wonder if we could recreate the scene in the stable today? Who would like to dress up as a king?

Activity

Dress up volunteers as Mary, Joseph and three wise men. Place Mary and Joseph around the manger with the baby in it. Ask each wise man to process down the aisle in turn with the gold, frankincense and myrrh, and then remain kneeling by the manger. By the end, you should have a living Epiphany tableau.

Storytelling

Encourage children to gather around you and the tableau for the storytelling. You will need one storyteller to tell the story and another to take the gifts from the tableau in turn and unwrap them as described below.

This is a scene we all recognise. But our story today is about the three gifts given to the baby Jesus. Mary and Joseph unwrapped these presents on the stable floor *(lay out brown cross)*. The first was heavy and bright: it was gold. *(Hold up the gold then unwrap it, unfolding the gold wrapping.)* Gold was a present fit for a king. *(Spread out the wrapping at the top of the cross, in the position of the sign at the crucifixion which read, 'The King of the Jews'.)*

The next present smelled wonderful. It was frankincense, made from the sap of an exotic tree. *(Unwrap the frankincense and pour out some grains into the palm of your hand for people to look at.)* When these hard little grains are sprinkled on burning wood or charcoal, they release a heavenly smell and pure white smoke. *(Hold up the long white wrapping.)* Frankincense looks and smells like holiness, so it is a gift which people offer to God. *(Unfold the white wrapping in the middle of the brown cross, forming a smaller cross like the figure of Christ.)*

The last present was myrrh. It was a sticky resin with a sweet, earthy smell which made people sad because it reminded them of death. A dead body was rubbed with myrrh to sweeten and preserve it. So the last present brought with it the shadow of a death which would come in the future. *(On the white cross where Christ's hands and feet would be, drop each red ribbon in a little pool and let it trail down.)*

Mary and Joseph looked at all these precious, important gifts. The gold for a king, *(place gold and the sign on one prayer station)* the holy white smoke of frankincense for God *(place frankincense and the sign on another prayer station)* and the myrrh for a dead body *(place myrrh and the sign on another prayer station)*. They kept them safe and treasured them through the years which followed, as their baby son grew into a man and went out into the world.

Music

We three kings

During this hymn, the tableau actors can remove their costumes and return to their seats.

Exploring

Today is called Epiphany: it means 'showing' or 'revealing'. The wise men came from different parts of the world and so their visit is seen as the moment when God showed himself to the world in the body of the baby Jesus. As we have seen in our story, their gifts reveal who he is in a clear and beautiful way. But what happened once the wise men left? What happened once they started to spread the news, and the truth of Jesus' birth was shown to the world?

We are going to explore this in a different way today – by making an imaginative leap from Israel, two thousand or so years ago, to the present day. I invite you to imagine what would happen if Jesus were born not in a stable, but in a garage behind a dilapidated hotel, somewhere in the modern Middle East. When important foreign visitors come to see him, how would they spread the news today? Where do we get our news from?

Elicit the answers and introduce the four media sheets: TV, the internet and newspapers.

If Jesus were born today, I wonder what we might see, hear and read about him in the media? For example, would there be paparazzi photographs of the garage? Would the wise men hold a press conference? Use your imagination as you look through these media sheets. Write or draw any ideas you have about how the Epiphany would be announced – how God would go public – in our modern world.

Allow plenty of time for people to circulate and generate ideas, then share some of the responses.

The Epiphany today would be big news. It would attract frenzied media attention of all kinds, from the most serious BBC reports to the silliest bloggers. That is the thing about publicity and exposure today – you don't get to choose how people treat you or your story. This was true of Jesus, too. As soon as news of his birth spread than people like the shepherds and the wise men came to worship him – but King Herod also sent soldiers to kill him. This is the reality of the Epiphany: it is when God exposes himself to all the riskiness and unpredictability of life. And he did it for us.

Music

What child is this

During this hymn, light the charcoal burner and add some incense; then pour a little myrrh oil into the dish.

Prayer action

In our prayers today, we will use four prayer stations. At each one there is an Epiphany gift which helps us to understand something about who Jesus is. As we learnt in our story, gold is a gift for the King of the Jews – but Jesus was born in a stable and spent his life serving whoever needed him, regardless of what they believed. Frankincense reminds us that Jesus is God – but he came into our world as one of us. Myrrh reminds us that Jesus died a real death – and yet he rose again. The fourth station uses our imaginary twenty-first century Epiphany to remind us that above all, Jesus gave himself to us by exposing himself to the best and the worst that life could offer. In a time of quiet, come forward and explore these gifts with all your senses: rest in God's presence and listen to what these things tell us about his Son.

In turn, the people look at the glow of the gold, smell some of the burning frankincense, rub a little myrrh oil on their palms and read the media pieces.

Let us pray.
Here is gold for a King born in a stable,
frankincense for God who became flesh and blood,
myrrh for the man who died but rose again.
Lord Jesus, Embracer of contradictions,
these gifts were given to you
but you gave yourself to us
so that we might have the gift
of everlasting life.
Open our hearts and minds
to receive you today.
Amen.

Music

The first Nowell

Conclusion

Turn the sheet of lining paper with footprints on it so that the footprints are facing towards the door of the church, or heading down the aisle.

Lord Jesus,
send us out into the world
to walk in your footsteps
and to follow your star wherever it may lead us.
Amen.

Give notices, announce the next all-age service and invite everyone to the feast.

Baptism of Christ

Theme	The Baptism of Christ
Scripture	Matthew 3:13–17

Running order	Total: 50 minutes
Welcome	Making footprints *(5 minutes)*
Introduction	Opening the theme
Activity	Watching a film clip – *O Brother, Where Art Thou? (5 minutes)*
Storytelling	Reading Matthew 3:13–17 with pictures *(5 minutes)*
Music	Christ, when for us you were baptised *(5 minutes)*
Exploring	Why was Jesus baptised? *(15 minutes)*
Music	Spirit of the living God *(5 minutes)*
Prayer action	Calendar prayers – confession *(5 minutes)*
Music	I am a new creation *(5 minutes)*
Conclusion	Footprints prayer

Resources

- A sheet of lining paper and felt-tip pens, in front of the altar
- DVD of the film *O Brother, Where Art Thou? (see appendix)*
- A laptop, projector, screen and speakers
- Recording of 'Down to the river to pray' *(see appendix)* and audio equipment to play it on
- Four pictures *(see appendix)*
  - The river Jordan
  - Newly baptised man
  - Dove in a radiant sky
  - Jesus emerging from the river
- Music and words
- A table with the following:
  - An apron
  - A bowl of water
  - Some soap and a towel
  - Bread, butter and jam
  - A plate and knife
- Blank pages from out-of-date diaries or calendars
- Lots of blank calendars for the coming year *(see appendix)*. Place these on the altar in front of the cross
- Two bowls: one to hand round with the calendar pieces and one placed in front of the altar

Leaders

Minimum: 2

- Leader
- Technician

Optimum: 6

- Leader *(Introduction and Conclusion)*
- Activity Leader/Technician
- Storyteller
- Music Leader
- Explorer
- Prayer Leader

Suggestions for additional music

- When Jesus came to Jordan
- Take this moment
- Morning has broken

Service

Welcome

Invite people to come up to the altar and draw round their feet on the sheet of lining paper as a way of saying, 'Here I am, Lord'.

Introduction

Today we celebrate the moment when John the Baptist (remember him?) baptised Jesus. Now in many Christian churches, baptism involves a sprinkling of water. But in Jesus' time, and in some Christian churches today, baptism meant getting a lot wetter than that. We are going to watch a clip from a film about three escaped prisoners who find themselves caught up in a baptism ceremony in a river. When John the Baptist was busy baptising people, it may have looked something like this.

Activity

Play the music, 'Down to the river to pray' and simultaneously play the baptism scene from 'O Brother, Where Art Thou?' with the sound turned down, so that you just have pictures with the music playing over (the dialogue contains some strong language). As the newly-baptised convict makes his way back through the water, turn the music down and the film soundtrack up, so that we hear his speech:

> Well that's it boys, I been redeemed! The preacher warshed away all my sins and transgressions. It's the straight-and-narrow from here on out and heaven everlasting's my reward![1]

Then immediately pause the film, leaving the picture on freeze-frame.

This clip gives us a beautifully clear picture of baptism. The water is a sign of God's loving forgiveness: whether you are sprinkled over the font or ducked in the river, you are as clean as a newborn baby, and like the man in the film clip, you can make a completely fresh start. No wonder crowds of people rushed to the river Jordan so that John could baptise them.

1. Ethan Coen and Joel Coen, *O Brother, Where Art Thou?* Universal Studios 2000.

Storytelling

This is the story of what happened when Jesus was baptised.[2]

Show picture of the river Jordan.

Then Jesus came from Galilee to John at the Jordan, to be baptised by him. John would have prevented him, saying, 'I need to be baptised by you, and do you come to me?' But Jesus answered him, 'Let it be so now; for it is proper for us in this way to fulfil all righteousness.' Then he consented.

Show picture of a newly baptised man, dripping water.

And when Jesus had been baptised, just as he came up from the water, suddenly the heavens were opened to him and he saw the Spirit of God descending like a dove and alighting on him.

Show picture of a dove in a radiant sky.

And a voice from heaven said, 'This is my Son, the Beloved, with whom I am well pleased.'

Show picture of Jesus emerging from the river.

Music

Christ, when for us you were baptised

Exploring

Today's story describes an important event in Jesus' life. We are going to explore together why his baptism was a big deal.

Show the picture of a newly baptised man, dripping water.

First of all, we have a big question to think about. Jesus is described in the Bible as being 'without sin'[3]: why, then, did he ask to be baptised? John the Baptist asks him this question, too. Everyone else came to John to have their sins washed away – so why did Jesus come, if he didn't have any sins? Take a few minutes to think about that, and perhaps to talk it over with someone else.

2. This reading is taken directly from Matthew's Gospel (NRSV): you may prefer to use a different translation.
3. Hebrews 4:15; 1 Peter 2:22; 2 Corinthians 5:21.

Allow a few minutes for discussion, then invite suggestions. Try to find some value in all contributions.

Jesus himself gives us a clue: he says he wants John to baptise him because it is the right thing to do. He shows that he is humble and obedient to God's will by being baptised. He has no sins to wash away, but instead of standing on the river bank watching everyone else get wet and saying, 'Not me – I don't need to!' he joins the queue and gets immersed like everyone else.

Show the picture of a dove in a radiant sky.

And what about the dove? The Bible reading tells us this is a shape taken by the Holy Spirit, and at the same time God's voice booms from heaven, saying, 'This is my Son, the Beloved, with whom I am well pleased.' At this moment, everything about Jesus is spelt out clearly. He is the Son of God, loved by God the Father and touched by God the Holy Spirit. In this Epiphany season, we see God showing himself to us, and in this story the Father, Son and Spirit – the three persons of the one God – are touched and heard and seen at the moment of Jesus' baptism.

Finally, there is another reason for Jesus' baptism which we will explore now. I need two big volunteers.

Give volunteer 1 an apron to put on and ask him/her to stand with hands behind his/her back, behind the table with the bowl of water and the sandwich ingredients. Stand volunteer 2 right behind 1, with his/her arms poking through the space by 1's elbows. In this position, 1 is armless and 2 provides the arms and hands, while being unable to see what is going on.

Now with a bit of co-operation here, we are going to help these two make a jam sandwich together. What is the very first thing our sandwich-maker needs to do?

Encourage contributions and instruct the sandwich-maker accordingly. The first action must be hand-washing; then take them through the (haphazard and messy!) sandwich-making process step-by-step, finishing with 1 taking a bite of the sandwich.

Now what does our sandwich-maker need to do before going back to his/her seat and picking up a hymn book?

Elicit the answer 'Wash their hands!' and finish the activity with hand-washing, then give the volunteers a round of applause as they return to their seats.

What was the first thing our sandwich-makers did before getting on with the job? And what was the thing they did before moving on to something new at the end?

Elicit the answer 'Wash their hands!'

Many religions in Jesus' time and today use washing rituals to mark the beginning of something new and important. People of faith may wash before meals, before prayers and to mark certain stages in life.

Show the picture of Jesus emerging from the river.

Jesus' baptism marks the beginning of a new stage in his life. After his baptism, he spent a long time alone in the wilderness and then began his public ministry of teaching and healing. Baptism marks a fresh start, a new beginning – and later, in our prayers, we will explore what this might mean for us at the start of this new year.

Music

Spirit of the living God

Prayer action

We have learnt that baptism means a fresh start – but what about those of us who want to make a fresh start but have already been baptised? Remember the escaped prisoner in the film clip who was so overjoyed to leave all his past wrongdoing behind him? He knew that his sins were forgiven. We may not have robbed a bank, but all of us have done things for which we are sorry.

We, too, can leave all our wrongdoing behind us by saying sorry to God and receiving his loving forgiveness. The start of a new year is a perfect time to confess past sins and look forward to a new beginning. *(Hand the calendar pieces round.)* In our prayers today, we are going to use these pieces of old diaries and calendars which represent all our messed-up yesterdays. In a moment of quiet, take a piece and as you do so, call to mind everything for which you want to say, 'Sorry'. *(Pause)* Then come forward, tear it up and throw the bits in this bowl in front of the altar, as a sign of handing all those things over to God. Let him take away all our sins and regrets. Then in front of the cross you'll find something to take away with you which represents the fresh start which God offers all of us.

Make your own confession and encourage others to come forward, throw their pieces in the bowl and take their new calendars. When everyone is seated, gather them together in prayer:

Lord of life and time,
forgive what we were yesterday,
renew what we are today and
bless what we will be tomorrow,
in Jesus' name,
Amen.

Music I am a new creation

Conclusion *Turn the sheet of lining paper with footprints on it so that the footprints are facing towards the door of the church, or heading down the aisle.*

Heavenly Father,
send us out into this new year
washed clean by your love
to make a new beginning.
Amen.

Give notices, announce the next all-age service and invite everyone to the feast.

One for All

Presentation in the temple

Candlemas

Theme	The presentation of Christ in the temple
Scripture	Luke 2:22–40

Running order	Total: 50 minutes
Welcome	Blessing candles *(5 minutes)*
Introduction	Opening the theme
Activity	Recognising his name *(10 minutes)*
Storytelling	Dramatised reading of Luke 2:22–40 *(10 minutes)*
Music	The kingdom of our God is here *(5 minutes)*
Exploring	Hot-seating – what is meeting Jesus like? *(10 minutes)*
Prayer action	Interactive prayer *(5 minutes)*
Music	Lord, the light of your love *(5 minutes)*
Conclusion	Closing prayer and invitation

Resources

- Enough candles for everyone to have one to take home. Try to give something bigger and longer-lasting than a tea-light or a thin votive candle: white household candles are good
- Matches and tapers
- Music and words
- 15 letters, spelling *Jesus the Messiah*, each on a piece of white card and written with white wax crayon or a white candle. Hide them around the church before the service begins
- Four signs, written in white wax as above: *SURE*, *SURPRISED*, *AWE*, *HOPE AND FEAR*
- Ink wash and brushes *(see appendix)*
- A table covered with newspaper
- Baby Jesus doll, wrapped in blankets
- Small covered box with air holes in it
- Four chairs

Leaders

Minimum: 5

- Leader/Explorer
- Cast x 4

Mary, Joseph, Simeon, Anna (all wearing traditional or modern dress)

Optimum: 9

- Leader *(Introduction and Conclusion)*
- Cast x 4
- Explorer
- Music Leader
- Prayer Leader

Suggestions for additional music

- Hail to the Lord who comes
- Colours of day

Service

Welcome

Invite everyone to take a candle, light it and return to their seat.

Today is called Candlemas. In some churches, it is the custom for the priest to bless candles today for people to light in their homes throughout the year. Today, we will pray for God's blessing on these candles which we will each take home with us. Let us pray:

Lord of light,
we ask for your blessing on these candles.
May their light shine in our homes
as you shine in our hearts.
In all that we say and do,
may our lives show your light to others.
Amen.

Blow out the candles.

Introduction

Candlemas marks the occasion when Mary and Joseph presented the baby Jesus in the temple in Jerusalem. There they encountered two people who had been waiting all their lives to meet Jesus. We will hear their story today: the Son of God is recognised in this face-to-face meeting in the temple.

Activity

Before our story, we have an activity which involves revealing and recognising. Hidden around the church are 15 pieces of white card: can you find them for me?

Volunteers hunt for the letters and bring them to the table at the front.

Now each card has an invisible letter which I have written with a white candle. To reveal the letter, you need to brush the card with this ink and the letter will appear . . .

Brush over a letter and show it once it has appeared. Encourage your volunteers to reveal the other letters, then lay them randomly out on the floor.

All these letters spell out three words which are an important name: can you rearrange the letters and spot what the name is?

Ask for everyone's help in sorting out the letters, giving clues as necessary, to reveal: Jesus the Messiah.

In all that jumble of letters, we recognised a name we knew – Jesus. 'Messiah' means God's Chosen One, and today's story is about two people who recognise Jesus the Messiah among all the crowds in the temple that day.

Storytelling

We need to imagine a very grand place of worship, crowded with people and priests who are coming and going. Here comes an ordinary-looking couple who have travelled down from their little country town with their baby. Their names are Mary and Joseph.

Mary and Joseph stand nervously at the front, clutching a covered box and a baby doll wrapped in blankets. Simeon and Anna are seated with the congregation.

Joseph — We are here to present our firstborn son to the Lord, as the law requires. Here are two young pigeons for the sacrifice.

Mary — And this is –

Simeon — *(Jumping up from his place and speaking to the baby)* Master!

He walks to the front and holds the baby.

Master, now you are dismissing your servant in peace,
according to your word;
for my eyes have seen your salvation,
which you have prepared in the presence of all peoples,
a light for revelation to the Gentiles
and for glory to your people Israel.

(To Mary and Joseph) May the Lord bless you both. Mary, this child is destined for the falling and the rising of many in Israel, and to be a sign that will be opposed so that the inner thoughts of many will be revealed – and a sword will pierce your own soul too.

Anna — *(Jumping up from her place and moving to stand by the baby)* Hallelujah! This is the Messiah I have been waiting all these years to see! This is the child who is chosen by God to save us all! Hallelujah!

Music The kingdom of our God is here

Exploring *Bring the characters to sit in four chairs at the front, like an interview panel.*

Let's ask our characters a few questions about this important event in their lives. Simeon, babies are brought to the temple all the time by their parents. How did you know this one was special?

Simeon: God told me that I would see the Messiah before I died, and I am old now so I knew I would meet him soon. Then, today, I suddenly knew that I had to come to the temple. I felt as if a strong wind was pushing me along and my heart was burning with the certainty that there was someone here I had to meet. And here he is – the Saviour.

Explorer: Anna, you are 84 years old and you never leave the temple. You worship here with fasting and prayer night and day and people know you as a wise prophet. What did you see in this baby?

Anna: He wasn't what I expected. All these years I've waited, I thought the Messiah would be a confident young man – perhaps a priest or a prince – who would march in here and boldly proclaim that he was God's Chosen One. I didn't expect this little baby with his shy parents from the north country. But when I saw him – I just knew it was him.

Explorer: Mary, Joseph: how did you feel when Simeon and Anna recognised your son?

Joseph: Even before he was born, people have said extraordinary things about Jesus. He's just a baby – but people call him 'Master' and 'Messiah'.

Mary: I know great things are in store for my son – that is God's will. But it won't be easy, and I won't forget Simeon's words: 'a sword will pierce your own soul too'. I wonder what will happen to us all.

Explorer: *(Have your four signs to hand.)*

So what do these people teach us about where we may meet Jesus and how we can recognise him? Now, I need some helpers to reveal some words for me. Each word describes how each person felt when they met Jesus.

Helpers get busy with the ink wash on the first blank sign. Reveal 'SURE' and give the sign to Simeon.

Simeon felt sure that he was face-to-face with Jesus, and sometimes we can feel that, too. The feeling may not make sense to us, but sometimes we can just know that we are in the presence of God.

What about Anna?

Helpers reveal 'SURPRISED'; give the sign to Anna.

Anna met Jesus in an unexpected place. She was surprised to see him in the arms of a poor country couple – and most of all, she was surprised to meet a little baby and not a powerful man. God is full of surprises, and we too may see him at work in the most unexpected places and people.

What about Mary and Joseph?

Helpers reveal 'AWE' and 'HOPE AND FEAR'; give the signs to Joseph and Mary respectively.

Joseph was awestruck at the way strangers responded to Jesus, and for Mary, the promise of her son's greatness was mixed with dread about what might be in store for them all. Whenever God works in our lives we may experience feelings like these. We may be full of awe, like Joseph, or torn between hope and fear for what lies ahead, like Mary.

All these feelings are at work in the Candlemas story, and we may experience them in our own lives. Remember how Simeon was sure and Anna was surprised; remember Joseph's awe and Mary's hope and fear: these feelings might help us to recognise Jesus when we meet him, too – wherever that might be.

Prayer action

Our prayer today is an active prayer to help us think about how Jesus is active in the world today. When you hear the word 'body', cross your hands over your chest like this *(demonstrate action)*. When you hear the word 'hands', open your hands in front of you like this *(demonstrate action)*. When you hear the word 'feet', stamp your feet once like this *(demonstrate action)* and when you hear the word 'eyes', point to your eyes *(demonstrate action)*. Let's practise *(do the actions together)*: 'hands', 'body', 'feet', 'eyes', 'hands', 'feet'. Now listen closely for those words as we pray together:

Christ, you have no **body** now on earth but ours,
no **hands** but ours,
no **feet** but ours.
Ours are the **eyes** through which your compassion
is to look out on the world.
Ours are the **feet** by which you are to go about doing good,
and ours are the **hands** with which you are to bless us now.[1]
Lord Jesus, show us how to be your **body, eyes, hands** and **feet** in the world.
Amen.

Music Lord, the light of your love

Conclusion Master,
may we now depart in peace.
May our eyes be opened to see your light in the world
and may we be ready to recognise you
in everyone we meet.
Amen.

Give notices, announce the next all-age service and invite everyone to the feast.

1. Adapted from St Teresa of Ávila (1515–1582).

One for All

Ash Wednesday

Saying sorry

Theme	Repentance
Scripture	John 8:1–11

Running order	Total: 50 minutes
Welcome	Writing in the sand *(5 minutes)*
Introduction	Opening the theme
Storytelling	News report from the temple *(5 minutes)*
Music	God forgave my sin *(5 minutes)*
Exploring	What is God's forgiveness like? *(5 minutes)*
Music	I'm accepted, I'm forgiven *(5 minutes)*
Prayer action	Bonfire – active confession *(10 minutes)*
Music	Give thanks with a grateful heart *(5 minutes)*
Activity	Ashing *(10 minutes)*
Conclusion	Closing prayer and invitation

Resources

- Some soft sand *(see appendix)*
- A large tray or piece of sheeting to spread the sand on
- Music and words
- Lots of plain lolly sticks *(see appendix)*
- Felt-tip pens
- A small, contained fire, lit outside in a brazier, barbeque or garden incinerator. It is helpful if there is a lid which can be closed down to make the fire safe while the service continues inside
- Ashes in a dish *(see appendix)*
- Wet wipes

Leaders

Minimum: 5

- Leader
- Cast x 3
- Fire warden

Optimum: 8+

- Leader *(Introduction and Conclusion)*
- Cast x 3, wearing modern dress
  Reporter, wearing smart clothes and holding a microphone
  Shimon, wearing robes
  'Mary', barefoot and wearing a dress
- Activity Leader(s)
- Music Leader
- Explorer
- Prayer Leader(s)/Fire warden

Suggestions for additional music

- O for a heart to praise
- Forgive our sins as we forgive

Service

Welcome

Spread the sand out on the tray or sheeting. Invite people to write or draw something in the sand: their name, a prayer or something they want to say sorry for. Every so often, wipe the sand smooth.

Introduction

Today is the beginning of Lent. It is a special time for those of us who are not perfect – and that's all of us. Lent is a time for saying sorry to God and making amends for whatever we have done wrong. In ancient times, a sign of repentance was to cover yourself in ashes: that is why this day of confession and repentance became known as Ash Wednesday. We'll be using some ashes later on – but first, here's today's big story. Let's go live to the scene in Jerusalem. It's 30 AD and although it's still early in the morning there has already been some trouble in the temple. Our reporter is on the spot.

Storytelling

The reporter and Shimon arrive at the front. Mary remains unseen.

Reporter — Good morning and I'm here now with one of the Pharisees here at the temple. Shimon, you're an expert on religious law, is that right?

Shimon — I am, yes.

Reporter — And today's trouble started off with someone breaking the law. Tell us what happened.

Shimon — Well – there was this woman. She's a married woman, but she was caught with another man – not her husband. And the law says that we should stone her to death. So some of us started collecting stones, and then someone said, 'Why don't we take her to Jesus and tell him what she's done? He's in the temple right now. The law is quite clear – Moses said people like her deserve stoning to death. If Jesus doesn't back us up then we've proved he's not fit to teach the law.' So we dragged this woman to the temple – but things didn't quite work out as we'd planned.

When we told Jesus what the woman had done, at first I thought he wasn't really listening. He was just drawing with his finger in the sand and dust on the ground. I got annoyed, and in the end I shouted at him, 'So what do *you* think we should do with her?' Then he stood up and looked at me. He was very calm. He looked round at all of us, and at the woman who was in a heap on the ground. And he said, 'If any one of you can honestly say you have never done anything wrong, then you can be the first to throw a stone. Be my guest.' And he just bent down and carried on doodling!

Now he'd got us. I knew I couldn't honestly say I had never done anything wrong – I'm only human – so in the end I just walked away. What else could I do? Some of the others got it straight away – they walked off, too. Some of our young bloods hung about, holding on to their stones, trying to work out a way round what Jesus had said, but even they gave up in the end. I just went home – I don't know what happened to the woman.

Shimon leaves.

Reporter That was Shimon, the Pharisee. Now I have managed to get exclusive access to the woman concerned – let's call her Mary (that's not her real name).

Mary enters.

Mary, tell us what happened.

Woman I thought I'd had it. They'd caught me red-handed, and people were starting to pick up stones and take aim. I don't know why they took me to Jesus. He barely looked at me – just doodled in the sand. Everyone else was shouting and I just sat there watching his finger making loops and shapes and lines, like I was in a sort of trance. I don't know what he said to them, but I snapped out of my daze when he suddenly stopped writing and looked straight at me. 'Where have they gone?' he said. He had a very gentle voice. 'Hasn't anyone condemned you?' And I looked around – and they'd all gone. There was just me and him. He said to me, 'I don't condemn you, either. Off you go – but you've got to make some changes in your life. Do the right thing.' And that was it! I felt like a huge weight had been lifted off my shoulders. I'd thought I was going to be killed – but now I feel like I've been given a new chance to live.

Music God forgave my sin

Exploring Let's see what Jesus did in our story. First of all, everyone stand up. *(Everyone stands – including you.)* Sit down if you have ever said anything you shouldn't have. *(Sit down yourself and continue talking.)* Now sit down if you have ever not bothered to do something which you know you should have done. And finally, sit down if you have ever done anything at all for which you had to say, 'Sorry.' *(By the end, all should be sitting down!)*

Of course – that's all of us. We're only human. That is how Jesus made sure that no one in our story could throw a stone at the woman, because even the religious leaders who accused her knew that they were only human, too, and that they sometimes did something wrong.

Who was the only person in our story who never did anything wrong? *(Invite responses until someone says, 'Jesus'.)* Jesus was not only human – he was God, too, and so he was perfect. So he was the only one who could have thrown stones at the woman – but he didn't. Instead, he did not condemn her and told her to go and lead a better life. He showed her, and us, how wonderful God's forgiveness is.

Music I'm accepted, I'm forgiven

Prayer action The woman in our story was brought before Jesus and everything she had done wrong was laid out before him. He saw it all and forgave her, giving her a fresh start. It is good for us to bring to God all the wrong things we have done and all the good things we have failed to do. In our prayers today, we are going to turn away from our sins completely by reducing them to ashes. You are all invited to take these lolly sticks and write on them anything for which you want to say sorry. You can write it, draw it or just put the word, 'Sorry'. Then take it outside and throw it onto the fire. Watch the flames consume it, just as God's love takes your sin away completely and gives you a fresh start.

Pass round the sticks and pens.

Let us rest in God's presence now and call to mind all those things for which we are sorry.

Pause and leave plenty of time for people to write. Then lead the way outside. All throw their sticks on the bonfire then gather around as you say:

Holy Lord,
may the warmth of your love
take away all our sins.
'Forgive what we have been,
sanctify what we are
and order what we shall be,'[1]
in Jesus' name,
Amen.

Then lead everyone back inside for the hymn.

Music Give thanks with a grateful heart

Activity In many churches today, people receive ash on their foreheads in the shape of a cross, as a sign that they, like us, have said sorry to God. If you would like to do this, too, come forward and receive the ashes.

As people come forward, dip your thumb in the ash mixture and draw a cross on each forehead. As you do so, say:

Receive this ash as a sign that you have said sorry to God and are ready to make a fresh start.

Conclusion Jesus did not condemn the woman in the story, but he did tell her to stop doing what was wrong and to turn her life around. Now we have said sorry to God, let's take from here a new resolution for Lent: let's do the right thing. Let us pray:

Forgiving Lord,
send us out into the world with a new determination
to do what is right.
Make in us a clean heart, O God,
and renew a right spirit within us.[2]
Amen.

Give notices, announce the next all-age service and invite everyone to the feast. Hand round wet wipes for those who want to clean off their ashes.

1. Source unknown, *The SPCK Book of Christian Prayer*, 1995, p.243.
2. From Psalm 51:11.

Palm Sunday

Palms and praise

Theme	Welcoming Jesus and the story of the Passion
Scripture	Matthew 21:1–11; 26:14–27:66

Act of Witness*	Carrying the cross and palms through the parish
Running order	Total: 50 minutes
The Palms	
Welcome	Receiving palm crosses *(5 minutes)*
Introduction	Opening the theme
Storytelling 1	Interactive retelling of Matthew 21:1–11 *(10 minutes)*
Prayer action	Laying out the red carpet *(5 minutes)*
Music	Give me joy in my heart *(5 minutes)*
The Passion	
Activity/Exploring	What story do these things tell? – exploring the Passion story through objects *(10 minutes)*
Storytelling 2	Uncovering the story of the Passion *(10 minutes)*
Music	You are the King of Glory *(5 minutes)*
Conclusion	Closing prayer and invitation

* This is a suggestion to accompany each act of all-age worship in Holy Week. It could take place before or after the service.

Resources

- Palm crosses, enough for one each
- Laptop and projector *or* OHP and screen *or* big cards displaying the Crowd's lines *(see appendix)*
- A volunteer dressed in white, with bare feet, carrying a large wooden cross
- Leaders should wear something red or have some red pieces of cloth so that they can start off the 'red carpet'[1]
- Music and words
- Six stations around the church with the following:
  - A plate of pitta bread; some wine or red grape juice in a jug, plus cups
  - A bag of silver coins *(see appendix for Tempted)*
  - Something to represent Roman soldiers: a helmet, a picture of an army, a sword *(see appendix)*
  - A bowl of water
  - A wooden mallet and some big nails (perhaps a crown of thorns as well)
  - Some myrrh oil and strips of cotton or muslin *(see appendix for Epiphany)*
- A sign for each station: The Last Supper; Betrayed; Arrested; Condemned; Crucified; Buried

Leaders

Minimum: 2

- Leader/Storyteller 1
- Reader: Jesus/Storyteller 2

Optimum: 7+

- Leader *(Introduction and Conclusion)*
- Storytellers x 2
- Reader: Jesus
- Activity Leader/Explorer
- Music Leader
- Prayer Leader(s)

Suggestions for additional music

- Clap your hands, all you people
- Ride on, ride on in majesty
- We have a King who rides a donkey

1. This prayer action is the work of many hands. The original inspiration came from a symbolic action suggested by the Iona Community (*Stages on the Way*, Wild Goose Publications, 1998, p.73). It was changed and developed by the all-age worship team at St John's, Ivybridge and I have further adapted the form we used there to create this version.

Service

Act of Witness

Carrying the cross and palms/palm crosses through the parish.

This traditional feature of Palm Sunday is a natural all-age, all-sorts occasion – especially if a live donkey is involved! The Walk of Witness has inspired the other acts of witness which I have suggested for each of the Easter services.

Welcome

If you have not already done so before the Walk of Witness, hand out palm crosses as people arrive.

Introduction

Welcome to our Palm Sunday service which marks the beginning of Holy Week. Let's begin by hearing today's story – and we will need everyone's help to tell it.[2]

The congregation will play the part of the Crowd. Display their lines and rehearse them in chorus, encouraging loudness, cheering etc. The last two lines should be divided between the two sides of the congregation, with one asking the question and the other answering it. When you are ready, bring your Storyteller and the person reading the part of Jesus to the front.

Storytelling 1

Storyteller 1 When they had come near Jerusalem and had reached Bethphage, at the Mount of Olives, Jesus sent two disciples.

Jesus Go into the village ahead of you, and immediately you will find a donkey tied, and a colt with her; untie them and bring them to me. If anyone says anything to you, just say this, 'The Lord needs them.' And he will send them immediately.

Storyteller 1 This took place to fulfil what had been spoken through the prophet, saying,

'Tell the daughter of Zion,
Look, your king is coming to you,
humble, and mounted on a donkey,
and on a colt, the foal of a donkey.'

2. The lines are taken directly from Matthew's Gospel (NRSV): you may prefer to use a different translation.

The disciples went and did as Jesus had directed them; they brought the donkey and the colt, and put their cloaks on them, and he sat on them. A very large crowd spread their cloaks on the road, and others cut branches from the trees and spread them on the road. The crowds that went ahead of him and that followed were shouting:

Crowd — Hosanna to the Son of David!
Blessed is the one who comes in the name of the Lord!
Hosanna in the highest heaven!

Storyteller 1 — When he entered Jerusalem, the whole city was in turmoil.

Crowd A — Who is this?

Crowd B — This is the prophet Jesus from Nazareth in Galilee.

All cheer.

Prayer action

When Jesus entered Jerusalem, he was treated like a celebrity. The people cheered and laid down palm leaves to cover his path: this was their equivalent of laying down the red carpet for him. If Jesus came here today, would we give him the red-carpet treatment? What would we lay down for him to walk on? Today we will reflect on this as we pray an active prayer. *(Indicate your pre-arranged volunteer standing at the back of the church.)* Here we have our representative of Jesus with his cross: in a moment of quiet, consider what you will lay down for him to walk on. Will it be your coat or scarf? Will it be a bag or a hat? If it is red, then so much the better for making a red carpet, but it could be anything of any colour which you would willingly lay down.

The people lay down their things in the aisle and 'Jesus' walks barefoot across them to take his cross up to the altar.

Living Lord,
what will we give you?
Will we lay out the red carpet for you?
What will we lay down before you
as you walk into our lives?
(Pause.)
Come, Lord Jesus.
Amen.

Music Give me joy in my heart

Activity/Exploring

Palm Sunday is the start of Holy Week. During the week we will remember the events which led up to Jesus' death and his resurrection on Easter Day. Today we remind ourselves of what he suffered: this is called the story of his Passion. Around the church are six stations which mark stages in the Passion story. There is a collection of objects for you to look at, feel, smell, listen to and even taste. We will tell the whole story together later: for now, take some time to explore each station and to think about the things you find there. What story do they tell?

Allow plenty of time for people to move around the stations and explore. When you are ready, gather everyone around the first station: the bread and wine.

Storytelling 2

Jesus and his friends were Jewish. The last meal they shared together was at the Jewish festival of Passover. There was bread on the table and Jesus blessed it. He said that the bread was his body. He broke the bread and shared it with his friends. Then he took some wine and said that the wine was his blood. He poured it out and shared it. This meal was called the Last Supper. *(Place the sign, 'The Last Supper', on the station then move to the next one: the bag of coins.)*

One of Jesus' friends had a secret. He had accepted money from the powerful people who wanted to get rid of Jesus. After supper he went out to find them and their soldiers, and showed them where Jesus was so that they could arrest him. That was when Jesus was betrayed. *(Place the sign, 'Betrayed', on the station then move to the next one: the Roman armour and weapons.)*

Soldiers arrived with swords and an angry mob, but Jesus didn't fight or try to escape. The soldiers arrested him and all his friends ran away. *(Place the sign, 'Arrested', on the station then move to the next one: the bowl of water.)*

The Roman governor had to decide what to do with Jesus: should he let him go or put him to death? He was afraid of the angry crowds, so he ordered his soldiers to kill Jesus. Then he washed his hands to show that he didn't want to be blamed for condemning an innocent man. *(Place the sign, 'Condemned', on the station then move to the next one: the hammer and nails.)*

Jesus was crucified: soldiers nailed him to a cross and left him to die. *(Place the sign, 'Crucified', on the station then move to the next one: the myrrh and the cloth.)*

When he was dead, Jesus' friends took his body down from the cross and rubbed it with bitter myrrh and wrapped it in cloths. They buried him in a cave which was sealed with a huge rock. *(Place the sign, 'Buried', on the station.)*

Music

You are the King of Glory

Conclusion

On Palm Sunday we remember that the crowds who cheered when Jesus arrived in Jerusalem were the same crowds who jeered when he was killed on Good Friday. But that was not the end: three days later, a new, joyful story began and that is what we will be celebrating next Sunday on Easter Day. Let us pray:

Living Lord,
as we go out into the world,
may we remember the events of this Holy Week.
May we follow you to the cross and into the garden
and share with you the joy of new life.
Amen.

Give notices, announce the next all-age service and invite everyone to the feast.

Maundy Thursday

Washing feet

Theme	Loving and serving each other
Scripture	John 13:1–17, 31b–35

Act of Witness*	Foot-washing and food-sharing
Running order	Total: 50 minutes
Welcome	Opening the theme
Introduction	Sketch – Laying the table *(5 minutes)*
Storytelling	Sketch – Jesus washes his friends' feet *(5 minutes)*
Exploring	Why did he wash their feet? *(2 minutes)*
Music	The world is fully of smelly feet *(5 minutes)*
Prayer action	Foot-washing *(10 minutes)*
Activity 1	Sharing the feast *(10 minutes)*
Music	Meekness and majesty *(5 minutes)*
Activity 2	Stripping the altar *(8 minutes)*
Conclusion	Solemn prayer

* This is a suggestion to accompany each act of all-age worship in Holy Week. It could take place before or after the service.

Resources

- Several tables placed end-to-end at the front of church
- A long tablecloth
- A pile of napkins
- Three plates with flat bread such as pitta
- Three plates of cold roast lamb, cut into chunks
- Three bowls of parsley and/or rocket
- Three jugs of wine and/or red grape juice
- Lots of cups
- Music and words
- One or two large bowls
- Jugs full of water
- One large towel, big enough to tie around the waist
- Lots of small towels

Leaders

Minimum: 6

- Leader
- Cast x 5

Optimum: 11+

- Leader *(Introduction and Conclusion)*
- Storyteller/additional Prayer Leader
- Cast x 5 in modern or traditional dress
  Senior servant
  Junior servant
  Jesus
  James
  Simon Peter
  (Optional – an additional 10 disciples, non-speaking, to sit around the table)
- Explorer
- Music Leader
- Prayer Leader
- Activity Leader(s)

Suggestions for additional music

- Lord Jesus Christ
- Brother, sister, let me serve you

Service

Act of Witness Foot-washing and food-sharing.

As a witness and an example of service, take a team of volunteers to a central place in your community, such as the shopping centre or outside the town hall. Offer foot-washing or hand-washing to passers-by and have a large tray of pitta breads stuffed with lamb and rocket to give away.

Welcome Welcome to our Maundy Thursday service. The word 'Maundy' comes from a Latin word which means 'commandment': we'll be finding out all about that later, but first we need to tell the story of what happened on this day in Jesus' life. Let's go now to an upstairs room in Jerusalem. It is the Jewish feast of Passover and two servants are preparing the table for Jesus and his friends.

Introduction *The two servants lay out the items as they are mentioned.*

Senior servant: Now our guests will be here soon for their special Passover meal. We must make sure everything is ready. Best tablecloth?

Junior servant: Check.

Senior servant: Best napkins?

Junior servant: Check.

Senior servant: Flat bread?

Junior servant: Check. Why is it flat? Didn't they put any yeast in it?

Senior servant: No – that's the point, apparently. In the old days, their people were slaves in Egypt and the night they escaped, they had to make a quick getaway so they didn't have time to wait for the bread rations to rise. Now – roast lamb?

Junior servant: Check. Wouldn't a nice bit of beef have been nicer?

Senior servant: Had to be lamb, apparently – their God's orders. Next – bitter herbs?

Junior servant: I bet there's a reason for that, too.

Senior servant To remind them of their bitter experiences when they were slaves, I'm told. Finally, red wine – it's to do with the earth's fruitfulness. There must be something we've forgotten – oh yes, the water. They do insist on having a good wash before they eat – that'll be your job. They'll all need their feet washing – and there's at least thirteen of them.

Junior servant Thirteen? Have you seen how dusty the streets are with all these crowds? They'll be filthy!

Senior servant You're the youngest servant here – it's your job, so you'd better get used to it!

The junior servant stands to one side, holding the water and the towel.

Storytelling

The table is all prepared. Here is Jesus – and here are all his friends.

Jesus enters and sits at the head of the table. The servant bows. James enters and sits down to have his feet washed. The junior servant ties the towel around himself and kneels down with the bowl.

Jesus Wait a moment!

He goes to the servant and takes the bowl from him.

Let me – I'll do that.

Junior servant But!

Jesus No – really. *(He ties on the towel and kneels down)*

James *(As Jesus washes one foot)* But – teacher!

Jesus *(Ignoring his protests)* Give us your other foot, then.

James' feet are washed.

You're next, Peter.

Peter You're not going to wash my feet too?! No – no way.

Jesus If I don't wash you, you can't share this meal with me.

Peter *(Sitting down)* Well wash my head and my hands as well, then!

Jesus *(Washing his feet)* You're quite clean enough, now that I've washed your feet.

Exploring

What was Jesus doing? It was a servant's job to wash guests' feet before a meal. Those feet would have been dusty, sweaty and smelly. Jesus amazed his friends by getting down on his knees and washing their feet himself. He did this to show that rather than lord it over each other, we should help and serve other people, as he did. He spelt it out for them, so there could be no mistake. This is what he says in John's Gospel:

Jesus — So if I, your Lord and Teacher, have washed your feet, you also ought to wash one another's feet. For I have set you an example, that you also should do as I have done to you . . . I give you a new commandment, that you love one another. Just as I have loved you, you also should love one another.

Explorer — Jesus washed his friends' feet to give them a practical demonstration of his new commandment: 'Love each other'. As he had done all his life, he didn't just rely on words to make his point, but showed them love in action – and that is the message of Maundy Thursday.

Music

The world is full of smelly feet

Prayer action

Today we will pray an active prayer that we might learn to love and serve each other as Jesus did. We will take it in turns to wash each other's feet or hands. As you do so, and as your own feet or hands are washed, pray that God might speak through this simple action.

The Leader holds the first person's foot or hand over the bowl and pours a little water over it, then dries it. Then the first person washes the second person's foot or hand, and so on. If you have a large congregation, you may need more than one foot-washing station. When everyone has finished, gather people together.

Let us pray:
Foot-washing Lord,
you knelt with wet hands and rolled-up sleeves.
May our washing of feet and hands
be for us a reminder that we should love and serve one another,
in your name.
Amen.

Activity 1

It is time to share the feast. This simple food reminds the Jewish people of their history; it reminds us of the bread and wine which Jesus blessed at this meal and which Christians share together. But it is also good food which was shared with friends around a table. Come and eat.

Everyone gathers round the table to eat and drink.

Music

Meekness and majesty

Activity 2

The meal Jesus shared that night is called the Last Supper because it is the beginning of the end. One of Jesus' friends leaves the table and goes off to betray him. Jesus knows he will soon be arrested, condemned and killed. When Jesus was handed over to the soldiers, he was stripped of everything. To remember that moment when Jesus lost all he had, we will strip our altar and our table of all its decoration.

Volunteers take everything off the altar, leaving only the cross and the candles. Blow out the candles. Clear the table and fold up the cloth.

Conclusion

The story of Holy Week continues tomorrow, on Good Friday – but it doesn't end there. This story has a happy ending which we will celebrate on Easter Sunday. Until then, let us pray:

Bread-breaking, self-giving Lord,
having loved your own who were in the world,
you loved us to the end.
Give us hearts to love one another
as you loved us.
Amen.

Give notices and announce the next all-age service. (The feast has already taken place and the service ends on a quiet, solemn note.)

Good Friday

Jesus on the cross

Theme	Jesus' death
Scripture	John 18:1–19:42

Act of Witness*	Pilgrimage with the cross
Running order	Total: 50 minutes plus time beforehand to make the Easter Garden
Welcome	Making the Easter Garden *(before the service begins)*
Introduction	Opening the theme
Activity 1	'Jesus lived with us' – three interactive areas *(15 minutes)*
Music	My song is love unknown *(5 minutes)*
Activity 2/Storytelling	'Jesus died for us' – following the Stations of the Cross trail *(9 minutes)*
Exploring	Why is Good Friday 'good'? *(1 minute)*
Music	There is a green hill far away *(5 minutes)*
Prayer action	Leaving our burdens at the cross *(5 minutes)*
EITHER	*(If you are holding an all-age service on Easter Day)*
Conclusion	Candlelit vigil including the Taizé chant *(5 minutes)*
Music	Jesus, remember me *(5 minutes)*
OR	*(If you are not holding an all-age service on Easter Day)*
Conclusion	Cress crosses and the good news of life *(5 minutes)*
Music	Now the green blade riseth *(5 minutes)*

* This is a suggestion to accompany each act of all-age worship in Holy Week. It could take place before or after the service.

Resources

NB Some advance planning needed!

- About 10 days before this service, sow a large cress cross *(see appendix)*

You will also need:

- All the equipment for your church's Easter Garden
- Three areas around the church with the following signs and items:
  - *Jesus had a home and a family like us*: objects which might have been in Jesus' home *(see appendix)*
  - *Jesus met ordinary people in ordinary places*: several large sheets of sugar paper, each with a picture of Galilee or old Jerusalem in the middle; lots of local newspapers; scissors and glue-sticks *(see appendix)*
  - *Jesus died on the cross – but that was not the end*: equipment for sowing cress crosses *(see appendix)*
- Music and words
- Stations of the Cross *(see appendix)*
- At the back of church, place a collection of heavy, solid objects, each labelled 'Sorry'. Wrap them in plain paper to disguise them or cover any printing: for example, bricks, large stones, big tins, boxes, pieces of wood. Try to avoid anything which rattles
- A large cross to stand or lie on the floor in front of the altar. Next to it, place:
  - A collection of palm crosses, enough for one each
  - *(Only if using the first Conclusion)* Tea-lights, matches and tapers

Leaders

Minimum: 2

- Leader
- Easter Garden Co-ordinator

Optimum: 7+

- Leader *(Introduction and Conclusion)*
- Easter Garden Co-ordinator(s)
- Activity Leader 1
- Activity Leader 2/Storyteller
- Explorer
- Music Leader
- Prayer Leader

Suggestions for additional music

- Beneath the cross
- You spoke and worlds were formed
- From the falter of breath

Service

Act of Witness

Pilgrimage with the cross.

Many churches make some kind of Good Friday pilgrimage: this one should be explicitly a walk for one and all, advertised in the community as well as in the church. Either pick a local hilltop as your destination and walk there from your church, carrying a large wooden cross between you, or walk from the centre of your community to a local church. At the end of the walk, offer a (well-publicised!) feast of hot cross buns.

Welcome

About 30 minutes before you plan to start the service, invite everyone to help you make the Easter Garden, according to your church's custom. Emphasise hands-on interactivity: it is more important to involve people, especially children, in the creative process than it is to fashion a 'perfect' garden.

Introduction

Welcome to our Good Friday service. Today we will be thinking about Jesus and what happened to him on Good Friday. We will try to answer the question that people often ask: 'Why is Good Friday called "good"?'

Activity 1

Here we have three areas to explore which will help us to think about Jesus' life and death. The first is called, 'Jesus had a home and a family like us,' and it is like the Home Corner which many of you may have in school. Come in and play with the sort of toys Jesus might have played with when he was a boy; try dressing up in the sort of clothes he might have worn.

The second area is called, 'Jesus met ordinary people in ordinary places.' Here are lots of pictures of places which may look exotic to us – but they were places which Jesus would have known as well as we know our local streets and shops. Around each of these pictures, we can stick pictures of our own everyday places and familiar people, by cutting them out of these local newspapers.

The third area is called, 'Jesus died on the cross – but that was not the end.' Here we can plant cress seeds to make crosses which will live and grow.

Take some time now to explore each of these three areas.

Music

My song is love unknown

Activity 2/Storytelling

Now we come to the story of what happened on Good Friday. Jesus was in trouble with powerful people because they were afraid he would take away their power. One of his friends told them where they could find Jesus and he was arrested and taken to the Roman governor of Jerusalem – a man called Pontius Pilate. So our story today begins with Jesus and Pilate, and Pilate has a decision to make: will he let Jesus go, or will he condemn him to death?

The Good Friday story is often told in pictures. These are called the Stations of the Cross and they mark the different stages of Jesus' journey. There are usually fourteen of them, but today we have seven and they are spread all around the church. Can you find picture number one?
Find the picture and gather round it.
The Roman governor decided that Jesus would have to be killed. Jesus didn't say anything.

Can you find picture number two?
Find the picture and gather round it.
Jesus had to carry his big, heavy, wooden cross through the streets.

Can you find picture number three?
Find the picture and gather round it.
The cross was so heavy that sometimes Jesus fell down.

Can you find picture number four?
Find the picture and gather round it.
The soldiers took Jesus' clothes.

Can you find picture number five?
Find the picture and gather round it.
The soldiers nailed Jesus to the cross.

Can you find picture number six?
Find the picture and gather round it.
Jesus said, 'It's finished.' Then he died.

Can you find picture number seven?
Find the picture and gather round it.
Jesus' friends laid his body in the grave.

Exploring

The events of Good Friday are so horrible and sad that people often ask, 'Why is Good Friday called "good"?' It is good because it is all about love. Because Jesus loves us, he wants to be close to us – so he became a human being like us and had all the ordinary, wonderful, difficult and amazing experiences of growing up in this world. So he knows what every bit of life is like because he has been through it, too – and on Good Friday he went through death as well, so he knows what dying is like. He did that to share it all with us, because he loves us.

Because Jesus loves us, he also wants us to be close to God, our Father. The bad things we all do – because we are only human – keep us separated from God. So Jesus gave his life for us so that we can get right with God and be close to him forever.

Music

There is a green hill far away

Prayer action

When he died on the cross, Jesus made it possible for us to leave all our wrongdoing behind us. We need this because the messes we have made and the wrongs we have done can be like a heavy weight, dragging us down. Jesus said he would take these burdens from us; in return, we receive God's forgiveness which gives us a completely fresh start. In preparation for our prayers today, let us all take a moment to think of anything we have done or failed to do which still weighs heavy on our hearts. *(Pause.)* At the back of the church, there is a pile of heavy weights which represent those things for which we need to say sorry. You are invited to take a weight and leave it at the foot of the cross, as a sign that you have left your burden in Jesus' hands. In return, take away with you this little cross as a sign of God's love and forgiveness.

Give people enough time to think before carrying the weights forward. When all have returned to their seats with a cross, end with the following:

Loving Lord,
may this cross be for us
a reminder that you have taken away all our sins
and a sign of your everlasting love for us.
Amen.

<u>EITHER</u> *(If you are holding an all-age service on Easter Day)*

Conclusion

In many churches on the night before Easter, a vigil is held as people sit quietly in the dark church, waiting for the dawn of Easter Day. We will finish our service today with an opportunity to sit quietly for a time and simply wait. Come forward and light a candle. If you would like to join in the song, the words are simple: 'Jesus, remember me when you come into your kingdom.' The robber who was crucified next to Jesus said this, and we can all ask the same thing: 'Jesus, remember me when you come into your kingdom.'

Turn the lights off, light the candles and after a short period of silence, begin the Taizé chant. Begin quietly, grow louder and then end quietly.

Music

Jesus, remember me

<u>OR</u> *(If you are not holding an all-age service on Easter Day)*

Conclusion

But this cross is not the end of the story. After he died, Jesus came alive again! The good news which we celebrate on Easter Day is the best news ever: death is not the end. Because God loves us so much, he sent Jesus to break down the barrier of death so that after we die, we can follow him into heaven and live forever with God.

Bring forward some cress crosses, including the one you planted earlier.

That is why we made these cress crosses. Take your cross home, water it and watch it grow: let it be a living reminder that God's gift to us at Easter is the gift of life. Let us pray:
Father, we thank you for your everlasting love
which, through your Son,
has given us everlasting life.
Amen.

Music

Now the green blade riseth

Give notices, announce the next all-age service and invite everyone to the hot cross bun feast.

Easter Day

Jesus is alive!

Theme	Resurrection
Scripture	Matthew 28:1–10

Act of Witness*	Bonfire and fireworks
Running order	Total: 40–50 minutes
	(In its shorter form, this service could be part of a service of Holy Communion.)
Welcome and introduction	Bringing lit candles into a dark church *(5 minutes)*
Music	Jesus Christ is risen today *(5 minutes)*
Storytelling	Dramatisation of Matthew 28:1–10 *(10 minutes)*
Music	All in an Easter Garden *(5 minutes)*
Exploring	Why did Jesus rise from the dead? – visual explanation *(5 minutes)*
Prayer/Activity	Living crosses *(5 or 15 minutes)*
Music	Led like a lamb *(5 minutes)*
Conclusion	Alleluia and invitation

* This is a suggestion to accompany each act of all-age worship in Holy Week. It could take place before or after the service.

Resources

- Paschal candle or other large candle
- Votive candles
- Matches and tapers
- *(Optional)* Worship flags/angel wings *(see appendix)*
- Music and words
- Percussion instruments for general use
- Stop/go sign (like road-menders use – a lollipop with a red 'Stop' on one side and a green 'Go' on the other)
- Large 'living cross' *(see appendix)*

Either

- Lots of small 'living crosses' *(see appendix)*, placed on the altar in baskets

Or

- The raw materials for these crosses *(see appendix)*
- Wool or twine
- Scissors and secateurs

Leaders

Minimum: 5

- Leader
- Readers/Cast x 4

Optimum: 8 *(or 9)*

- Leader *(Introduction and Conclusion)*
- Readers/Cast x 4
  Mary
  Guard
  Angel
  Jesus
  (If using costume and props, dress all in plain tunics – white for the Angel and Jesus. Mary holds a small box, the Guard has a sword and the Angel has worship flags/angel wings)
- Explorer
- Music Leader
- Prayer Leader
- Activity Leader *(Optional)*

Suggestions for additional music

- Thine be the glory
- Now the green blade riseth
- All heaven declares

Service

Act of Witness

Bonfire and fireworks.

This is most effective at a Dawn Rise service at 5 am, but could also be used before the main morning service. Light a contained fire at least 30 minutes before the start of the service: a garden incinerator is good for this purpose, especially as it has a lid which will keep the fire safe while the service continues inside. Fireworks announce Easter with a bang; sparklers around the fire are also a wonderful way to welcome the light.

Welcome and introduction

Begin the service outside the church with the Paschal candle. Distribute votive candles among the people.

Jesus is the light of the world;
his light conquers the darkness.

Light the Paschal candle and the votive candles, then carry the Paschal candle into the dark church with the people following. When everyone is inside, turn all the lights on and blow out the candles.

The Lord is my strength and my song,
and he has become my salvation.

Welcome to our celebration of Easter. There is a word which is especially appropriate for today: 'Alleluia!' It means, 'Praise God!' Let's raise the roof with our 'Alleluia!' after this opening sentence:
Jesus Christ is risen today.
Alleluia!

Music

Jesus Christ is risen today

Storytelling

(NB This section can be adapted depending on your time and resources. It can simply be read from the front by different voices, rather like a radio play, letting the words and sound effects paint the pictures. Or it could be read from the front and enhanced by visual effects (the gravestone/angel wings) and by some symbolic action, such as Mary falling at Jesus' feet. Alternatively, it could be performed in full costume by actors who have learnt their words and rehearsed their actions. My directions are for this kind of presentation – they can be adapted as required.)

At the front, a large circle of white fabric represents the circular stone in front of the tomb. It conceals the Angel, who is holding two semi-circular worship flags/angel wings together to form the stone. The Guard stands in front of it.

Mary *(Walking down the aisle, talking to the congregation)* It's dark and cold this morning. No one about – even the sun isn't up yet. I've got a basket full of spices for Jesus. It's three days since he died – three days since they nailed him to the cross. What with the Sabbath in between, I couldn't have come any sooner. But I've come now with some spices for his poor body – the last and the least I could do for him, now that he's in his grave. Come with me.

Guard *(Talking to the congregation)* 'Stand guard,' they told me, so that no body-snatching goes on. We want none of those tall tales about dead men walking. This bloke Jesus – he must be special, because the Guv'nor himself ordered an armed guard. So that's why me and the boys got sent down here with strict instructions to seal this stone in front of his grave – and that's why we've been out here all night. So move along please. There's nothing to see.

Mary Now that I'm nearly there, I realise that I didn't think this through. Jesus' body is in that cave, behind that huge stone. There's no way I can move it on my own. What am I going to do? Come with me.

Guard Who goes there? Oh, it's only a woman. You're not going in there, love. More than my job's worth. It's only a body – keep away, please. There's nothing to see.

A tremendous sound: a loud, low chord on the organ, a drum roll or similar. The circular stone breaks apart and becomes angel wings beating around a white-robed figure. The Guard runs off.

Angel Don't be frightened! You're looking for Jesus, but he's not here. He's not dead any more – he's alive! He's alive! He's ALIVE!

The angel swiftly walks the length of the aisle, moving his wings.

Jesus walks to the front and turns, arms outstretched.

Jesus Mary – it's me.

Mary My Lord! *(She falls at his feet)*

Music All in an Easter Garden

Exploring *If using the angel wings, position the Angel at the front again, with the wings making the circular stone as before. Stand in front of the stone.*

When Jesus died, his round gravestone was like a full stop and it looked as if his grave was a dead end.

Show the 'Stop' sign.

Being human, he had lived and died like us – but, being God, Jesus was greater than death and he came alive again. Jesus turned that dead end into a gateway which can lead us all into everlasting life with God.

The gravestone opens into angel wings; you stand in front with the 'Go' sign.

Because he loves us, God wants us to be close to him forever, so he sent Jesus to give us the greatest gift of all: the gift of life. Our good news on Easter Day is the best possible news: death is not the end because God loves us with an everlasting love and he is always, always with us. Alleluia!

Prayer/Activity *Hold up the large 'living cross'.*

Today, the cross that Jesus died on has become the cross of life. This cross reminds us of that good news. It was made from branches which looked like dead wood. But now this cross is starting to come alive again – there are new buds and leaves on it. It is a living reminder of the good news of Easter: life and death are followed by life again.[1]

Then either this *(If they are finding ready-made crosses)*

All around the church there are living crosses like this – enough for one each. Who can help me find them?

Allow enough time for the crosses to be found and distributed.

1. See John Moses, *The Sacrifice of God*, The Canterbury Press Norwich, 1992, p.201.

Or this

(If they are making their own crosses)

Here are some budding twigs and some spring flowers. If you would like to, come forward and use these things to make a living cross of your own.

Allow enough time for people to complete their crosses and return to their seats.

Make sure everyone has a living cross, then gather the people together in prayer:

Take your living cross home and place it in water: as the leaves begin to unfurl, they will remind you that God's gift to us at Easter is the gift of life. Let's hold these living crosses for a moment in prayer.

Pause.

Our Easter prayer over these living crosses begins and ends with a big 'Alleluia'. Let us say together:
Alleluia!
From this dead wood, new life springs green;
from the empty tomb leaps the risen Lord;
from Friday's cross grows the gift of eternal life.
Alleluia!

Music

Led like a lamb

Hand out the percussion instruments and encourage general participation! The Angel should also move around the church waving the angel wings, which now become worship flags.

Conclusion

This is the day that the Lord has made;
we will rejoice and be glad in it.
Alleluia!

Give notices, announce the next all-age service and invite everyone to the feast.

The Annunciation

The angel's visit

Theme	Mary's obedience and God's care
Scripture	Luke 1:26–38

Running order	Total: 50 minutes
Welcome	Drawing round our hands *(5 minutes)*
Introduction	Opening the theme
Storytelling	Dramatised dialogue – Luke 1:26–38 *(5 minutes)*
Exploring	What might Mary have replied? Speech bubbles *(10 minutes)*
Music	For Mary, mother of our Lord *(5 minutes)*
Activity	Handmade angels *(15 minutes)*
Prayer action	Carried on angels' wings – creative prayer *(5 minutes)*
Music	The Virgin Mary had a baby boy *(5 minutes)*
Conclusion	Angel prayer

Resources

- Either set up the church with tables and chairs, café-style, or place a number of tables to one side. On each of the tables, you should have the following:
  - Pieces of white A4 card
  - Pens, pencils, crayons
  - Scissors
  - Sellotape or white address labels
- Music and words
- Angelic sound effect (e.g. a chord on the organ or a special effect on an electronic keyboard – aim for something loud, lovely and unearthly)
- Pieces of A4 paper, each one covered with a large, empty speech bubble
- Whiteboard / flip chart / large piece of board covered with a large speech bubble which contains the words, 'Here I am – God's servant. Let everything happen to me just like you said'
- Marker pens for whiteboard / flip chart
- Angel templates *(see appendix)*
- Lots of cardboard tubes (from toilet rolls)

Leaders

Minimum: 3

- Leader
- Cast x 2

Optimum: 8+

- Leader *(Introduction and Conclusion)*
- Storyteller
- Cast x 2
  Mary, wearing something plain, with bare feet
  Gabriel, wearing something bright or white, with trainers
- Explorer
- Music Leader
- Activity Leader(s)
- Prayer Leader

Suggestions for additional music

- The angel Gabriel from heaven came
- Magnificat

Service

Welcome

As people arrive, give them a piece of thin A4 card and invite them to draw around their hands, cut out the handprints and write their name on them, then leave them at the altar as a way of saying, 'Here I am, Lord'.

Introduction

Today we will be hearing the story of the angel Gabriel's visit to Mary. We celebrate this occasion on the 25th March because it is exactly nine months before Christmas: today was the day when Mary learnt that God had chosen her to give birth to his Son. This is what happened.

Storytelling

This took place in Nazareth, a small town in Galilee. God sent the angel Gabriel to a young woman who was soon to be married. Her name was Mary.

Angelic sound effects as Gabriel enters.

Gabriel: Greetings, favoured one! The Lord is with you.

Storyteller: Mary was completely stunned. She wondered who this unearthly creature was and what he was talking about.

Gabriel: Don't be frightened, Mary, because God is very pleased with you. So you are going to become pregnant and have a son, and you will call him Jesus. He will be great: he'll be called the Son of the Most High, and God will make him king of the Jews. He will reign over God's people for ever, and his kingdom will never end.

Mary: How can I have a baby? I'm a virgin!

Gabriel: The Holy Spirit will come upon you, and the power of God will overshadow you; your child will be holy; he will be called the Son of God. Your relative Elizabeth is also expecting a son. She's six months pregnant, even though she thought she was far too old to have children. You see – nothing is impossible with God.

Exploring

Cut into the scene: the storytellers freeze.

Before Mary answers the angel, let's just pause the action. If you were in her shoes, what would you say to the angel Gabriel? Here are lots of empty speech bubbles: gather round them all and think what *you* would say at this point.

Hand round the speech bubbles. Allow plenty of time for people to think and write (the storytellers may join in too) then invite everyone to sit back down.

Here are some of the things we might have said in Mary's position: *(read out some contributions.)*

Now, let's rewind our scene slightly and see what she actually said.

Gabriel — The Holy Spirit will come upon you, and the power of God will overshadow you; your child will be holy; he will be called the Son of God. Your relative Elizabeth is also expecting a son. She's six months pregnant, even though she thought she was far too old to have children. You see – nothing is impossible with God.

Mary — Here I am – God's servant. Let everything happen to me just like you said.

Show the board with the large speech bubble containing Mary's words.

Let's take a moment to think about what Mary said. What words would you use to describe Mary now? What do you think about the answer she gave the angel?

Let people think and talk for a short time before asking for their answers. Try to find value in them all and write them around the speech bubble.

We often take Mary for granted because her story is so familiar to us, but today is the occasion when we remember just what a momentous thing she agreed to. God chose her for his most important job – being the mother of his Son – and she accepted. So we have Mary as well as God to thank for Jesus being born into the world.

Music

For Mary, mother of our Lord

Activity

What about the other character in our story? The angel Gabriel makes quite an entrance. In school Nativity plays, Gabriel is often played by a blonde girl in a sparkly white dress, but he must have been rather more unearthly and terrifying. He suddenly appears in

Mary's kitchen and announces that the Lord is with her: no wonder the next thing he says is, 'Don't be frightened!' Mary is clearly shocked and speechless in the presence of this messenger from God.

However, after this first life-changing appearance, God's angels pop up quite regularly in the lives of Mary and Joseph. As Mary's pregnancy progresses, an angel reassures Joseph, and later directs the shepherds to the stable; angels warn Mary and Joseph that Herod's soldiers are coming to kill Jesus, and another angel tells them when it is safe to go back home. So from the minute his life began to the time when he settled in Nazareth to grow up, Jesus was watched over by God's angels who intervened in his life in very practical ways.

Today we are going to make our own practical angels to remind us that God can help us, too, in our daily lives.

Show the angel templates.

Here is a practical angel who has come to do God's work. This figure is surrounded by a heavenly glow – but he or she also has rolled-up sleeves and something sensible on his or her feet. Take some time now to make this angel look like someone who could get God's work done.

Hand round the angel templates. Allow plenty of time for drawing and decoration. Then get your cardboard tube and demonstrate the next stage.

Now cut out your angel along the dotted lines and fold and stick it around the cardboard tube, like this, to make it stand up.

Hand round the cardboard tubes and give people time to do this.

Now, what's missing? *(Elicit the response, 'Wings!')*

Do you remember the handprints we each left at the altar at the beginning of the service? If you go and find yours now, you can fit them together to make a perfect pair of wings – like this.

Demonstrate by sticking on your own cut-out handprints, then allow plenty of time for people to collect and stick on their handprints.

Prayer action

Now we can use these practical angels in our prayers today. Take some time now to think of anyone you know who is particularly in need of God's care and guidance at the moment. *(Pause.)* Now write or draw those people on your angel's wings.

Allow some time for people to complete their prayers, then encourage them to take their prayer-angels up to the altar. Offer the prayers with these words:

Almighty God,
your angels watched over your Son from his very beginning.
May you hold all these people in your care,
watching over those we remember today,
those we have forgotten
and all of us, now and always.
Amen.

Music

The Virgin Mary had a baby boy

Conclusion

Take your prayer-angels home and use them to encourage your prayers, but remember that you don't need a prayer-angel or a real angel to bring you close to God. Picture these wings made of your hands. *(Hold your hands out together, fanned in the position of the angel wings.)* You just need to put those hands together *(demonstrate)* and pray. Let us pray:

God of all angels and all of us,
you chose Mary to bear your Son – and she said, 'Yes.'
As we go about our daily lives,
may we listen for your call
and have the courage to answer as she did.
Amen.

Give notices, announce the next all-age service and invite everyone to the feast.

The Ascension

Theme	Christ's Ascension – Mission: Universal
Scripture	Acts 1:1–11

Running order	Total: 50 minutes
Welcome	Incense prayers *(5 minutes)*
Introduction	Opening the theme
Storytelling 1/Activity	The Ascension told interactively with puppets *(15 minutes)*
Music	All heaven declares *(5 minutes)*
Storytelling 2	The disciple's tale *(5 minutes)*
Exploring	'Why did Jesus have to go back up into heaven?' Visual exploration *(5 minutes)*
Music	Christ triumphant, ever reigning *(5 minutes)*
Prayer action	Balloons – interactive intercessions *(5 minutes)*
Music	Majesty, worship his majesty *(5 minutes)*
Conclusion	Closing prayer and invitation

Resources

- A packet of incense *(see appendix)*
- A small charcoal brazier for use outside, or a thurible or other incense-burner for use inside. If you have lots of people, the outside option is preferable, as too much incense at once will choke a small burner
- Charcoal and matches
- A sign which reads, *O Lord, let my prayer be counted as incense before you*
- Puppets or cut-outs; performance cloth *(see appendix)*
- Music and words
- A cardboard sun, covered with shiny gold foil or glitter
- Ordinary latex balloons, filled with helium *(see appendix)* and tied with a long string
- Marker pens

Leaders

Minimum: 6

- Leader
- Cast x 4
- Storyteller / Disciple 3

Optimum: 11

- Leader *(Introduction and Conclusion)*
- Cast / puppeteers x 5
  Jesus
  Disciple 1 handling group 1
  Disciple 2 handling group 2
  Disciple 3 handling group 3
  Angels also handling the cloud
- Storyteller (Simon), wearing a simple robe or tunic
- Explorer
- Helper with high-powered torch
- Music Leader
- Prayer Leader

Suggestions for additional music

- Meekness and majesty
- Crown him with many crowns
- Jesus shall reign where'er the sun

Service

Welcome

Place your small charcoal burner and dish of incense granules next to the sign which reads, *O Lord, let my prayer be counted as incense before you*. As people arrive, a helper should be on hand to light the charcoal and help people add a few grains of incense as a sign of their prayer.

Introduction

Today, as our incense prayers are lifted up to heaven, we come together to celebrate the Ascension: this was the moment when the resurrected Jesus was lifted up into heaven. The Ascension is a dramatic story: let's find out exactly what happened.

Storytelling 1/Activity

Jesus — Now listen – you must stay in Jerusalem and wait. I promise you that any day now, you will be given great power: the power of God's Holy Spirit.

Disciple 1 — Great power?

Disciple 2 — Us?

Disciple 3 — Wow!

Disciple 1 — What's your plan, then, Jesus?

Disciple 2 — Does that mean you are going to save Israel now?

Disciple 3 — What is our mission?

Jesus — I can't tell you – God's in charge of all that. But I can promise you the power of the Holy Spirit, and when you receive that power your job is to be my representatives and spokespeople not just here, in this city and this country, but all over the world. My work on earth is your work, now. That's the plan.

The cloud comes down and Jesus disappears behind it. The cloud lifts Jesus up and out of sight.

Disciple 1 — Where's he going?

Disciple 2 — He's up in that cloud!

Disciple 3 — Don't leave us!

Angel — Men of Galilee, why are you gawping at the sky? Jesus has gone back up into heaven, where he belongs, and one day he'll come back the same way.

Disciple 1 — What do we do now?

Disciple 2 — Who's running the mission now?

Disciple 3 — How can we do it on our own?

Music

All heaven declares

Storytelling 2

My name is Simon and I was – am – one of Jesus' disciples. What I loved about him when I first met him was that he was the Man with the Plan. When he was alive, it all seemed pretty clear: he was the Saviour, the Messiah, who had come to make everything right. Then he was killed on the cross and we were all left wondering, 'So what's happened to the plan? What do we do now?' Before we even had time to think of an answer to that one, Jesus came back! He rose from the dead and appeared to us, and kept on appearing. He was no ghost, either: he shared meals with us, we touched him and felt the fresh wounds left by his crucifixion. He talked to us, like in the old days, and gave us instructions. At last we could ask him about the plan: what was going to happen now? Was he going to stay with us and make everything right with the world?

That was when Jesus dropped the bombshell: he couldn't tell us when anything was going to happen, but we, the disciples, would receive the power of God's Holy Spirit, and then it would be all down to us! Our job was to be witnesses for Jesus across the world. He said, 'Here's the plan: you, my disciples, are going to do my world-changing work yourselves. With God's help, *you* are going to make it happen.' And before we know it, there's a cloud, some angels and he's gone!

Jesus had left us, but we remembered his promise. We stayed in Jerusalem, like he told us to, and waited for this amazing power he said he would send us. It was an exciting time, but also rather terrifying. What would the Holy Spirit's power be like? Could we really be given the strength to do Jesus' work without him?

Exploring

Stand behind the performance cloth, behind which your helper with the torch is hiding.

Those poor disciples – they had just got used to Jesus being with them again, when he disappeared into heaven. They must have asked themselves, 'Why?' and that is the question we are going to explore now. Why did Jesus have to go back up into heaven?

When Jesus was on earth, his influence was local, restricted to first-century Jerusalem, Judea, Galilee and the surrounding area. In heaven, Jesus is one with God the Father and God the Holy Spirit and his power can go global: he can reach out across the world, across time and space, into the lives of individuals and the life of his church.

Think of it like this. *(Hold your shiny sun so that it just pokes above the performance cloth; your helper targets it with a beam of torchlight.)* If the sun didn't rise, but stayed just above the horizon all day, a few beams of sunlight would reach a few trees and houses while the rest of the landscape stayed in shadow. But if the sun rises to the place where it belongs, high up in the sky, *(lift the sun up; your helper illuminates it fully)* then it can give light to all of us, everywhere.

When Jesus ascended into heaven, God the Son took his rightful place alongside God the Father and God the Holy Spirit. The disciples may have felt that Jesus had left them with 'Mission: Impossible' but in fact he was planning 'Mission: Universal' and the first part of that plan was his return to heaven, whence he would send the Holy Spirit to inspire and empower his disciples. That is why we celebrate his Ascension today.

Music

Christ triumphant, ever reigning

Prayer action

Hand round the helium-filled balloons.

Today we remember Jesus being physically lifted up into heaven, and we will use this idea in our prayers. In a moment of quiet, let us call to mind a person or a situation in need of our prayers. *(Pause.)* Write your prayer intention on this balloon which is ready to rise up.

Allow enough time for everyone to complete their prayer, then gather outside with the balloons.

We will offer these prayers together: as we say 'Amen', release the balloons.
Heavenly Father,
may the wind of your Holy Spirit lift these prayers to you
in Jesus' name.

Release the balloons into the sky.

Amen!

Music Majesty, worship his majesty

Conclusion Almighty God,
as we go out into the world,
may we remember that there is nothing and no one
beyond the reach of your power and love.
Help us to do your work of love in the lives of others,
in Jesus' name.
Amen.

Give notices, announce the next all-age service and invite everyone to the feast.

Pentecost

Wind and Fire

Theme	The Holy Spirit
Reading	Acts 2:1–12, 41

Running order	Total: 50 minutes
Welcome	Lighting votive candles *(5 minutes)*
Introduction	Opening the theme
Activity	Flame crowns *(15 minutes)*
Music	The Spirit lives to set us free *(5 minutes)*
Storytelling	Interactive retelling of Acts 2:1–12, 41 *(5 minutes)*
Music	All over the world *(5 minutes)*
Exploring	What is the Holy Spirit like? Brainstorming with visual aids *(5 minutes)*
Prayer action	Bubble-blowing – active intercessions *(5 minutes)*
Music	Spirit of the Living God *(5 minutes)*
Conclusion	Closing prayer and invitation

Resources

- Tea-lights, matches and tapers
- Large Bible
- Music and words
- Pots of bubble mixture
- Electric pedestal fan
- For the flame crowns: *(see appendix)*
  - Strips of card
  - Red and yellow acetate or card
  - Scissors
  - Sellotape or stapler

Leaders

Minimum: 1

- Leader

Optimum: 6+

- Leader *(Introduction and Conclusion)*
- Activity Leader
- Storyteller
- Music Leader(s)
- Explorer
- Prayer Leader

Suggestions for additional music

- Colours of day
- Lord, pour out your Spirit

Service

Welcome

As people arrive, invite them to light a candle and place it on the altar, as a way of saying, 'Here I am, Lord'.

Introduction

Today is the festival of Pentecost. Amazing things happened to Jesus' friends on this day, and we'll be hearing their story later on. It is a special story because it tells us about the super-powerful actions of God's Holy Spirit. Today's service is called 'Wind and Fire' because although no one knows what God's Holy Spirit looks like, in the Pentecost story he appears in two weird and wonderful ways: he arrives as a wild wind which blows inside a house, even though all the doors and windows are shut, and he appears as a fire which touches people but doesn't burn them. The first thing we are going to do today is make ourselves some fiery crowns which won't burn us.

Activity

Everyone makes a flame crown *(see appendix for illustration)*. Use a long strip of card to make a simple circlet, then cut out flame shapes and attach them. Stick or staple the tips of big flames together to make them stand up.

Music

The Spirit lives to set us free

Storytelling

When everyone has completed their flame crowns, invite them to gather round. Open a large Bible.

Today's story – the story of Pentecost – happened after Jesus had gone up to heaven. His friends waited for what would happen next. They waited and waited, because Jesus had promised that he would give them God's power – the power of the Holy Spirit. But he didn't say exactly when, so all the disciples sat in the same house and prayed and waited together. They must have got fed up with waiting.

Encourage everyone to flop about as if they are bored and tired of just sitting around.

Then: guess what? Even though all the doors and windows were shut, a big wind started to blow inside the house.

Encourage everyone to make the sound of a wind.

It got stronger and stronger . . .

Encourage everyone to make the sound of a hurricane.

Then: guess what? Jesus' best friend, Peter, suddenly had flames coming out of the top of his head – but they didn't burn him at all. The fire caught each of the friends in turn, until every one of them had a fire over his head.

All put on flame crowns.

The amazing thing was, this fire didn't hurt them, any more than these flames hurt us. Instead, the fire of the Holy Spirit made Jesus' friends feel strong and powerful, as if they were wearing crowns.

Encourage everyone to sit or stand tall, as if they were all-powerful kings and queens.

Then: guess what? They rushed outside into the city's main square and stood up in front of a huge crowd of pilgrims and tourists. And Jesus' friends started telling everyone about Jesus – in all kinds of foreign languages! None of the disciples even knew how to count up to ten in another language, but suddenly a family from Greece heard them speaking Greek and a woman from Rome heard them speaking Latin.

Everybody heard all about Jesus and wanted to join his disciples. Three thousand people were baptised, and this was when the Church began. Everything that we now know as the Church was kick-started by God's Holy Spirit. That day – Pentecost – was the Church's birthday.

Music All over the world

Exploring

The story of Pentecost can help us discover what the power of God's Holy Spirit is like. What is one way in which the Holy Spirit appears?

When someone says 'wind', turn on the electric fan.

What is the wind like?

Invite answers, drawing out those things which are like the Holy Spirit, too, such as:

- You can't see it, but you can feel it and you can see what it does.
- It can be strong or gentle.
- It generates energy (wind turbines).

How else does the Holy Spirit appear in today's story?

When someone says 'fire', light the taper and then a line of 12 tea-lights.

What is fire like?

Invite answers, drawing out those things which are like the Holy Spirit, too, such as:

- It's catching.
- It's a powerful form of energy. For Jesus' disciples, the Holy Spirit gave them new energy: they felt fired up and ready to do God's work.

Prayer action

The word which the Bible uses for Spirit is the same word it uses for both 'wind' and 'breath'. And the word 'Spirit' gives us words like 'inspiration'. The Holy Spirit is like God's breath, breathing on us and inspiring us with new energy and strength. There is a Pentecost hymn which contains this prayer:

Breathe on me, breath of God,
fill me with life anew.[1]

For our prayers today, we're going to use our breath.

1. Edwin Hatch (1835-1889).

Produce pots of bubble mixture with blowers.

Breathe onto these bubble blowers and watch the bubbles fill with your breath: as you do so, think about anyone you know who feels tired or sad and who really needs to feel energetic, strong and inspired. Let's pray for the Holy Spirit of Pentecost to breathe into our lives.

Everyone blows bubbles. Then as the bubbles are still floating, gather round to say the closing words.

Breathe on us, breath of God,
fill us with life anew.
Amen.

Music

Spirit of the Living God

Conclusion

May we know God's powerful Holy Spirit
moving among and between and within us all,
now and always.
Amen.

Give notices, announce the next all-age service and invite everyone to the feast.

Trinity Sunday

Father, Son and Holy Spirit

Theme	The Trinity; the work of the Church
Scripture	Matthew 28:16–20

Running order	Total: 50 minutes
Welcome	Paper-chain prayers – triple loops *(5 minutes)*
Introduction	Opening the theme
Activity	Exploring the Trinity shape and stations *(15 minutes)*
Music	I bind unto myself today *(5 minutes)*
Storytelling	Reading Jesus' words in Matthew 28:18–20 *(2 minutes)*
Exploring	'What is the job of the Church?' – three interactive areas *(13 minutes)*
Music	Father, we love you *(5 minutes)*
Prayer action	Trinity twist – creative prayer *(5 minutes)*
Conclusion	Closing prayer and invitation

Resources

- Strips of paper
- Pens, Sellotape and scissors
- Trinity Activity *(see appendix)*
- Interactive areas for Exploring *(see appendix)*
- Music and words
- Lengths of cord or wool in gold, white and red, knotted together at one end. A 20 cm length should make a 10 cm plait with enough for a knot and a 'tail' at both ends. (You may like to use something longer and more substantial, such as fabric strips, for your demonstration plait.) You should order the colours from left to right as follows: white, red, gold. Make sure that there is enough for everyone to make a plait

Leaders

Minimum: 1

- Leader

Optimum: 6

- Leader *(Introduction and Conclusion)*
- Activity Leader
- Storyteller
- Explorer
- Music Leader
- Prayer Leader

Suggestions for additional music

- To God be the glory
- Lord of all hopefulness

Service

Welcome

As people arrive, invite them to write their prayer intentions on three strips of paper and join them together as a mini paper-chain, in which the last link goes through both the first and second loops, forming an inseparable triple loop of prayer. Your Prayer Leader will need to help with this.

Introduction

Today we celebrate Trinity Sunday, which is the day in the Church year when we especially remember the Holy Trinity. There is only one God, but he has three persons: God the Father, God the Son and God the Holy Spirit. God the Father created us; we observed the events of his Son's life throughout Christmas and Easter, and at Pentecost, we celebrated the coming of the Holy Spirit and the birth of the Church. So today is when we pause and consider this wonderful mystery, our Three-in-One God.

Activity

Christians have tried to explain the mystery of the Trinity in many different ways. Some of those ways are laid out here for us to explore today. Take your time to visit each station, where you will find a collection of symbols which represent Father, Son and Holy Spirit. There are three stations, but they are held together in unity by this pattern, just as there are three persons of the one God. You may also like to walk the path which outlines this Trinity pattern. Like God, it has no beginning and no end.

Allow plenty of time for people to explore the Trinity Activity stations and walk the path.

Music

I bind unto myself today

Storytelling

Matthew's Gospel ends with Jesus' words to his disciples. As he leaves them, he gives them a job to do. Listen to what he said:

Read Jesus' words in Matthew 28:18–20.

Exploring

The disciples were the first Christians, so the job which Jesus gave them to do is the job of the Church – and that means it is our job, too. But what exactly is the job of the Church in the world? Around our church today are three interactive areas which may help us to explore some answers to this question. Take your time in visiting each area and thinking about what you find there; keep asking yourself the question, 'What is the job of the Church?'

Allow plenty of time for people to explore each interactive area, then gather them together and invite answers to this question. If people are hesitant, you might suggest some discussion in pairs and groups to get ideas flowing.

Music

Father, we love you

Prayer action

On this Trinity Sunday, we remember that many Christians bless themselves in the name of the Trinity, often by making the sign of the cross, like this: *(demonstrate by crossing yourself whilst saying,* 'In the name of the Father, and of the Son, and of the Holy Spirit.'*)* Today we are each going to make our own Trinity blessing in the form of a plait. *(Show the three coloured cords.)* Here is gold for God the Father, white for God the Son and red for God the Holy Spirit. Plait them together like this and as you do so, say: 'In the name of the Father' *(bring in the gold cord)*, 'and of the Son' *(bring in the white cord)*, 'and of the Holy Spirit' *(bring in the red cord. Repeat this once more.)*. Now let us call to mind those people and situations we would like to bring before God. Hold your prayer in your heart and as you do so, make your Trinity plait and pray in the name of the Father, and of the Son, and of the Holy Spirit.

Everyone begins their plait, repeating the words as they do so.

Conclusion

As we go out into the world to do God's work,
may the grace of the Lord Jesus Christ,
the love of God, and the communion of the Holy Spirit
be with all of us,
now and always.[1]
Amen.

Give notices, announce the next all-age service and invite everyone to the feast.

1. From 2 Corinthians 13:13.

The Transfiguration

Theme	The Transfiguration
Scripture	Matthew 17:1–9

Running order	Total: 50 minutes
Welcome	Lighting votive candles *(5 minutes)*
Introduction	Opening the theme
Storytelling	Visual retelling of Matthew 17:1–9 *(5 minutes)*
Activity	Drawing portraits – what does God look like? *(5 minutes)*
Music	You are the King of Glory *(5 minutes)*
Exploring	What does the Transfiguration reveal? *(15 minutes)*
Prayer action	Amen! Interactive prayer of adoration *(5 minutes)*
Music	Lord, the light of your love *(5 minutes)*
Conclusion	Sparklers *(5 minutes)*

Resources

- As many candles and votive candle stands as can safely stand on or around the altar
- Matches and tapers
- Laptop, projector and screen
- Three pictures *(see appendix)*
  - The mountains
  - Shining Jesus
  - The bright cloud
- The words of the prayer *(see appendix)*
- Music and words
- Pieces of paper printed with picture frames *(see appendix)*
- Outlines of Jesus and his friends *(see appendix)*
- Pens, pencils and crayons
- Tables to work at
- Indoor sparklers *(see appendix)*
- A bucket of sand

Leaders

Minimum: 1

- Leader

Optimum: 6+

- Leader *(Introduction and Conclusion)*
- Storyteller
- Activity Leader(s)
- Music Leader
- Explorer
- Prayer Leader(s)

Suggestions for additional music

- 'Tis good, Lord, to be here
- Majesty, worship his majesty
- My God, how wonderful you are

Service

Welcome

Invite everyone to light at least one votive candle when they arrive, so that by the time the service begins the altar is ablaze with light.

Introduction

Today we remember a special event in Jesus' life called the Transfiguration. This means 'change' or 'transformation' and the story of how Jesus was changed is an amazing one. This is what happened.

Storytelling

Show the mountain picture.

'Come with me!' said Jesus to his friends, Peter, James and John. They were used to following him when he called them, so they went – but they weren't expecting the hike that followed. Through the towns and villages, through the fields, up into the hills and up, up to the highest point for miles around. For once, there were no eager crowds pressing in around them – just the three friends and Jesus, alone on the mountain.

Suddenly, Jesus changed. His face began to shine until it was too bright to look at and his clothes became dazzling white.

Show the picture of a shining Jesus.

The three friends shielded their eyes as if they were looking at the sun, but then in the dazzling brightness they saw two other people who seemed to be having a conversation with Jesus. They could see that they were two wise, old men who shone with a holy light of their own – and suddenly they knew that here were Moses and Elijah the Prophet, the great men whom every Jew remembered and honoured.

Peter felt he had to do something to mark this momentous occasion. 'Lord!' he cried out, 'It's a good job we came! We can build each of you a special shelter up here! One for you, one for Mos –'

Show the picture of the bright cloud.

But he didn't get to finish. A bright cloud overshadowed them all and a voice from inside the cloud said, 'This is my Son, the beloved; with him I am well pleased; listen to him!'

The friends fell to the ground and hid their faces in terror. The next thing they knew, Jesus was kneeling beside them looking like his ordinary self again. He shook them gently and said, 'Get up – don't be frightened.'

When they stood up, the light and the cloud had gone, and there was nobody there except the four of them. They walked down the mountain in stunned silence, wondering how they would explain all this to the others, and whether anyone would believe them. As if he had read their minds, Jesus said, 'Don't tell anyone about this until I have died and risen again.'

Activity

Today's story, the Transfiguration, is revealing. We are going to think first about what it reveals about God, because this is one of those dramatic Bible stories where we get a glimpse of God himself. What did we see and hear of God in our story? *(Invite responses.)* The friends hid their eyes because they didn't dare to see God face-to-face – but they must have wondered what they might have seen. What God looks like is a mystery to all of us, but that doesn't stop us wondering. *(Show paper with the picture frame.)* Here we have a fancy frame for a portrait: I wonder whether each of us can fill it with a picture of what we think God might look like? You might like to write a description instead.

Allow plenty of time for people to complete their pictures.

Music

You are the King of Glory

Exploring

Spread out the outlines of Jesus and his friends on some tables, with pens.

Our story also reveals something important about Jesus and about human reactions to God, as represented by Jesus' friends on the mountain. Think back to the story and see if you can fill in something in these empty outlines *(show outlines of Jesus and his friends.)* What does the story show us about Jesus, and what does it show us about his friends?

Allow plenty of time for people to think and write.

So what does this story show us about Jesus? *(Read out/invite some responses, trying to find value in them all.)* It is one of those rare occasions when God steps in and makes it absolutely clear who Jesus is – his beloved Son, someone who is even more important than those great men who were so close to God, Moses and Elijah.

And how about his friends? What do they do? *(Read out/invite some responses.)* You get the feeling that poor Peter is floundering, and he clutches at an idea which was part of Jewish history – building a special tent to cover something holy. He recognises that he is in the presence of great holiness, and thinks, 'I don't know what to do – I know, we'll make some special tents! One each!' It is just the kind of well-meaning fumbling that any of us might resort to in the face of an overwhelming religious experience.

Finally, what does this story show us about God? *(Hold up some of the portraits.)* These portraits are as different as each of us from each other, but – like our story – they all reflect something true about God: the fact that he is an amazing, awe-inspiring mystery which our minds can never grasp. No wonder the friends fell on their faces in terror! Because getting even a tiny glimpse of the reality of God is an extraordinary experience and it is completely natural to hide, or to stand with our mouths open in fear and wonder. If we are not completely speechless, we might manage to say 'O!' or 'Wow!' These are the feelings expressed by the words of our prayer today.

Prayer action

The only ones who are not lost for words in God's presence are the angels. On the contrary, the angels in the Bible are a noisy lot. While we are used to prayer being something we do quietly or silently, the angels sing God's praises at full volume and cry out in loud voices. Today we will use a prayer which the angels sang, and we will praise God as loudly as we possibly can.

Get everyone to stand up and practise by yelling 'Amen!' together after a countdown of '3 – 2 – 1 – AMEN!', then try it a second time, more loudly if possible. Then introduce the words of the prayer, either on screen or on cards. Invite the people to read them through in unison in normal voices, thinking about what these words of praise mean. Suggest that those who can't yet read save all their energy for a big 'AMEN!' at the beginning and end.

Now let's raise the roof with this prayer:
Amen! Blessing and glory and wisdom
and thanksgiving and honour
and power and might
be to our God for ever and ever!
Amen![1]

Music Lord, the light of your love

Conclusion We are going to end today with a prayer to remind us of Jesus' bright and shining appearance on the mountain.

Gather in a circle and hand round the sparklers. As you light them, say:
Shine, Jesus, shine
so that the dazzling light of your glory fills the world.[2]
Amen.

Give notices, announce the next all-age service and invite everyone to the feast.

1. Revelation 7:12.
2. Adapted from Graham Kendrick, 'Lord, the light of your love is shining' © 1987 Make Way Music.

God our Father

Known to God

Theme	How God knows each of us
Scripture	Genesis 21:8–21; Matthew 10:29–31

Running order	Total: 50 minutes
Welcome	Salt dough prayers *(5 minutes)*
Introduction	Opening the theme
Storytelling	Retelling the story of Hagar and Ishmael, with visual aids *(10 minutes)*
Music	Do not be afraid *(5 minutes)*
Activity	Knowing your own pebble *(10 minutes)*
Music	There are hundreds of sparrows *(5 minutes)*
Exploring	How does God know each one of us? Picking your pebble from a pile *(10 minutes)*
Prayer action	Votive pebbles and a chant – 'God to enfold you' *(5 minutes)*
Conclusion	Closing prayer and invitation

Resources

- Salt dough *(see appendix for Crib Service)*. Colour one half blue and the other green and form them into a rough sphere to suggest the earth
- Pictures *(see appendix)*
  - Nomad tents in the desert
  - A tree in the desert
  - A spring in the desert
- A laptop, projector and screen
- Music and words
- Lots of pebbles (or beads/shells – adapt the script accordingly) which are similar but all slightly different
- Table
- A large candle or Paschal candle and matches

Leaders

Minimum: 1

- Leader

Optimum: 6+

- Leader *(Introduction and Conclusion)*
- Activity Leader
- Storyteller
- Music Leader(s)
- Explorer
- Prayer Leader

Suggestions for additional music

- Lord, for the years
- God be with you till we meet again

Service

Welcome

As people arrive, invite them to create something out of salt dough as a sign of their prayer.

Introduction

Today's story comes from the beginning of the Bible and it is about two little boys for whom God had big plans. They are still remembered as the fathers of the Jewish and Arab nations.

Storytelling

Show the picture of the nomad tents.

This story begins in the desert. Tents made of rugs and cloths are clustered around a spring; a few trees cast a little shade. All around the camp stretches the big, hot desert – nothing but sand and stones for miles and miles.

Two young boys were playing in and out of the tents. Their names were Isaac and Ishmael. Isaac was the only son of Abraham and his wife, Sarah. He would one day inherit everything they had. But Sarah was uneasy because Ishmael was also Abraham's son. His mother was the slave, Hagar, and Sarah didn't like to see the two boys playing as equals, so she told Abraham to get rid of Ishmael and his mother.

Abraham didn't want to lose his son, so he asked God what to do. God told him to do as Sarah asked, and not to worry about his sons because they would both become fathers of great nations. So Abraham very sadly sent Hagar and Ishmael into the desert.

Show the picture of the desert and the tree.

They took some bread and a skin full of water and then wandered off, not knowing where they were supposed to go. Soon the bread ran out, and then the water ran out, too. The desert sun was beating down and Hagar felt herself and her son getting weaker. Soon, Ishmael couldn't walk any further. Hagar laid him down gently under a little tree, where at least he had some shade. She went and sat behind a rock where she cried to God, because she couldn't bear to see her son die.

God heard Hagar and sent an angel to her. The angel said, 'What's the matter, Hagar? Don't be frightened: God has heard the voice of the boy where he is. Come on, pick him up and hold his hand tight, because God will make him the father of a great nation. Come and look!'

Show the picture of the spring.

Then God's angel showed Hagar that in the shadow of some rocks there was a cool, deep spring. Hagar ran to Ishmael and carried him to the water: they drank and knew that they were going to be all right. God continued to watch over Ishmael and he grew up in the desert to become a strong young man.

Music Do not be afraid

Activity In today's story, God intervened directly to help someone in need. The angel said, 'God has heard the voice of the boy where he is,' and suddenly, there was a spring full of water and Ishmael's life was saved. Our activity today will help us to consider how God knows about each of us, where we are.

Here is a collection of pebbles: they are all slightly different. Choose a pebble and take some time to get to know it. Notice everything about it: its size, texture, patterns and colour. Become an expert on your own, particular pebble.

Allow plenty of time for people to study their pebbles, then invite one or two people to describe everything they have noticed about theirs.

Music There are hundreds of sparrows

Exploring Who knows every tiny detail about their pebble? *(Invite a show of hands.)* I wonder if you could find it again if it was lost in the middle of a pile of other pebbles? Let's find out. Take one last look at your own, special pebble and then put it in the bowl.

Pass the bowl round and collect all the pebbles. Then spread them all out on a table.

Come forward now and see if you can find your own pebble.

Allow plenty of time for people to search through the pebbles. When some people have found theirs, invite comments.

How did you know that pebble was yours?

Ask those who are still looking to describe exactly what they are looking for. Then gather everyone together.

Each of us had a particular interest in finding our own pebble. We knew exactly what it was like and even when it was lost, we knew it was here somewhere and we kept on looking until we found it. Think of all the care and attention you have focused on that one small pebble. That is the way Jesus said God cares about you – and me, and every single one of us. He said:

> Are not two sparrows sold for a penny? Yet not one of them will fall to the ground unperceived by your Father. And even the hairs of your head are all counted. So do not be afraid; you are of more value than many sparrows.

Just as we know every line and lump on our pebbles, God knows every hair on our heads! It is mind-boggling to think how anyone could know and care so much, in so many different directions at once, but God does.

Now think back to your pebble in this pile: was it easy to find? *(Invite comments.)* Just because it was special to you, it wasn't magically protected from getting lost. When Jesus said that no sparrow fell without being noticed by God, the sparrow had still fallen. So bad things will sometimes happen, but it doesn't mean that God has stopped noticing or caring: whatever happens to us, God knows and loves us. He will keep looking out for us and he will never leave us. That is why Jesus tells us, 'Do not be afraid.'

Prayer action

Place the lit Paschal candle in the middle of the table or floor with a clear space around it. Turn off some lights.

Our prayer today is a blessing for all of us: that we will each be kept in God's sight. We will sing this simple chant together and pray for anyone who especially needs to be held in the light of God's love. As a sign of your prayer, place a pebble in the circle of light which spreads around this candle.

Begin the chant – 'God to enfold you' – and repeat it until everyone has offered their prayers.

Heavenly Lord,
may you keep us always in your sight
and in the light of your love.
Amen.

Conclusion

Father,
as we go out into the world,
help us to trust in your ever-watchful care,
for you are great and do wonderful things;
you alone are God.[1]
Amen.

Give notices, announce the next all-age service and invite everyone to the feast.

1. From Psalm 86:10.

God will provide

Theme	God is working his purpose out in our lives
Scripture	Genesis 22:1–14

Running order	Total: 50 minutes
Welcome	Tea-light cross *(5 minutes)*
Introduction	Opening the theme
Storytelling	Abraham and Isaac – dramatised dialogue *(10 minutes)*
Music	God is working his purpose out *(5 minutes)*
Activity	Following instructions for a mystery drawing *(15 minutes)*
Exploring	What was Abraham doing? – Thinking about how we carry out God's purpose for us *(5 minutes)*
Prayer action	Tangled knots – offertory prayer *(5 minutes)*
Music	Father, I place into your hands *(5 minutes)*
Conclusion	Closing prayer and invitation

Resources

- Tea-lights, matches and tapers
- A piece of board for the tea-lights to stand on
- Music and words
- Pieces of A4 card, squared off and numbered *(see appendix)*, enough for one each
- Eight tables around the church, each with one numbered square of the mystery picture on it plus the same square, already filled in *(see appendix)*. Put the numbers in a random order and put Table 8 in the most hidden-away spot
- Resources on each table as follows:
  - Tables 1, 2, 4 and 5: PVA glue and cotton wool
  - Table 3: old manila envelopes, scissors, glue-sticks and an example of folded and unfolded shapes *(see appendix)*
  - Tables 6 and 7: PVA glue, cotton wool and felt-tip pens
  - Table 8: PVA glue, cotton wool, felt-tip pens, old manila envelopes and scissors
- One piece of rope, tied in tangled knots
- Pieces of string, about 30 cm long, enough for one each

Leaders

Minimum: 4

- Leader
- Readers x 3

Optimum: 9

- Leader *(Introduction and Conclusion)*
- Storyteller
- Readers x 3 (no costumes required – read from the script like a radio play):

  God

  Abraham

  Isaac
- Explorer
- Music Leader
- Activity Leader
- Prayer Leader

Suggestions for additional music

- God moves in a mysterious way
- Take me, Lord, use my life

Service

Welcome

In front of the altar, lay out unlit tea-lights in the shape of a cross. As people arrive, invite them to light a candle as a sign of their prayer.

Introduction

The theme of today's service is 'God will provide'. These trusting words were spoken by Abraham in the middle of a life-and-death situation. Let's find out what happened.

Storytelling

Storyteller: God loved Abraham. He promised that Abraham and his son Isaac were the beginning of a great family. He would have more descendants than there were stars in the sky and they would be God's chosen people. Abraham knew that God had special plans for him, but he didn't know that God had decided to test him. God wanted to see just how much Abraham loved and trusted him.

God: Abraham!

Abraham: Here I am, Lord.

God: I want a blood sacrifice – a burnt offering. I want you to sacrifice your son for me.

Abraham: What? My precious boy, Isaac?

God: Yes.

Abraham: The miracle son you gave me, even though I'm an old man?

God: Yes.

Abraham: The boy you have such plans for – the father of a great nation?

God: Yes.

Abraham: *(Sighs. Pause)* I trust you, Lord. I'll do what you say.

Storyteller: So Abraham set off on a three-day journey with Isaac. They took the donkey, loaded with kindling, and a big knife for the sacrifice.

Abraham: If you're going to step in, Lord, now would be the time.

Storyteller — They were heading for a special mountain, and by the second day they could see it in the distance.

Abraham — If you're going to step in, Lord, now would be a good time.

Storyteller — When they reached the foothills, they tied up the donkey. Isaac carried the kindling and Abraham carried the big knife.

Isaac — Father!

Abraham — Here I am, my son.

Isaac — We've got everything we need except a lamb for the sacrifice.

Abraham — God will provide, my son.

(To God) If you're going to step in, Lord, right now would be the best time.

Storyteller — When they got to the top, they laid the fire for the burnt offering. They prepared the altar and the big knife for the sacrifice. But there was no lamb. Isaac himself was put on the altar and Abraham lifted up the big knife –

Abraham and Isaac — If you're going to step in, Lord, PLEASE DO IT NOW!

God — ABRAHAM, ABRAHAM!

Abraham — Here I am!

God — Stop right there! Don't hurt a single hair on your son's head. Now I know how much you love and trust me. And look what God has provided.

Storyteller — There was a ram caught in a bush, so Abraham made a sacrifice and a burnt offering, after all, then he and Isaac came back down the mountain together. Abraham gave the mountain a name which means, 'The Lord will provide'.

Music — God is working his purpose out

Activity — Today's story is a hard one to get our heads around. What was God *thinking* of? What was Abraham *doing*? What about poor Isaac? This story is difficult to come to terms with because it involves a kind of trust which most of us would find it hard to feel. God had promised

Abraham great things for his son, Isaac, and Abraham trusted God's promises absolutely. He could not have believed that God would really ask him to kill his son – even though for a while, it seemed as if that was exactly what God wanted him to do. As they walked up the mountain he said, 'God will provide' – he trusted that God would come up with something. Let's hope that Isaac, too, had that kind of trust, both in God and in his father; let's hope that he never really believed that either could want to hurt him.

So today's story gives us an extreme example of how Abraham trusted in God's bigger plan for him and Isaac, even when some parts of that plan seemed incomprehensible. Our activity today is about trusting in an overall purpose when all we have are step-by-step instructions which – in themselves – may seem strange. Around the church are some numbered tables. At each number there are instructions for something to fill in on your numbered sheet. Go round the church and visit the numbers in any order: at each number, fill in the corresponding section of your numbered sheet. Don't worry about what the overall outcome will be – don't try to turn it into anything – simply follow the instructions as carefully as you can until you have filled in the whole sheet.

Exploring

Invite comments on the activity, with questions like these:

What have you ended up with? Did you guess what it was? What did you think it was going to be? Did any bits of the plan really puzzle you?

This activity gives us a taste of what it can be like to try and follow God's plan for us. We faithfully take one step at a time – just as we tried to copy accurately each numbered part of the picture, even though the instructions seemed strange. Abraham knew that God wanted Isaac to be the father of his people, so it seemed to make no sense that God then demanded his sacrifice – but Abraham trusted that God had a purpose which was bigger than he could understand. We may not know what God's plan for us is, so it is even harder for us to see the sense behind some of the situations we find ourselves in. But remember that today's story was all about trust. We can trust that whatever happens, God loves us and wants us to become the best and the most we can be.

Prayer action

In our prayers today, we will bring before God those difficult things which make it hard to see God's purpose for us. *(Show the tangled rope.)* Sometimes our lives can seem so tangled and messy that we can't seem to straighten them out. All we can do is place the tangles, the mess and the difficulties into God's hands and say, 'Here you are. You'll have to sort this knot out, because it's too hard for me to untie by myself.' As we call to mind those people and situations we want to place in God's hands today, take a piece of string and tie it into big, messy knots. Then take the tangle to the altar and leave it there as a sign that you have entrusted it to God in prayer.

Hand round the pieces of string and allow plenty of time for people to complete their prayers.

Almighty Father,
as you work your purpose out in our lives,
guide us through the twists and turns we face.
May we put our trust in your steadfast love.[1]
Amen.

Music

Father, I place into your hands

Conclusion

God of all goodness,
whatever we need, may we look to you;
may we trust like Abraham that 'The Lord will provide'.
Amen.

Give notices, announce the next all-age service and invite everyone to the feast.

1. From Psalm 13:5.

Hide and seek

Theme	God always finds us
Scripture	Psalm 139:1–9

Running order	Total: 50 minutes
Welcome	Tea-light heart *(5 minutes)*
Introduction	Opening the theme
Activity	Finding the runaway bunnies *(10 minutes)*
Storytelling	Reading *The Runaway Bunny* and Psalm 139:1–9 *(10 minutes)*
Music	O God, you search me *(5 minutes)*
Exploring	Is there anywhere where God can't find us? Hide and seek *(10 minutes)*
Prayer action	Hidden prayers – active intercessions *(5 minutes)*
Music	Father God *(5 minutes)*
Conclusion	Closing prayer and invitation

Resources

- Tea-lights, matches and tapers
- An upright cross
- A piece of board for the tea-lights to stand on
- Hidden around the church, lots of toy rabbits or pictures of rabbits
- On the floor (perhaps on sheets of lining paper), lots of rabbit tracks *(see appendix)*
- A copy of *The Runaway Bunny* by Margaret Wise Brown *(see appendix)*
- Music and words
- Lots of little squares of paper (the blocks of paper sold as telephone memo pads are good for this)
- Pens and pencils

Leaders

Minimum: 1

- Leader

Optimum: 6

- Leader *(Introduction and Conclusion)*
- Storyteller
- Explorer
- Activity Leader
- Music Leader
- Prayer Leader

Suggestions for additional music

- In heavenly love abiding
- Our God is a great big God

Service

Welcome

In front of the altar, place a cross in the middle of a large heart-shape laid out in unlit tea-lights. As people arrive, invite them to light a candle as a sign of their prayer.

Introduction

Who likes playing hide and seek? Today's service is all about hiding and being found. I think some rabbits have been playing hide and seek in our church – have you noticed the paw prints all over the floor? I wonder if you could help me find all those runaway bunnies?

Activity

Children run around the church finding all the toy rabbits.

Storytelling

Our story today is about a runaway bunny.

Read The Runaway Bunny *by Margaret Wise Brown.*

Think about the story of the runaway bunny and his mother as we listen to today's Bible reading, which is all about how God knows us and loves us.

Read Psalm 139:1–9.

Music

O God, you search me

Exploring

Now it's going to be your turn to play hide and seek. Children, you need to find a hiding place while the grown-ups who are with you cover their eyes and count. Grown-ups, you need to look for your own children: if you find anyone else, leave them hiding there and keep on looking.

Allow plenty of time for the game of hide and seek to take place. You may consider playing it outside if your church does not offer much in the way of hiding places. Then gather everyone together and invite responses to the game with questions like these:

Who found a great hiding place? Who was really hard to find? Did you worry that no one would find you? Grown-ups – if you couldn't find the child you were looking for, would you give up?

When we played hide and seek, we kept on looking for the people we loved until we found them: nothing would have made us give up, no matter how good their hiding place was or how hard they were to find. In our story about the runaway bunny, the mother made her child a wonderful promise: 'If you run away, I will run after you. For you are my little bunny.' Wherever he went, whatever he changed into, she would stay with him: sometimes she was a tree which he could come home to, or a wind which would blow him where she wanted him to go; sometimes she took great risks by climbing mountains or walking across the air on a tightrope.

Our Bible reading today is a Psalm which reminds us that this is how God loves us, too. Sometimes we might feel lost and far away from God – but he loves us and will find us, wherever we are. Sometimes we might feel as if we want to hide from God, because we have done something we are ashamed of – but he loves us and wants to find us, wherever we are. No matter how far away we go – as the Psalmist said – God's hand shall lead us, his right hand hold us fast. God even risked his own Son because he loves us and wants us to stay with him forever.

Remember what happened at the end of the story. The mother rabbit didn't blame her child for wanting to run away: he decided that he wanted to stay and she accepted him with open arms – and gave him a carrot. Whenever we turn back to God, he will welcome us back like this, with loving acceptance and a gift – the gift of eternal life which is ours through Jesus.

Prayer action

Jesus told his disciples that God our Father sees what is done in secret.[1] However small, quiet or secret our prayers may be, God knows and understands them. Today we will offer our prayers in secret by writing or drawing them on a little piece of paper. Fold or roll it up as tightly as you can and find a little hiding place in church for your prayer. It may be a crack in the stonework or a little nook behind your seat. Tuck your prayer into its hiding place.

1. Matthew 6:1–17.

Hand out paper and pens and allow plenty of time for people to find a hiding place for their prayers.

Our Father,
we offer you our hidden prayers in secret,
trusting that you see and know everything about us,
and you know what we need before we even ask.
Amen.

Music

Father God

Conclusion

Loving Lord,
as we go out into the world,
may we know that you are with us
and will keep us wherever we go.[2]
Amen.

Give notices, announce the next all-age service and invite everyone to the feast.

2. From Genesis 28:15.

One for All

The Maker's mark

Theme	Giving to God the things that are God's
Scripture	Matthew 22:15–22

Running order	Total: 50 minutes
Welcome	Balloon prayers *(5 minutes)*
Activity 1	Finding the maker's mark *(10 minutes)*
Introduction	Opening the theme
Storytelling	Retelling Matthew 22:15–22 – the question about Roman taxes *(2 minutes)*
Music	Holy, holy, holy, holy *(5 minutes)*
Activity 2	Leaving our own maker's mark – making clay tokens *(15 minutes)*
Exploring	Whose image is stamped on us? *(3 minutes)*
Music	Abba, Father, let me be *(5 minutes)*
Prayer action	Clay tokens – active offertory prayer *(5 minutes)*
Conclusion	Closing prayer and invitation

Resources

- Balloons and a balloon pump
- Lengths of ribbon or string
- Scissors
- Permanent marker pens
- A fixture near the altar onto which balloons may be tied (have one or two already on there)
- Some Lego bricks
- Hidden around the church, objects which have the maker's name, trademark or country of origin stamped on them: for example, plastic toys, anything with a kite mark, china and glassware, clothes with labels. Search your house for suitable items! Pictures might include car adverts from magazines which show the company logo on the car, or sportswear adverts
- A few copper coins
- A large copy of a denarius *(see appendix)*
- Music and words
- A quantity of clay, Model Magic or salt dough *(see appendix)*
- Wipe-clean tables with some tools for making marks in clay, such as cocktail sticks and plastic cutlery

Leaders

Minimum: 1

- Leader

Optimum: 7

- Leader *(Introduction and Conclusion)*
- Activity Leaders x 2
- Storyteller
- Explorer
- Music Leader
- Prayer Leader

Suggestions for additional music

- Lord, I lift your name on high
- I will offer up my life

Service

Welcome

As people arrive, invite them to blow up a balloon and write or draw their prayer on it, then tie it with ribbon and add it to the bunch by the altar.

Activity 1

We begin today's service with a challenge. All around the church are objects which have special marks on them: these are words, symbols or pictures that show everyone which company, factory or country produced something. *(Show a Lego brick.)* For example, on every single knobbly bit on a piece of Lego there is a tiny stamp which says, 'Lego'. This is the maker's mark: can you find the maker's mark on anything in church today, or on anything of your own?

Allow plenty of time for everyone to investigate the objects and pictures provided, and to find a mark on things of their own. Then invite people to show what they found.

Introduction

Our service today is about the maker's mark. In the objects we have been looking at, the mark does two jobs: it shows who made something, and it also shows ownership. You can make a copy of a Lego brick, but you can't stamp it with the name 'Lego', because that design and name belong to the Lego company. The maker's mark is even more important when it comes to money. Whose head is on these coins?

Show the coins to the children and invite responses.

That's because they were made by the Royal Mint, and only coins which are made there and stamped with the Queen's head are legal money. In Jesus' time, Roman coins were stamped with the head of the Roman emperor. One of these coins is at the centre of our story today.

Storytelling

Jesus was making himself unpopular with the Pharisees – the religious leaders in Jerusalem. They saw him as a troublemaker and were looking for an excuse to get him arrested. Now, everyone had to pay Roman taxes and these were always resented: there had been riots in the past. If Jesus stirred up a riot about not paying taxes to the Romans, they would certainly arrest him! So the Pharisees tried to trap him with a question.

They began by flattering him. 'Teacher, we know you are a sincere, God-fearing man who treats everyone equally. We know you teach people about God's way. So can you tell us please, is it right for us to pay taxes to the Roman emperor, or not? Should we pay or shouldn't we?'

Jesus spotted the trap. They wanted him to say it was wrong to pay Roman taxes – but if he said it was right to pay then many of his own followers would lose heart, because they believed he had come to free them from the Romans. Thinking quickly, he said, 'Show me the coin which is used to pay tax.' They brought him a denarius. Here is a big version of what this little coin looked like.

Show the picture of the coin.

Jesus said to the Pharisees, 'Whose head is on this coin, and whose name?'

They replied, 'The emperor's.'

So Jesus answered, 'Well then – give to the emperor the things that are the emperor's, and give to God the things that are God's.' The Pharisees looked at each other in amazement and didn't know what to say.

Music Holy, holy, holy, holy

Activity 2 Before we explore our story further, we are going to have the chance to leave our own maker's mark. Use this clay to make a round, flat coin or token, then use the tools provided to make your mark on it: it could be your initials, or a picture of your head, or some other words or pictures which mark out this particular one as yours. Make as many as you like and mark them as your own.

Allow plenty of time for people to make and mark their clay tokens.

Exploring

These clay tokens carry our mark and they belong to us: the Roman coin in the story carried the image of the emperor, so Jesus said it belonged to the emperor. But the most interesting part of the story is the other half of what Jesus said: 'Give to God the things that are God's.' What carries God's image? What belongs to God? The answer lies right at the beginning of the Bible, in the story of the Creation. This story reminds us that God called everything into existence, from the light of the Big Bang onwards. Everything that was created and everything that has evolved bears his maker's mark. And as the icing on the cake of his creation, God made us. This is what the book of Genesis says:

> So God created humankind in his image,
> in the image of God he created them;
> male and female he created them.[1]

We bear God's image: like the coin which was imprinted with the head of the emperor, his image is carried by each one of us. By this we know that God made us and that we belong to him.

Think of your own clay token, which you carefully marked as yours: it is wonderful to think that this is how God made each one of us. However our lives have changed us, whoever and whatever we are, we will always carry God's image and he will always recognise us as one of his own.

When Jesus said, 'Give to God the things that are God's,' he was asking a lot of us. If everything in all creation is God's, then we should use this planet's wonderful resources wisely and share them generously, in God's name. If *we* are God's, then we should live our lives God's way, rather than thinking – as the song puts it – 'I did it my way'. What that means in practice will be different for each one of us, but let's each take this question away with us today: 'How can I do things God's way?'

1. Genesis 1:27.

Music Abba, Father, let me be

Prayer action We made these clay tokens and marked them to show that they belong to us. Let's take some time now to think about how we belong to God. Let's pray that we might show that belonging in our lives: as we do so, let's offer these tokens as a sign of our prayer.

Pause for a short time, then take your clay token up to the altar. Encourage others to do the same, then gather everyone together.

Father God,
you made us and you know us.
Show us how to offer our lives to you
in Jesus' name.
Amen.

Conclusion Creator God,
open our eyes to a world which bears your imprint.
Show us our Maker's marks in all that we have.
Amen.

Give notices, announce the next all-age service and invite everyone to the feast.

Jesus Christ

Living water

Theme	Jesus gives the water of life
Scripture	Exodus 17:1–7 and John 4:5–42

Running order	Total: 50 minutes
Welcome	Prayer pebbles in water *(5 minutes)*
Introduction	Opening the theme
Storytelling	Sketch – Water from the rock *(5 minutes)*
Music	As the deer pants for the water *(5 minutes)*
Activity	The Cream Cracker Challenge *(10 minutes)*
Exploring	What is the water of life? *(15 minutes)*
Music	Have you heard the raindrops *(5 minutes)*
Prayer action	Drinking water – interactive thanksgiving *(5 minutes)*
Conclusion	Pebble prayer

Resources

- Lots of small pebbles
- A half-filled jug of water standing in a large glass bowl
- The rock which gushes water *(see appendix)*
- Music and words
- A plate of cream crackers
- A stopwatch
- Three glasses of water on a tray
- Three tables with the following:
  - The rest of the cream crackers, a jug of water and lots of plastic cups
  - Desert photographs and facts *(see appendix)*
  - John 4:13, 14 – enlarged on a piece of card
- For the prayer action, use the water jug and the rest of the plastic cups from table 1, above

Leaders

Minimum: 7

- Leader
- Storyteller
- Cast x 5

Optimum: 11

- Leader *(Introduction and Conclusion)*
- Activity Leader
- Storyteller, wearing shades and a sunhat
- Cast x 5
  Moses, in a robe with a staff
  Israelites 1 and 2, (male and female)
  Israelite children 1 and 2, all wearing simple robes/head coverings
- Music Leader
- Explorer
- Prayer Leader

Suggestions for additional music

- Will you hide me in your shelter?
- Father, hear the prayer we offer

Service

Welcome

Place the half-filled jug of water in the bowl on the altar, with a pile of pebbles next to it. As people arrive, invite them to add a pebble to the water as a sign of their prayer.

Introduction

Today's service is about something which none of us can live without: water. Our story today is set in the desert, where God's people have been led by Moses out of slavery in Egypt.

Storytelling

Welcome to the Israelite camp at Rephidim. We're in the middle of the desert and it is really *really* hot. In fact, could someone get me a drink of water?

Israelite 1 — There isn't any! Moses has brought us to another dust-bowl.

Israelite 2 — What, again? We're going to die of thirst!

Israelite child 1 — Mummy, I want a drink of water!

Israelite child 2 — Dad, our sheep aren't looking very well – their mouths are all dry.

Israelite 1 — They're not the only ones!

Israelite 2 — Why did Moses bring us out of Egypt, with our children and our animals, just so we could die of thirst in the desert?

Israelite 1 — I think we should ask him!

Everyone — Yeah! Good idea! MOSES! MOSES! MOSES!

Storyteller — Moses is here and, understandably, he's looking a bit worried. Moses, the crowd seems to be turning nasty. Some of them look like they're getting ready to throw things. What are you going to do?

Moses — I'm going to ask the Lord.

He goes and kneels for a moment in front of the altar.

I need my staff. Now, all of you, see what the Lord has provided!

He hits the rock and water pours out.

Everyone — HOORAY!

They rush forward to fill their hands with water.

Music — As the deer pants for the water

Activity

Living in this rainy country, we don't very often feel really, really thirsty. We have lots of clean water in our taps whenever we need it, and however much we use there is always more. Today's activity may remind us how vital water is and how much we take it for granted. I'll need three volunteers to come forward and eat cream crackers – just plain cream crackers with no butter. Here's the challenge: you need to keep eating for as long as you can before you have a drink of water. The person who holds out the longest is the winner! Here's the stopwatch – now can I have some volunteers?

Invite your volunteers to the front and give them each a few cream crackers. Ask another volunteer to stand by with three glasses of water on a tray. Challenge the volunteers to start eating as you start the stopwatch. When each one reaches for the water, check the watch and announce the time. When all three have completed the challenge, announce the winner and let them all return to their seats, taking their drinks with them!

Exploring

I think our volunteers have been reminded of what it is like to be really, really thirsty! It is something which people in the Bible lands of the Middle East never forget. The desert is all around and in the days before piped water, wells and oases were the difference between life and death. Whenever Jesus talks about water, we have to remember that he is talking in this context.

Indicate the three tables.

Today we have three areas to explore together. The first is the 'Cream Cracker Challenge', for anyone who would like to remind themselves what it feels like to really need water. The second is the 'Desert Experience', with lots of photos and facts about life in the desert. And the third area has the words of Jesus himself, who had been walking in the desert all day when he stopped at a well. He talked about water to the woman who gave him a drink. This is what he said:

> Everyone who drinks of this water will be thirsty again, but those who drink of the water that I will give them will never be thirsty. The water that I will give will become in them a spring of water gushing up to eternal life.

Take some time now to try the cream cracker challenge, to imagine life in the desert and to ask yourself what Jesus meant when he talked about the 'living water' he would give us.

Allow plenty of time for everyone to visit each station. Then gather everyone together and invite responses to each. You may like to round off the discussion like this:

We drink ordinary water because our bodies need it to stay alive – especially when we are hot or our throats are dry. We use it up and we will be thirsty again. The 'living water' which Jesus gives us refreshes our thirsty spirits. It flows like a never-ending, life-giving spring. This is the way Jesus describes the gift he gives us: the everlasting gift of a living relationship with God.

Music Have you heard the raindrops

Prayer action In our prayers today we will say, 'Thank you,' to God for the water of life.

Give everyone a cup of water.

Lord of life,
thank you for the running water
which sustains our bodies;
thank you for your living water which saves our souls.
As we drink this water, we remember all those
who are thirsty in body, mind and spirit.
(All drink. Pause.) We pray that they will find
the water of life.
Amen.

Conclusion

Pour more water into the pebble-filled glass jug until it overflows into the bowl underneath.

Jesus, Spring of life,
may your living water pour into our lives
and overflow into the world.
Amen.

Give notices, announce the next all-age service and invite everyone to the feast.

The gate

Theme	Jesus is the gateway to life
Scripture	John 10:1–10

Running order	Total: 50 minutes
Welcome	Adding leaves to the living prayer tree *(5 minutes)*
Introduction	Opening the theme
Activity	Exploring Psalm 23 through visual and tactile stations *(10 minutes)*
Music	The Lord's my shepherd, I'll not want *(5 minutes)*
Exploring 1	'What is a gate for?' – looking at a real gate *(5 minutes)*
Storytelling	Reading John 10:1–10 *(5 minutes)*
Exploring 2	'I am the gate' – what does Jesus mean? Brainstorming *(10 minutes)*
Music	O let the Son of God enfold you *(5 minutes)*
Prayer action	Blessing – meditation montage *(5 minutes)*
Conclusion	Closing prayer and invitation

Resources

- A living 'prayer tree': some budding branches in a large pot or vase, filled with water and pebbles to weigh it down *(see appendix for Seeing and believing)*
- Prayer leaves *(see appendix for Seeing and believing)*
- Six stations, one for each verse of Psalm 23, with the verse displayed along with pictures and objects to encourage reflection *(see appendix)*
- Music and words
- A child's stairgate
- Luggage labels and pens, placed in the pews
- 2 large cards: '24/7' and '10:10'
- Audio-visual equipment: a laptop (see below) connected to a projector, a screen and a speaker system. If your church does not have these things in place, it can be done with a borrowed screen and projector (talk to local schools), domestic stereo speakers and lots of extension leads
- A volunteer who is confident with computers and photographic or video equipment. The brief is to create a 'meditation montage' *(see appendix)* on a laptop to be used as part of the Prayer action

Leaders

Minimum: 2

- Leader
- Prayer Leader/Technician

Optimum: 6

- Leader *(Introduction and Conclusion)*
- Activity Leader
- Explorer
- Storyteller
- Music Leader
- Prayer Leader/Technician

Suggestions for additional music

- The King of love my shepherd is
- Such love

Service

Welcome

Invite people to add prayer leaves to the living prayer tree as they arrive.

Introduction

Jesus gave us new life through his death and resurrection, and he often described himself as life: he said, 'I am the resurrection and the life,' and, 'I am the way, and the truth, and the life.' Today we will be looking at another of his great 'I am' statements, and wondering what it has to do with life: Jesus said 'I am the gate'. The kind of gate he was talking about was the sort that keeps sheep in the sheepfold; those sheep are where we start our service today, with the Psalm which begins, 'The Lord is my shepherd'.

Activity

Around the church we have lots of different stations which may help us think about how the Lord is our shepherd. Take your time to move round the stations in any order and reflect on the words, pictures and objects which you find there.

Allow plenty of time for people to circulate, think and discuss amongst themselves.

Music

The Lord's my shepherd, I'll not want

Exploring 1

Bring the stairgate to the front and hold it as you talk, demonstrating how it opens and shuts. You may need a helper for this.

Before we hear today's story, let's get in touch with what Jesus will be talking about. Here is a real gate. What is this used for? Is it just for keeping children in? Why does it open and close both ways?

Invite answers, using these or similar questions. Value all responses, drawing out the message that a gate is for letting people through as well as keeping them in and keeping others out. For example, some people may use such a gate to keep dogs out of their kitchen, and there may be useful comparisons to be drawn with wolves and the sheepfold.

Storytelling

Now let's hear what Jesus had to say about gates.

Read John 10:1–10.

Exploring 2

Let's think through what Jesus said, remembering what we said about our gate and its uses. What did Jesus mean when he talked about the sheepfold and said 'I am the gate'? Let's use these labels to brainstorm as many ideas as we can and tie them onto this gate.

Allow plenty of time for people to write and then tie their luggage labels onto the gate. Then read out some of the ideas.

Jesus is the gate which leads us into life. Through him we can have everlasting life with God in heaven. But Jesus wasn't just talking about life after death: the sheep in his story come in and go out through the gate, and find pasture. They are not stuck in the sheepfold, safely penned in with no freedom, and they are not left to wander in the wilds, with no rest or refuge. Jesus is the gate which gives the sheep a safe place to come home to *and* the freedom to go out and explore. This may, for us, be another meaning of his wonderful promise, 'I came that they may have life, and have it abundantly'. He wants us to have life – not just a bare-minimum life, but abundant life, life in all its fullness. This is a life which involves lots of activity, exploration and discovery – like the sheep wandering far and wide in search of good grass to eat. But life needs balance: it needs rest and peacefulness after busyness, and that is like the peace which settles on sheep which have been safely penned up for the night.

That balance of rest and activity is something which eludes many of us. We have become a 24/7 society *(hold up the card with these numbers)* – TV, the internet and many businesses now keep going 24 hours a day, 7 days a week and many of us find it hard to stop working, too. Jesus said, 'I came that they may have life, and have it abundantly': these words from today's reading may be found in chapter 10, verse 10 *(hold up the card with these numbers)* of John's Gospel. *(Show the numbers in each hand.)* So instead of 24/7 living, let's try

10:10 living: let's balance work and Sabbath, our daily busyness with the peace of Christ, so that we may not merely exist but have life and have it abundantly.[1]

Music

O let the Son of God enfold you

Prayer action

In our prayers today, we will reflect on finding Christ's peace in the midst of life. Rest in God's presence as we hear the words of this old Scottish blessing, accompanied by some pictures.

Turn the lights off and play the montage, which might look something like this:

Deep peace of the running wave to you,
(pictures of the sea and waves)
deep peace of the flowing air to you,
(pictures of clouds and wind-blown trees or fields of grass)
deep peace of the quiet earth to you,
(pictures of moorland or close-ups of shoots and growing plants)
deep peace of the shining stars to you,
(pictures of the sky at night or outer space)
deep peace of the Son of Peace to you, for ever.[2]
(picture of the risen Christ)

Pause for a moment of quiet, remaining focused on the last picture.

Conclusion

Lord of life,
may you make us lie down in green pastures
and lead us beside still waters.
May you refresh our souls
and lead us into life.
Amen.

Give notices, announce the next all-age service and invite everyone to the feast.

1. This idea is cited by Rosemary Lain-Priestly, *The Courage to Connect*, SPCK 2007, p.69.
2. Source unknown (Early Scottish).

One for All

The way, the truth, and the life

Theme	Jesus is the Way
Scripture	John 14:1–14

Running order	Total: 50 minutes
Welcome	Adding leaves to the living prayer tree *(5 minutes)*
Introduction	Opening the theme
Activity	Exploring the maze *(15 minutes)*
Music	Father, hear the prayer we offer *(5 minutes)*
Exploring/Storytelling	Reading the words found at the centre of the maze and asking: 'I am the way, and the truth, and the life' – what did Jesus mean? *(15 minutes)*
Prayer action	Labyrinth of life – reflective prayer *(5 minutes)*
Music	We are marching in the light of God *(5 minutes)*
Conclusion	Closing prayer and invitation

Resources

- A living 'prayer tree': some budding branches in a large pot or vase, filled with water and pebbles to weigh it down *(see appendix for Seeing and believing)*
- Prayer leaves *(see appendix for Seeing and believing)*
- A maze laid out on the floor or outside *(see appendix)*
- Gold envelope, labelled 'A secret and a promise', containing a card with the Scripture reading *(see Storytelling)*
- Maps of the maze, showing the way through
- Music and words
- Lots of copies of a small maze with a cross in the middle *(see appendix)*

Leaders

Minimum: 2

- Leader
- Activity Leader

Optimum: 6

- Leader *(Introduction and Conclusion)*
- Activity Leaders / Maze organisers x 2
- Explorer
- Music Leader
- Prayer Leader

Suggestions for additional music

- Come, my Way, my Truth, my Life
- Guide me, O thou great Redeemer

Service

Welcome

Invite people to add prayer leaves to the living prayer tree as they arrive.

Introduction

Today we will be thinking about one of Jesus' great 'I am' statements: 'I am the way, and the truth, and the life', and we will begin by trying to find our way.

Activity

Today we have a challenge for you. We have made our own maze and you are all invited to try and find your way through it. There are mazes like this to be found in churches all over Europe, and some of them are very old. Ours is brand new – can you find your way to the centre? There is some gold waiting there . . .

Allow plenty of time for everyone to walk the maze. The first person to the centre takes the gold envelope. Ask them to keep the envelope and read out the contents later.

Music

Father, hear the prayer we offer

Exploring

Use the following questions or similar to explore the idea of the maze. Try to value all contributions – there is no 'right' answer here.

- What was it like in the maze?
- How did you feel when you were trying to get to the middle?
- I wonder why so many churches and cathedrals have mazes?
- I wonder what mazes have to do with God?

As we think about these questions, let's find out what was in that gold envelope we found at the centre of the maze. What's so special about it? It says on the front that this envelope contains a secret and a promise.

Invite your winner to open the gold envelope and read Jesus' words.

Storytelling

Jesus said, 'Do not let your hearts be troubled. Believe in God, believe also in me. I am the way, and the truth, and the life. No one comes to the Father except through me. If you know me, you will know my Father also. From now on you do know him and have seen him.'

Exploring (cont'd)

Jesus tells us a great secret. Although no one has ever seen God, or can fully understand what he is like, Jesus knows and he tells us the secret: God is Jesus-shaped. If we know Jesus and believe in him, then we know and believe in God.

Now for the promise: Jesus says, 'I am the way, and the truth, and the life. No one comes to the Father except through me.' This is where we remember our experience in the maze. Our lives can be a bit like mazes: sometimes we know which direction we're heading in, but sometimes we can feel hopelessly lost and confused. Jesus is the way: he is like a set of directions to help us through the maze.

Hand out the maps for the maze.

Let's use these directions to help us through the maze again, and see what it is like when we are shown the way.

Allow plenty of time for people to follow their maps through the maze.

What was it like being in the maze with a map?

Invite contributions.

Even with a map, we still had to find our way through the maze, following different paths. If we follow Jesus, our life's twists and turns don't magically disappear, but we do have a true guide as we try to find our way through. In what Jesus said and did, he showed us the way. We also have the promise of a wonderful prize when we get to the end, which is the gift of everlasting life with God. Jesus makes all this possible: he is the way, the truth and the life.

Prayer action

As we find our path through the labyrinth of life, Jesus shows us the way. For our prayers today, you are invited to take a maze and in a time of quiet, reflect on its twists and turns. Remember Jesus' words, 'Do not let your hearts be troubled.' Rest in God's presence now and follow the path with the cross at its centre, because this will lead you home.

Allow enough time for people to reflect on the maze and find their way through it.

Father, we thank you that your Son leads us to you.
His living and his dying on the cross
have shown us the way.
Amen.

Music

We are marching in the light of God

Conclusion

Living Lord,
may you be our closest companion as we go out into the world:
our way when we need direction;
our truth when we don't know what to believe;
our life, now and forever.
Amen.

Give notices, announce the next all-age service and invite everyone to the feast.

One for All

Christ the King

The Servant King

Theme	Serving Christ and his kingdom
Scripture	Matthew 25:31–46

Running order	Total: 50 minutes
Welcome	Crown of light – lighting votive candles *(5 minutes)*
Introduction	Opening the theme
Storytelling	Sketch – the King on the throne of his glory *(5 minutes)*
Exploring 1	What is different about this King and his kingdom? Brainstorm and visual aids – the upside-down face *(10 minutes)*
Music	From heaven you came *(5 minutes)*
Activity	King / servant game *(10 minutes)*
Exploring 2	How are we called to serve? Analysing the King / servant activity *(5 minutes)*
Music	Brother, sister, let me serve you *(5 minutes)*
Prayer action	Standing, sitting, kneeling – attentive prayer *(5 minutes)*
Conclusion	Closing prayer and invitation

Resources

- Votive candles arranged as a 'crown of light' *(see appendix)*
- Matches and tapers
- A large chair draped to resemble a throne
- Pictures of people in need *(see appendix)*
- A laptop, projector and screen
- Music and words
- Flip chart or whiteboard plus marker pens
- One large copy of the upside-down face and lots of small copies to hand out *(see appendix)*
- Several lightweight chairs
- A large, clear space for the King/servant game

Leaders

Minimum: 4

- Leader
- Cast x 3

Optimum: 10+

- Leader *(Introduction and Conclusion)*
- Storyteller
- Cast x 3+

  Jesus, wearing white and a crown or a 'royal robe' (something velvet or richly coloured)

  People on the right and left, wearing their own clothes. Only one of each needs to speak. Invite others to form a group behind the spokespeople on each side
- Activity Leader
- Explorers x 2
- Music Leader
- Prayer Leader

Suggestions for additional music

- Christ triumphant
- When I needed a neighbour

Service

Welcome

As people arrive, invite them to light a candle in the crown as a sign of their prayer.

Introduction

Today we are thinking about Jesus as the King who reigns over heaven and earth. We also think about his kingdom which will come at the end of time. But what will that kingdom be like? Jesus told many stories to explain the kingdom: our story today is one of the last he told, and it features Jesus himself as the King.[1]

Storytelling

Storyteller

When the Son of Man comes in his glory, and all the angels with him, then he will sit on the throne of his glory. *(Jesus sits on the throne.)* All the nations will be gathered before him, *(indicate the congregation)* and he will separate people one from another as a shepherd separates the sheep from the goats, and he will put the sheep at his right hand and the goats at the left.

Jesus

(Jesus calls forward the people on his right-hand side.) Come, you that are blessed by my Father, inherit the kingdom prepared for you from the foundation of the world; for I was hungry and you gave me food, I was thirsty and you gave me something to drink, I was a stranger and you welcomed me, I was naked and you gave me clothing, I was sick and you took care of me, I was in prison and you visited me.

Person on the right-hand side

Lord, when was it that we saw you hungry and gave you food, or thirsty and gave you something to drink? And when was it that we saw you a stranger and welcomed you, or naked and gave you clothing? And when was it that we saw you sick or in prison and visited you?

Jesus

Truly I tell you, just as you did it to one of the least of these who are members of my family, you did it to me.

Show the pictures of people in need. The people on the right come and sit around the throne.

1. The lines are taken directly from Matthew's Gospel (NRSV): you may prefer to use a different translation.

(Turning to those on the left) You that are accursed, depart from me; for I was hungry and you gave me no food, I was thirsty and you gave me nothing to drink, I was a stranger and you did not welcome me, naked and you did not give me clothing, sick and in prison and you did not visit me.

Person on the left-hand side — Lord, when was it that we saw you hungry or thirsty or a stranger or naked or sick or in prison, and did not take care of you?

Jesus — Truly I tell you, just as you did not do it to one of the least of these, you did not do it to me.

The people on the left walk sadly away down the aisle.

Exploring 1

Very few of us have ever met a king or a queen, but we have encountered many of them in stories and in our study of history. Let's think about what we expect a king to be like. What does a king wear?

Invite responses and draw the king as suggested on the flip chart or whiteboard. Then draw or write additional attributes of the king and his kingdom, prompted by questions such as these:

- *Where does a king live?*
- *What does a king's throne look like?*
- *Who is allowed in a king's palace?*
- *What does a king do?*
- *What did kings used to do to people who disobeyed them?*
- *How do people behave when they meet a king?*
- *How do kings show their power and importance?*

We have built up a detailed picture of what a typical king is like. Is Jesus like this?

Invite responses.

Jesus the King is the all-powerful ruler of heaven and earth, but he said that this is where we meet him:

Show the pictures of people in need again.

We meet Jesus in hungry and thirsty people, in strangers, in people who have lost everything, in those who are sick or in prison. In other words, he is a King, but we find him where society's powerless and rejected people are.

Show the upside-down face and turn it round so that the king turns into a poor, ragged man.

All this makes Jesus a very unusual sort of king – a kind of topsy-turvy king, like this upside-down face. *(Hand out copies of the face.)* When we look at what Jesus himself said about his kingdom, we learn how that, too, turns our expectations upside-down. The kingdom of God does not always appear grand: it can be small and humble-looking, like yeast or a mustard seed, but it can grow into something great. It may be small but it is incredibly precious, like a single, perfect pearl or a pot of buried treasure. The kingdom of God does not always seem fair by our standards: people who assume they have a place there are shut out, and those who we might think don't merit the honour are welcomed with open arms. Those who expect to be the least important find they are the most important – and vice versa. The kingdom of God does not distribute wealth fairly, either: the King is crazily generous and lavishes riches on all sorts of people, regardless of whether or not they deserve them. The kingdom of God is not a fortress for those who want to keep themselves safe within its walls: it is entered by those who risk everything. Finally, the kingdom of God is not governed by a tyrant who demands and enforces obedience. The only people who don't get in are those who choose not to – who reject or ignore the generous invitation which the King offers to everyone.

Music From heaven you came

Activity As we are thinking today about kings and servants, I'd like to give you all the chance to be a king – and a servant. Could I have some volunteers in pairs?

Invite your volunteers forwards and give one of each pair a chair to carry. Explain that the chair-carrier is the servant: their job is to follow the king closely, wherever he/she goes, and to be ready with the chair the minute the king wants to sit down. It is the king's job to walk wherever he/she wants and to sit down whenever he/she pleases, without turning round. Demonstrate first with one pair. Then set off all the volunteers; after a time, tell the kings and servants to swap roles.

Exploring 2

What was it like being a servant in that last activity?

Invite responses.

Jesus calls us to serve him by serving each other, particularly those people who are most in need. Our activity gave us an insight into what that kind of service might involve. There is hard work: carrying the chair around was not easy, and helping other people can be difficult, time-consuming and frustrating, as well as rewarding and fulfilling. But when the servants in our activity were not actually busy putting the chair in position, they were still serving because their attention was absolutely focused on the king's needs. Was he about to sit down? He hadn't sat down for a while – so would he want the chair soon? The servants had to pay attention to little details: if the king stopped walking, or started to bend over, that might mean they had to be there, ready, with the chair. This is the other side of serving others: not only doing the work, but also being attentive, watching and waiting, considering another person's needs above all else.

This kind of service is an expression of love. Just think of how naturally we focus our attention on another person and their needs when we love them: new parents watch over their baby, attending to every smile and whimper; couples who have fallen in love have eyes for no one else. Old friends seem to sense when we particularly need help or a shoulder to cry on. This is how Jesus served us when he lived among us and died for us, and it is the example of service which he asks us to follow, so that we might join him in his kingdom. Loving and serving other people like this won't always be easy – but we are called to try.

Music

Brother, sister, let me serve you

Prayer action

You may like to demonstrate these different positions yourself, or ask for a volunteer.

If we were to meet a king, we would be expected to bow or curtsey. Subjects have always shown respect for a king's power by some kind of physical gesture: they might bow their head, kneel, remain standing or even lie face down on the floor. All these physical positions have been used in prayer, too, because they help us to acknowledge God's power and authority over us. Today, as we think of Christ the King sitting on the throne of his glory in heaven, surrounded by angels, let's choose a position for our prayers: we could bow our heads, kneel, stand or lie down.

Allow time for everyone to choose a position in which they are comfortable.

In a moment of quiet, let's call to mind all those who need someone to love and serve them.

Pause for a short time.

Let us pray.
Heavenly King, we come before you now.
Show us how to serve you by serving one another
in your name.
Amen.

Conclusion

Invite everyone to stand.
Jesus, our Servant King,
as we go out into the world,
grow in us the habit of attentiveness.
Teach us to serve and lead us in the ways of your kingdom.
Amen.

Give notices, announce the next all-age service and invite everyone to the feast.

God's Kingdom

Sowing the seed

Theme	Growing God's kingdom
Scripture	Matthew 13:1–9, 18–23

Running order	Total: 50 minutes
Welcome	Salt dough prayers *(5 minutes)*
Introduction	Opening the theme
Storytelling	The sower's story *(5 minutes)*
Exploring	How can we grow God's kingdom? – Thinking about the birds, the stony ground, the thorns and the healthy crop *(15 minutes)*
Music	We eat the plants that grow from the seed *(5 minutes)*
Activity	Sowing the seeds of love – cress hearts *(10 minutes)*
Prayer action	'In the hollow of his hand' – interactive blessing *(5 minutes)*
Music	He's got the whole world in his hand *(5 minutes)*
Conclusion	Closing prayer and invitation

Resources

- Salt dough *(see appendix for Crib Service)*. Colour one half blue and the other green and form them into a rough sphere to suggest the earth
- A bowl of seeds (sunflower will do, or you can buy wheat grain from health food shops)
- Music and words
- Lots of sheets of kitchen roll
- Scissors
- Small plastic plates, or paper plates with a square of tin foil on them
- Cress seeds
- A couple of small watering cans
- Lots of carrot seeds. Have plenty to spare so that children who lose theirs may still have some to take home
- A couple of dishes for the carrot seeds
- Four tables or areas around the church, with the following:
- Pictures *(see appendix)*
  - crows in a ploughed field
  - a field ripe for harvest *or* (instead of a picture) some real ears of wheat
- A little heap of stony soil with a wilting plant sticking out of it
- A heap of brambles or other weeds

Leaders

Minimum: 1

- Leader/Storyteller

Optimum: 6+

- Leader *(Introduction and Conclusion)*
- Storyteller (with simple props or costume to suggest a farmer: a hat, a waterproof jacket, etc.)
- Explorer
- Music Leader
- Activity Leader
- Prayer Leader

Suggestions for additional music

- Jesus Christ, perfect love
- Your love reaches out to me

Service

Welcome

As people arrive, invite them to create something out of salt dough as a sign of their prayer.

Introduction

Jesus loved telling stories. He used them to tell people about God and about God's way of doing things. Today's story is about a farmer sowing seeds: it is told to us by the farmer him/herself.

Storytelling

Storyteller is dressed as a farmer, holding a bowl of seeds.

This seed is precious to me. I have kept it safe and dry since last harvest and I've watched over it to make sure that rats and birds don't steal it. I want it to grow and thrive; I want it to root in good soil and become the biggest, best crop I have ever grown.

I want to sow this seed as generously as I can. That way, I have the best chance of a good yield. I can't stint on the sowing, so I will scatter all the seed I have.

We farmers are realistic, mind you. There is an old saying for sowing-time: 'One for the rook, one for the crow, one to let rot and one to let grow'. I know that the birds will steal some of my seeds before they even have a chance to take root.

The farmer then moves to each area in turn. First, sprinkle seeds in front of the picture of crows.

I know that some seeds will take root where the soil is stony, and the little seedlings won't be strong enough to withstand the full heat of the sun.

Sprinkle seeds in front of the stony soil and the withered plant.

I know that some seeds will grow well, only to be choked by weeds.

Sprinkle seeds in front of the weeds.

But I still pin all my hopes on the seed which escapes the crows and the stones and the weeds – the seed which falls where the soil is ready and waiting. I picture this field turning from green to waving gold; I picture a barn piled high with grain, a hundred times fuller than before.

Sprinkle seeds in front of the ears of wheat/the picture of a field ripe for harvest.

This is my hope for my seed: this is what I know it can become.

Exploring

Jesus used the story of the sower to tell people about God's kingdom. He said that this seed is 'the word of God's kingdom'. But what does that mean? The simplest explanation is that 'God's kingdom' means 'God's way of doing things'[1] – and God's way is all about love. If the seed in our story is the word of God's kingdom then that word must be Love.

Today we are going to think about the seed in our story as God's love which he wants to grow in the world. Here are the four areas where seed has been sown.

Indicate the table with the seed and the picture of crows.

Here, birds have snatched the seed away. I wonder what stops love taking root in the world?

Indicate the stony soil and the withered plant.

Here, stony soil has stopped the roots becoming deep and strong, so the plant withers in the hot sun. I wonder what makes it hard for love to thrive?

Indicate the weeds.

Here, the growing plants are choked by weeds. I wonder what pressures and concerns crowd out love in the world?

Indicate the ears of wheat/the picture of a field ripe for harvest.

1. Keith White in *Through the eyes of a child*, ed. Anne Richards and Peter Privett, Church House Publishing 2009, p.48.

Here, the plants have taken root in good soil and they have grown strong and tall; they promise a huge harvest. I wonder what difference love makes in the world, if it has a chance to grow and thrive?

Take some time now to visit each of these areas and think about what you find there. Ask yourself, 'What am *I* doing to help God's love grow in the world? And what may be stopping that growth?'

Allow plenty of time for people to visit each area. You may like to invite comments at the end.

The seed in our story is the word of God's kingdom, and that word is Love. God wants that little word to take root in the world, to grow and flourish. He wants his word of love to grow stronger than the thorns of greed and deeper than the shallow soil of self-interest. He wants his word of love to yield so abundantly that all the hatred in the world cannot steal it away. God wants us to help his love grow in the world. Whenever we say or do something out of love, we are helping God's love – God's kingdom – to thrive.

Music

We eat the plants that grow from the seed

Activity

Our activity today will remind us about sowing the seeds of love in the world. Cut the shape of a heart from several layers of kitchen roll, place it on a plastic plate and water it lightly. Then sprinkle cress seeds onto the heart. Put it on a sunny window sill at home, then watch it grow. If it is kept well watered, your cress heart will soon be a living reminder that we need to do all we can to grow God's love in the world.

Allow plenty of time for people to cut out and sow their heart shapes. Five or six sheets on top of each other can be cut out together, making a good bed for the seeds.

Prayer action

Just as God wants his love to grow in the world, he wants us to grow, too: he wants us to blossom into the best people we can be. Our prayer today is an old Celtic blessing which prays that God might hold us all, like tiny seeds, in the hollow of his hand. As a sign of our prayer, we will give each other a tiny carrot seed. This represents new life and growth which need to be nurtured: if you take your seed home and plant it, you'll water it and hope to see it thrive. Let us pray that in this growing season, God will help us all to grow in love.

Invite everyone to stand and, if numbers allow, to gather in a circle.

May the road rise to meet you,
May the wind be always at your back,
May the sun shine warm upon your face,
May the rains fall softly upon your fields.
Until we meet again,

Turn to the person next to you and place a seed in their open palm, saying:

May God hold you in the hollow of his hand.[1]

Each person repeats this line as they give a seed to their neighbour, and so on, round the circle until the last person gives a seed to you. Then all say together:
Amen.

Music

He's got the whole world in his hand

Conclusion

Lord of all life and growth,
nurture the seed of your kingdom within us
and help us to grow your love in the world.
Amen.

Give notices, announce the next all-age service and invite everyone to the feast.

1. Source unknown (Celtic).

Small things and great treasure

Theme	The kingdom of heaven
Scripture	Matthew 13:31–33, 44–52

Running order	Total: 50 minutes
Welcome/Activity	Bread-making *(20 minutes)*
Introduction	Opening the theme
Storytelling 1	The mustard seed – visual, interactive storytelling *(5 minutes)*
Exploring 1	How can we help God's kingdom come? *(2 minutes)*
Music	The kingdom is upon you *(5 minutes)*
Storytelling 2	The pearl – visual storytelling *(5 minutes)*
Exploring 2	What is the promise of God's kingdom? *(3 minutes)*
Music	O, heaven is in my heart *(5 minutes)*
Prayer action	Yeast-prayers – contemplative prayer *(5 minutes)*
Conclusion	Prayer and invitation followed by cooking and eating the fresh bread

Resources

- Ingredients for bread-making *(see appendix)*, plus one quantity of fresh, ready-made dough
- Wipe-clean tables with extra flour for dusting, baking trays and clean tea towels
- Some aprons (child and adult sizes)
- If your church has no bathroom, provide bowls of water and towels for hand-washing
- If your church has no kitchen, take the rolls home and bake them, then freeze them and serve them at the next all-age service. For today's feast, provide some rolls which you made earlier
- Music and words
- Some mustard seeds
- A piece of plastic sheeting / small, folded tarpaulin
- Some soil
- A small watering can
- Green shoots, leaves, a leafy twig and some branches
- Some paper birds *(see appendix)*
- A piece of velvet cloth
- Lots of loose pearl-effect beads (try charity shops for cheap pearl-effect necklaces)
- One larger bead or pearly, opaque marble
- Some gold coins *(see appendix for Tempted)*
- Copies of pearls on card *(see appendix)*, hidden around the church
- Some dishes of dried yeast

Leaders

Minimum: 2

- Leader
- Baker / Activity Leader

Optimum: 6

- Leader *(Introduction and Conclusion)*
- Baker / Activity Leader
- Storyteller
- Explorer
- Music Leader
- Prayer Leader

Suggestions for additional music

- If you believe and I believe
- God of life, God of love

Service

Welcome/Activity

As everyone arrives, invite them to join in with the bread-making by kneading the dough and shaping it into small rolls. Begin with one quantity of ready-mixed dough: it will then need about 10 minutes of kneading. If lots more people are ready to join in, have the ingredients ready to mix another quantity of dough from scratch. Have your baking trays to hand for the finished rolls. Cover them with damp tea towels and leave them to rise in a warm place during the service. Allow enough time at the end of the bread-making for people to wash their hands. Switch on the oven to pre-heat during the service.

Introduction

Jesus spent a great deal of time teaching people, and one of his most important lessons was about the kingdom of God, which is also called the kingdom of heaven. He used lots of different images to help people understand what God's kingdom is like: we will explore some of those images today.

Storytelling 1

The growing tree may be laid out flat on the floor or held upright, depending on how well people can see it from where they are sitting.

This is a story about how things grow.

Spread out the sheet and the soil.

Once upon a time there was a tiny seed.

Show the mustard seed.

This is where it began.

Place the mustard seed in a small amount of soil and sprinkle water on it.

This is what happened next: a tiny shoot appeared.

Place a small shoot coming from the soil.

Then there was a little leaf – then another, and another.

Place a few small leaves.

Then the shoot grew stronger . . .

Replace the shoot and leaves with a thin twig.

and stronger . . .

Replace the twig with a bigger, longer branch.

and then there were more shoots and twigs and branches and leaves all over the place . . .

Invite children to help spread out all the branches and hold them in a tree shape.

until at last there was a great big tree. In its shady branches, there's room for lots of birds to make their homes.

Invite children to help put the birds in the branches.

And all of this started with one tiny little seed.

Show a mustard seed again.

Exploring 1

Jesus told a story about a tiny seed like this: a mustard seed. He said that it reminded him of the kingdom of God – in other words, 'God's way of doing things.'[1] And God's way of doing things is all about love. Just like this tree, love can start as something really small, like a kind word, and turn into something much, much bigger which spreads out into the lives of many other people. It could turn into a wonderful friendship or a family; it could turn into a peace treaty or a worldwide charity.

The mustard seed story shows us that God's kingdom is something which we can help to build here and now,

1. Keith White in *Through the eyes of a child*, ed. Anne Richards and Peter Privett, Church House Publishing 2009, p.48.

on earth. We help the kingdom come by trying to do things God's way – and that way is love. Remember this great big tree and think: is there some small, kind thing I could do or say today which might grow into something great?

Music The kingdom is upon you

Storytelling 2 Here is another story Jesus told about God's kingdom.

Spread out the velvet cloth.

Once upon a time, there was a man who bought and sold pearls for a living.

Scatter the pearls on the velvet cloth.

He travelled far and wide looking for the finest pearls in the world.

Pick up and examine different pearls as you talk – encourage the children to do so, too.

He knew exactly how to judge the shape and lustre of pearls, how to pick the best from the rest, how to find the perfect pearl among a lot of also-rans. He became very rich.

Scatter the coins on the velvet.

Then one day, everything changed.

Hold the special pearl in the palm of your hand.

He found a pearl so extraordinary and so valuable that he knew he had to have it. He couldn't rest until it was his. So he gathered together all his money *(scoop up the coins)*, all his other pearls *(scoop up the pearls)* and everything he had *(fold up the velvet cloth)* and gave all of it in exchange for that one, precious pearl.

Put all the other props away and hold the special pearl in both hands in front of you. Pause for a moment.

Exploring 2

Jesus said that the precious pearl was like the kingdom of heaven. His story shows another way of understanding God's kingdom: it is the kingdom which is promised to us at the end of time, when everything in creation will become subject to God's way of doing things. This kingdom is like a precious pearl because it is where God will gather us all in and keep us close to him forever. What does this mean for us? Let's find out. Hidden around the church are lots of big pearls. Can everyone find one?

Allow some time for everyone to find a pearl.

This pearl is yours to keep and treasure, because these words from the Bible spell out God's wonderful promise to us:

> Neither death, nor life, nor angels, nor rulers, nor things present, nor things to come, nor powers, nor height, nor depth, nor anything else in all creation, will be able to separate us from the love of God in Christ Jesus our Lord.

When God's kingdom comes, nothing will separate us from his love – and that precious promise is worth more than anything on earth.

Music

O, heaven is in my heart

Prayer action

If the rolls are well risen by now, bring them out and use them as a focus for this prayer.

We began this service by making bread, and since then the dough has been magically growing and rising. Our rolls are twice the size they were when we made them. Does anyone know why? *(Invite contributions.)* Yeast is the little ingredient which makes a big difference: it turns stodgy dumplings into round, fluffy rolls. That is why Jesus said that yeast is like God's kingdom, God's loving way of doing things. If we mix a bit of love into our lives and the lives of others, it makes all the difference in the world.

For our prayers today, we are going to take some dried yeast and think about the difference it can make.

Pass round the dishes of dried yeast and invite everyone to take a pinch and to hold it in their open palm.

Look at how insignificant this yeast seems. It hardly weighs anything and it's a dull beige colour. But if you smell it, there is a faint promise of what yeast can do. As we hold this yeast, let's rest in God's presence and ask whether there is any seemingly small, insignificant thing we could say or do which has the potential to make a big difference. Let us pray that, like this yeast, we might be agents of change in the world.

Pause for a moment of silence.

We pray for ourselves, but also for our church, remembering that we are one body. Let's gather all our yeast together now and pray that together, as a church, we might be God's agent of change in our community.

Everyone comes forward and puts their yeast back in the dishes. If your congregation is large, two or more dishes could be passed among the people instead.

God of small things and great changes,
however humble our efforts,
help us to grow your kingdom in the world.
Amen.

Put the rolls in the oven now!

Conclusion

Father God,
may we help your kingdom come on earth
and look forward to the promise
of your eternal kingdom,
in Jesus' name.
Amen.

Give notices, announce the next all-age service and invite everyone to a feast of fresh bread rolls in about 10-15 minutes.

One for All

Fruits of the kingdom

Theme	Growing the kingdom of God
Scripture	Matthew 21:33–46

Running order	Total: 50 minutes
Welcome	Natural treasures *(5 minutes)*
Introduction	Opening the theme
Storytelling	Dramatised dialogue – the parable of the tenants in the vineyard *(5 minutes)*
Music	For the fruits of his creation *(5 minutes)*
Activity	Finding the fruits of the kingdom – treasure hunt *(10 minutes)*
Exploring	What can we do to produce the fruits of the kingdom? – active reflection *(15 minutes)*
Music	Put peace into each other's hands *(5 minutes)*
Prayer action	Sharing the fruits – active offertory prayer *(5 minutes)*
Conclusion	Closing prayer and invitation

Resources

- Natural treasures such as shells, polished stones, feathers, conkers and bright autumn leaves, attractively displayed – perhaps on a velvet cloth, or in a collection of little jewellery boxes
- A sign next to the treasures: 'The earth is the Lord's and all that is in it'
- A plate with two or three bunches of grapes
- Music and words
- Some bare branches
- Bunches of grapes (outlines on card) *(see appendix)*:
  - 11 bunches labelled with the fruits of the kingdom: hide all except 'Justice' and 'Righteousness' around the church
  - Lots of blank bunches
- Pens
- Green or brown wool
- Scissors

Leaders

Minimum: 4

- Leader
- Cast x 3

Optimum: 9

- Leader *(Introduction and Conclusion)*
- Storyteller
- Cast x 3 (in modern or traditional dress)
  Jesus, wearing white
  Two chief priests, wearing smart clothes or robes
- Activity Leader
- Explorer
- Music Leader
- Prayer Leader

Suggestions for additional music

- Christ is our cornerstone
- Come and see the shining hope

Service

Welcome

As people arrive, invite them to spend some time in quiet contemplation of the natural treasures you have displayed.

Introduction

Show a bunch of grapes.

Who likes grapes? *(Invite a show of hands.)* Where Jesus lived, grapes grew as easily as apples do in this country, and lots of people either owned vineyards or were hired to work in them. Our service today begins with a story Jesus told about a vineyard.

Storytelling

Let's set the scene. We are in the temple in Jerusalem. All of us here are pilgrims who have crowded into the courtyards. Some of us have come to pray, but all of us are hoping to get a glimpse of Jesus who was here yesterday, causing trouble. Rumour has it that he smashed up the market stalls here in the temple and shouted at the chief priests! If he comes back again today, there might be something worth watching. Look – here come the chief priests, looking very serious. *(The two chief priests enter at the front.)* And there he is! There's Jesus! *(Jesus walks down the aisle.)*[1]

Jesus — Listen to another parable. There was a landowner who planted a vineyard, put a fence around it, dug a wine press in it, and built a watch-tower. Then he leased it to tenants and went to another country. When the harvest time had come, he sent his slaves to the tenants to collect his produce. But the tenants seized his slaves and beat one, killed another, and stoned another. Again he sent other slaves, more than the first; and they treated them in the same way. Finally he sent his son to them, saying, 'They will respect my son.' But when the tenants saw the son, they said to themselves, 'This is the heir; come, let us kill him and get his inheritance.' So they seized him, threw him out of the vineyard, and killed him. Now when the owner of the vineyard comes, what will he do to those tenants?

1. The following lines are taken directly from Matthew's Gospel (NRSV): you may prefer to use a different translation.

First chief priest — He will put those wretches to a miserable death . . .

Second chief priest — . . . and lease the vineyard to other tenants who will give him the produce at the harvest time.

Jesus — Therefore I tell you, the kingdom of God will be taken away from you *(pointing at the priests)* and given to a people that produces the fruits of the kingdom. *(He gestures towards the congregation.)*

Storyteller — The chief priests looked at each other. How dare he? They wanted to arrest him, but they were afraid to do anything in front of the watching crowds. The people were on Jesus' side – who knew what they might do if the priests laid a finger on the people's hero?

Music

For the fruits of his creation

Activity

Bring the bare branches forward.

In his story, Jesus compared the kingdom of God to a vineyard which would be 'given to a people that produces the fruits of the kingdom.' If God's kingdom is God's way of doing things,[2] then what are its fruits? If we do things God's way, then what do we have to show for it? The Bible has a lot to say about vineyards and fruits. The Old Testament describes the Jewish people as God's vineyard, and says that the harvest which God expected was justice and righteousness[3] – so these are two results of doing things God's way, two fruits of the kingdom.

Add the bunches of grapes labelled 'Justice' and 'Righteousness' to the branches.

In the New Testament, Paul gives a long list of what he calls, 'the fruit of the Spirit'[4]: these are also signs that we are doing things God's way. There are lots of these fruits hidden around the church: can you find them?

People find the nine labelled bunches of grapes: read them out as you add them to the branches.

2. Keith White in *Through the eyes of a child*, ed. Anne Richards and Peter Privett, Church House Publishing 2009, p.48.
3. Isaiah 5:7.
4. Galatians 5:22.

Exploring

Jesus told his story in terms which would have been familiar to his audience. Many were farmers, used to planting crops and anticipating harvest; lots of ordinary people found seasonal work helping to pick the grapes in local vineyards. Although we are less familiar with these things, Jesus' story does demonstrate to us that the kingdom of God is not just something we have to wait and hope for at the end of time. It is also something we can work for here and now: like the grape harvest, it requires our hands-on involvement and good, honest labour.

So how can we work to produce the fruits of the kingdom, like justice, peace and generosity? What can we do, in our daily lives, to demonstrate God's way of doing things? For example, is there an argument which could be resolved if we said sorry? Do we know someone who needs a friend? Take some time now to think and talk about this. *(Show the blank bunches of grapes.)* Then write down some specific things we could do to produce the fruits of the kingdom: fill in as many of these bunches of grapes as you can and add them to the branches.

Allow plenty of time for people to think, discuss and add bunches of grapes. You may like to invite people to share their contributions.

Music

Put peace into each other's hands

Prayer action

'Put peace into each other's hands . . . Put Christ into each other's hands' – the words of our hymn inspire our prayer action today. We pray for the grace to share the fruits of God's kingdom with one another and with the world. As a sign of our prayer, we will share these grapes. Take one and give it to the person next to you as we pray.

Hold the plate and give a grape to your neighbour, then say the words of the prayer as the plate is passed among the people and the grapes are shared.

Loving Lord, may we put peace into each other's hands.
May we put love into each other's hands.
May we put joy into each other's hands.
May we put patience into each other's hands.
May we put kindness into each other's hands.
May we put generosity into each other's hands.
May we put faithfulness into each other's hands.
May we put gentleness into each other's hands.
May we put self-control into each other's hands.
May we put justice into each other's hands.
May we put righteousness into each other's hands,
in Jesus' name,
Amen.

Conclusion

Heavenly Father,
as we go out into the world,
may we work to produce the fruits of your kingdom.
Amen.

Give notices, announce the next all-age service and invite everyone to the feast.

An open invitation

Theme	God calls everyone to his kingdom
Scripture	Matthew 22:1–14

Running order	Total: 50 minutes
Welcome	Holding crosses *(5 minutes)*
Introduction	Opening the theme
Storytelling	Interactive dramatisation of the parable of the wedding banquet *(10 minutes)*
Music	The King is among us *(5 minutes)*
Exploring	Who is invited to the kingdom? Visual exploration *(10 minutes)*
Prayer action	Open arms – active praise *(5 minutes)*
Music	I come with joy *(5 minutes)*
Activity	Sharing the feast *(10 minutes)*
Conclusion	Closing prayer and invitation

Resources

- Holding crosses *(see appendix)*. You may like to spread these out on a rug, with cushions for people to sit on
- At the front of church, some long tables (no chairs) laid end to end and laid as if for a banquet: white cloths, fancy glasses, lots of cutlery, flowers, etc.
- Props: a mobile phone, a hanky splashed with red food colouring
- 'Party clothes' for everyone: fancy robes or cloaks, party hats, party masks, tinsel scarves etc. – whatever you can find
- Music and words
- Invitations *(see appendix)* placed under every seat
- Pens in every pew / under every seat
- A picture of Christ the Redeemer – the statue in Rio de Janeiro – together with the song words *(see appendix)*
- A recording of 'Come as you are' *(see appendix)*, plus sound equipment to play it on
- Party food on plates

Leaders

Minimum: 3

- Leader / ***King*** or ***Personal Assistant*** (PA)
- Cast x 2

Optimum: 8

- Leader *(Introduction and Conclusion)*
- Cast x 3
  King, wearing formal clothes and a crown
  PA, wearing a suit
  Ungrateful Guest (non-speaking), dressed in ordinary clothes and sitting with the congregation
- Explorer
- Music Leader
- Prayer Leader
- Activity Leader

Suggestions for additional music

- Rejoice, the Lord is King!
- There's a place where the streets shine

Service

Welcome As people arrive, invite them to spend some quiet time handling the holding crosses.

Introduction We all know how lovely it is to get a party invitation – and how sad we feel if we are not invited. We feel even worse if we throw a party and none of our guests turn up. Today's story is about a very grand party: it is a party fit for a prince, but it didn't turn out exactly as planned.

Storytelling

Personal assistant: Pray silence for his majesty, the king!

The PA leaves.

King: *(Addressing the congregation.)* Today is a very special occasion. My son the prince is getting married and I am giving a wedding banquet in his honour. All the finest, most important people in the land have been invited. *(He moves round the table, indicating places.)* These seats here are for Lord and Lady Muck; this is for a Premiership footballer; several A-list celebrities will be sitting here. I only want the best for my boy. But I wonder where they are? The invitations said 7pm and it's already a quarter to eight. My chef tells me that dinner is ready to serve – where can my guests have got to? I've sent my personal assistant to find out.

PA: Your majesty, I couldn't find them – but Lord and Lady Muck rang to say they had a crisis at their country estate, so they can't come.

King: What about the footballer? He's my son's favourite. Go and find him.

The PA leaves.

Hang on, I'm getting a text. *(The king consults his mobile.)* It's those celebrities: they've all had to go to a showbiz party, apparently.

The PA returns, clutching a blood-stained hanky to his/her nose.

PA: The footballer's not coming. He punched me in the face.

King WHAT?! From now on, he's a nobody as far as I'm concerned. And the rest of them, the ungrateful lot. They're all dead to me. But this feast is ready, and the guests who were invited don't deserve it. So I want you to go out there, into the streets, *(indicating the congregation)* and invite everyone to my banquet.

PA *(Looking dubiously at the congregation.)* What – everyone?

King Everyone.

The PA invites people to come forward and gather around the table. The Ungrateful Guest, currently incognito, should be among them. The king addresses everyone – those around the table and those still seated in the congregation.

Welcome, one and all! Please accept these wedding clothes as a gift from me.

The king distributes cloaks, party hats, tinsel scarves, etc. to everyone. The Ungrateful Guest leaves his on the floor. The king spots him.

Friend, how come you are not wearing the wedding clothes I gave you?

The Guest looks awkward.

Get out! Security – throw him into the streets!

The Ungrateful Guest runs off.

Everybody else – enjoy the party! The feast will begin shortly.

Music

The King is among us

During the hymn, people return to their seats – but they can keep their party hats and clothes on if they wish!

Exploring

Our story of the wedding banquet is an updated version of a parable which Jesus told. He used it to describe what the kingdom of heaven is like. What does this story have to tell us? Who is invited to God's kingdom? These are the questions we will be exploring today. Underneath your seats, you will each find an invitation for you. You might like to fill in your own name at the top.

Allow time for everyone to find their invitations and write their names.

These are like the second set of invitations sent out by the king in our story. The select group of important people didn't bother to turn up, so the king sent his servant out into the streets with that wonderful instruction, 'Invite everyone!' I wonder what the aristocrats and celebrities thought when they saw who the king had invited instead?

Invite responses.

How would we feel if we were in the supermarket and were suddenly given an invitation to a royal banquet at Buckingham Palace?

Invite responses.

Jesus said that this is what God's kingdom is like. Let's look at Jesus more closely as we explore what he meant by this.

Hand out the picture of Christ the Redeemer, the statue with open arms.

Jesus was a Jew and his people were waiting for the Messiah – the Saviour whom God had promised to send to his chosen people. When Jesus came, he outraged his neighbours in Nazareth by telling them that he was the Saviour and that he would help and save all sorts of non-Jewish people too. In Jesus' ministry, he demonstrated time and time again that anyone was welcome to come to him for help, whether they were a Roman centurion, women from Samaria or Canaan or someone suffering from leprosy. None of these was accepted by Jesus' people, but Jesus himself stepped across the boundaries and reached out to them.

In the same way, he reaches out to all of us. Another way of looking at Jesus' arms, stretched out on the cross, is to see him making a huge welcoming gesture to us all *(hold out your own arms in welcome)*. This famous statue of Jesus in Brazil *(indicate the picture)* looks just like this. When he predicted his death, he said, 'And I, when I am lifted up from the earth, will draw all people to myself.'[1] By opening his arms on the cross he says to us all, 'Come to me!' Like the king in the story, he invites everyone. He wants us all to be with him in his kingdom.

But there is someone in this story who doesn't get a happy ending. What about the wedding guest who was thrown out for not wearing the right clothes? Surely the kingdom of heaven doesn't have a strict dress code, does it?

Hold up a fine robe.

This part of the story seems rather cruel until we discover what actually happened at the sort of banquets Jesus was describing. Historical evidence suggests that these royal feasts were hosted with lavish generosity. The king presented his guests with special wedding robes to wear – so the person in our story who wasn't wearing one had rejected a generous gift offered by his royal host.

Throw the robe aside.

What about us? What does this story tell us? It reminds us that we are all invited to God's kingdom *(show the invitation)*. It tells us to accept the love which God offers us in his Son, because it is the precious gift of life *(put on the robe)*. Most of all, this story shows us that whoever and whatever we are, Jesus opens his arms to us and says, 'Come to me, just as you are.'

Show the picture of Christ the Redeemer again and play the opening part of the song, 'Come as you are', following the words from the chorus.

Prayer action

Hold out your arms in welcome.

We will use this open, welcoming gesture in our prayers today, as we pray with our bodies as well as

1. John 12:32.

with words. Our prayer will begin, 'Heavenly King': raise your hands up like this *(stretch your arms up, palms facing upwards).* When I say, 'You welcomed us to your kingdom with open arms,' open your arms like this *(stretch your arms open wide).* When I say, 'Your love', cross your hands over your heart *(demonstrate the action)* and when I say, 'May we welcome others,' spread your arms open wide as if welcoming everybody *(stretch your arms forwards and then open them outwards).*

You may wish to practise these actions once more. Say the words of the prayer slowly and thoughtfully as you all perform the actions.

As we call to mind God's all-embracing love, let us pray.
Heavenly King,
on the cross you welcomed us to your kingdom with open arms.
Your love is an open invitation:
may we welcome others in your name.
Amen.

Music I come with joy

Activity *Bring out plates of food and cover the banqueting table with them, then invite everyone to come and join the feast!*

Conclusion Generous Lord,
in our church, in our work and in our lives,
help us to share the good news
that your love welcomes everyone.
Amen.

Give notices and announce the next all-age service.

One for All

The wealth of the kingdom

Theme	God's generosity and using our talents
Scripture	Matthew 25:14–30

Running order	Total: 50 minutes
Welcome	Natural treasures *(5 minutes)*
Introduction	Opening the theme
Storytelling	Sketch – the Boss and his money *(10 minutes)*
Exploring/Activity	What should we do with our talents? Written brainstorm and TV talent show clip *(15 minutes)*
Music	Take my hands, Lord *(5 minutes)*
Prayer action	Counting blessings – creative thanksgiving *(10 minutes)*
Music	Be bold, be strong *(5 minutes)*
Conclusion	Closing prayer and invitation

Resources

- Natural treasures such as shells, polished stones, feathers, flowers and leaves, attractively displayed – perhaps on a velvet cloth, or in a collection of little jewellery boxes
- 5 copies of the large cheque *(see appendix)*
- Underneath every seat, an envelope containing a pen and the outline of a person *(see appendix)*
- *Optional*: a clip from a TV talent show, plus equipment to show it on
- Music and words
- On tables around the church:
  - Lots of beads, buttons or sequins of different colours and shapes
  - Thread or thin jewellery wire

Leaders

Minimum: 5

- Leader
- Cast x 4

Optimum: 9

- Leader *(Introduction and Conclusion)*
- Cast x 4, all wearing smart business clothes

  Boss, with a holiday shirt or sun hat for his/her second entrance

  Chief executive, with a laptop and a mobile phone

  Deputy chief executive, with two mobile phones

  Third executive
- Activity Leader
- Explorer
- Music Leader
- Prayer Leader

Suggestions for additional music

- I will offer up my life
- Lord of the future

Service

Welcome

As people arrive, invite them to spend some time in quiet contemplation of the natural treasures you have displayed.

Introduction

Our service today is all about a story that Jesus told which has become known as 'The parable of the talents'. Before we tell it, we need to do a little bit of translating – and some maths. In Jesus' time, a talent was a large amount of money – it was worth six thousand times the daily wage of a labourer. Today, a factory worker might earn about £50 a day[1], so in today's money a talent would be worth £50 x 6000, which is . . . ? *(Invite responses.)* One talent equals £300,000 in today's money! That is one sum of money mentioned in our story.

Show the big cheque for £300,000.

But our story also involves two more sums of money. What would two talents be worth today? *(Invite responses.)* Two talents equal £600,000! That is the second sum of money mentioned in our story.

Show the big cheque for £600,000.

Finally, there are five talents. What is 5 x £300,000? *(Invite responses.)* £1.5 million! That's the biggest sum of money mentioned in our story.

Produce the big cheque for £1,500,000.

Now we're ready for our story: an updated version of Jesus' parable of the talents.

Storytelling

These characters can be male or female. Substitute 'Ma'am' for 'Sir' as necessary.

Boss: I'm the Boss. I'm a self-made multi-millionaire. I've built my business empire out of nothing in six years. I've taken some risks, played the stock market and

1. Based on an 8-hour shift at 2010 minimum wage level – adjust as necessary.

made my money multiply itself. Now things are looking good. I deserve a break, so I'm off overseas for an extended holiday – but I need to leave some people in charge of my business, to protect my interests.

Chief executive: Good morning, sir.

Boss: Ah, my chief executive. Just the person. I want you to look after this for me while I'm away.

Hands over the cheque for £1.5 million.

Chief executive: Sir, I'm honoured that you'd give me such an opportunity! I won't let you down.

Deputy chief executive: Good morning, sir.

Boss: Now, my deputy chief executive. I want you to look after this for me while I'm away.

Hands over the cheque for £600,000.

Deputy chief executive: Sir, thank you for this responsibility. I won't let you down.

Third executive: *(Entering nervously)* G – Good morning, sir.

Boss: The new kid on the block, eh? Here's your chance to show me what you're made of. Look after this for me while I'm away, will you?

Hands over the cheque for £300,000. The third executive looks appalled and says nothing.

Now don't let me down.

The Boss leaves.

Chief executive: *Gets out a laptop and begins tapping furiously.*

Now, investments, investments . . .

Takes out a mobile phone.

Hello, Susan. Put me through to Sir's investment bankers, would you?

Deputy chief executive: *Watches this then gets out two mobile phones and dials furiously.*

(Into the first phone) Hello, put me through to the London Stock Exchange, will you? I need to make an investment. *(Into the second phone)* Hello, is that the Financial Times?

Third executive *Looking helplessly at the cheque and the other two, then speaking to the congregation.*

What am I going to do? I'm worried about the recession, and banks going bust, and the credit crunch, and mounting debts. If I invest this, I might lose the lot, and then where would I be? I know my boss demands a good return on his investments. I'm terrified of disappointing him, so I think I'll just play safe and keep all the money tucked away until he gets back, then I'll return every penny to him and he won't have lost anything. That's the best plan.

Hides the cheque somewhere in the church.

All three executives leave.

The Boss returns, wearing a holiday shirt or a sun hat.

Boss Now, how hard have you been working for me since I left last year? Time to settle the accounts!

Chief executive Sir, I'm pleased to say that I've doubled your money to £3 million!

He hands over the cheque.

Boss Well done, you've proved your worth! I'd like to make you a partner in this business.

Chief executive Thank you, sir!

Deputy chief executive Sir, I'm delighted to tell you that I've doubled your money, too: here's £1.2 million!

He hands over the cheque.

Boss I'm impressed. I'm promoting you to chief executive.

Deputy chief executive Thank you, sir!

Boss What about you?

Third executive I – er – I – well, I know how demanding you are, sir, and I was afraid to lose a single penny of your money, so I kept it safe. It's all here.

He hands over the original cheque.

Boss WHAT? You should have invested this, like the others! I'm giving this to my partner as a bonus. *(He hands over the cheque.)* As for you, you've let me down, you've let the team down and you've let yourself down. You're fired!

Exploring/Activity

Jesus told his story to explain God's kingdom – to illustrate 'God's way of doing things.'[2] Some parts of the story may seem rather harsh: who did you feel sorry for?

Invite responses and ask people to explain their reactions.

Our task today is to explore this story and work out what it is telling us about God's way of doing things. First of all, let's look at those sums of money, called 'talents' in the original story. As the name suggests, they have come to represent our own God-given gifts which we are expected to use in God's service, just as the executives were expected to invest their boss's money and enrich his business empire. What our updated version shows is just how much money Jesus was talking about: hand-outs of £1.5 million, £600,000 and £300,000 – an absolute fortune! This suggests that God gives us gifts and talents in great abundance: he overflows with goodness and gives us each a generous portion of his riches.

I wonder what our own gifts and talents might be? Underneath every seat is an envelope. In it you will find an outline of a person and a pen. Take some time now to think about your own gifts and talents, and fill your person with words or pictures to describe what you are good at. Not everyone has a big, showy talent like singing or football: some people are gifted organisers or listeners; some people are blessed with a cheerfulness that is shared with everyone they meet. You don't need to show anyone else what you write: you can keep your ideas to yourself and put the person back in the envelope when you have finished.

Allow plenty of time for people to fill in their outlines and put them back in the envelope. Make sure you do this yourself, too.

Whoever we are, we are good at something: God has given us some gift or talent. But just having that gift is

2. Keith White in *Through the eyes of a child*, ed. Anne Richards and Peter Privett, Church House Publishing 2009, p.48.

not enough. Our story is about God's way of doing things, and it shows that God expects us to use our gifts and talents to make a difference, to make things better, to increase the sum of his world's goodness. But making that happen is not always easy. Our story was told against the background of banks in trouble and world-wide financial crisis, reminding us that life is full of uncertainty and risk. But the two who won their boss's approval were the two who dared to take a chance. They used their money, their talents, and risked failure and loss. Their gamble paid off, and the boss reserved his anger for the third one, who didn't dare take any chances at all.

Like the boss in our story, God wants us to use what he has given us, not just keep it safely hidden away. He wants us to take chances and risk failure, because only then do we stand a chance of increasing the store of riches he has given us in life. If we want a real-life example of people taking this kind of risk, we need look no further than the TV talent shows. Some people are embarrassingly bad, some are astonishingly good, but they have all taken whatever talent they have and risked exposing it to critical judges and public ridicule.

You may like to show a short clip of some good and bad contestants on current TV talent shows, or some archive footage: Susan Boyle singing 'I dreamed a dream' on Britain's Got Talent *would be an excellent example. After the clip, point out what the contestant(s) risked: stinging criticism, mockery or prejudice and the possibility of rejection.*

Let's peep inside our envelopes where we listed our own gifts and talents. Will they stay in there, safely hidden away? Or will we take a chance? Do we dare to put our gifts and talents to good use?

Music Take my hands, Lord

Prayer action Of course, the gifts which we have received from God amount to much more than the sum of our talents. All good things come from him, and sometimes it is easy to take these things for granted. We may enjoy something every day which someone else longs for, such as a safe place to sleep, a roof over our heads and enough food to eat. How often do we really appreciate our family and friends? Even if you are sad today, try to think of something to be glad about. Our prayers today are simple: we are going to say thank you to God by – literally – counting our blessings. Make yourself comfortable with a piece of thread and a collection of beads and take your time to count all those good things for which you can say, 'Thank you'. As you think of each one, add it onto the thread until you have a whole string of blessings.

Give everyone plenty of time to complete their strings, then invite them to gather with their counted blessings round the altar.

God of overflowing goodness,
we thank you for all these good things.
Show us how to increase these gifts
and make us bold in the service of your kingdom.
Amen.

Music Be bold, be strong

Conclusion Almighty God,
the riches of your grace make us wealthy indeed.
May we use them in Jesus' name,
Amen.

Give notices, announce the next all-age service and invite everyone to the feast.

Being disciples

Living in the light

Theme	Putting on 'the armour of light'
Scripture	Romans 13:11–14 and Matthew 24:36–44

Running order	Total: 50 minutes
Welcome	Lighting a votive candle each *(5 minutes)*
Introduction	Opening the theme
Activity	Stations – different kinds of light *(10 minutes)*
Storytelling	Visual retelling of the Scripture passages *(5 minutes)*
Music	This little light of mine or We are marching *(5 minutes)*
Exploring	How can we live in the light? *(15 minutes)*
Prayer action	Circle of light – interactive offertory prayer *(5 minutes)*
Music	Shine, Jesus, shine *(5 minutes)*
Conclusion	Closing prayer and invitation

Resources

- Votive candles and matches
- Three stations around the church: areas or tables labelled *Being ready*, *Being seen* and *Being the light of the world*
- Items which could belong at each station, placed around the church. For example:

  Being ready: torches and utility candles, a miner's lamp, a picture of a lighthouse, a camping lantern

  Being seen: high-visibility clothing (e.g. arm-bands, tabard, jacket) and reflective badges or stickers

  Being the light of the world: the Paschal candle or other large candle, votive candles, a print of 'The Light of the World' by Holman Hunt, an icon
- A dark-coloured blindfold
- A candle with a cross on it
- A sign for each station: *How can we be prepared?*, *How can we show ourselves clearly?* and *How can we be the light of the world?*
- A pack of Post-it notes per station, preferably in bright colours
- Pens and pencils
- Music and words
- Lots of tubes of glow-sticks *(see appendix)*

Leaders

Minimum: 2

- Leader
- Blindfolded volunteer, dressed in dark clothes

Optimum: 7

- Leader *(Introduction and Conclusion)*
- Activity Leader
- Storyteller
- Blindfolded volunteer
- Music Leader
- Explorer
- Prayer Leader

Suggestions for additional music

- Be bold, be strong
- Awake, awake
- Like a candle flame

Service

Welcome

Invite people to light a votive candle as they arrive.

Introduction

Today we will be thinking about Jesus as the Light of the world – and about what it means to live in the light.

Activity

Turn off the lights and introduce the stations and the scattered objects, picking out the packet of candles, the reflective arm-bands and the Paschal candle.

All over the church there are objects which are bright and light. They do different jobs: some of them are about being prepared for darkness and perhaps danger, like these candles I keep in case of a power cut. Some of these objects help us to be seen in the dark – like these light-reflecting arm-bands. Some of these objects – like this candle – are used in churches to show Jesus as the Light of the world, shining in the dark places of our lives.

Being prepared; being seen and being the light of the world: three different ways of using these bright and shining things. Can you find them all and decide where they belong? Which things help us to be prepared for darkness? Which things help us to be seen in the dark? Which things reflect Jesus, the Light of the world?

Allow a few minutes for people to find the objects and put them where they think they belong. Turn on the lights.

Storytelling

Bring forward your volunteer dressed in dark clothes. Blind-fold them with a dark-coloured strip of fabric.

Sometimes we can lose ourselves in the dark. We can lose control of our lives, forget who we really are and regret what we have become. It can feel as if we are sleepwalking though life, fumbling about in the dark and not knowing where we are going.

Remove the blindfold as you say:

Because God loves us, he wants us to wake up and open our eyes. He doesn't want us to feel as if we have to hide any more. He wants us to live boldly in the light and not be afraid to be seen.

Dress your volunteer in the reflective tabard and high-visibility jacket.

Because God loves us, he wants us to be ready, too: ready to face whatever darkness and danger comes our way, confident that the light of his love is always with us, showing us the way forward. He wants us to be ready to meet him, too, and we never know when that might be.

Give your volunteer a big torch to hold in one hand.

Because God loves us all, he wants each of us to be ready to share his light with the world. If love is at the heart of all that we say and do, then we are each helping to shine the light of God's love into the dark places of our world.

Give your volunteer a candle with a cross on it to hold in the other hand.

This person is not afraid to be seen; he/she is ready for anything and is carrying the light of the world. The Bible calls this 'putting on the armour of light'. This is living in the light – and this is what God is calling us to do.

Music This little light of mine or We are marching in the light of God

Exploring So how can we live in the light? What does that actually mean? Let's look again at these three stations and ask ourselves a question at each one. First of all: what might we do, today and tomorrow, to help us be prepared for the darkness of life, and be ready to let Jesus in? For example, do we need to pray more often?

Attach sign: 'How can we be prepared?'

Secondly: what might we do in our lives to be visible and unafraid? Might that mean standing up for something we believe in, standing out from the crowd? What else might it mean for us?

Attach sign: 'How can we show ourselves clearly?'

Thirdly: how might we show Jesus' light to others? What can we do that would demonstrate his love?

Attach sign: 'How can we be the light of the world?'

Move around and visit each station and use the bright post-it notes there for your practical answers to each question. There is no such thing as a wrong answer here: write or draw as many bright ideas as you like.

Allow plenty of time for people to circulate, think and write, then call everyone together and perhaps read out a few sample answers (anonymously) for each question.

Prayer action

Our prayers today remind us that we are the light of the world. That light is like this glow-stick. *(Show the inactive glow-stick in your hand.)* The light in this stick is hidden – just as some of the goodness in us is hidden. We *could* do something kind, or helpful, or caring – but sometimes we choose not to, or we just can't be bothered. But when we *do* make the effort *(bend the glow-stick until the stuff inside it cracks, activating the light) then* the goodness in us breaks out, like this light, and shines around us. Today, we're going to use these glow-sticks to help make our prayers.

Invite everyone to form a circle and take a glow-stick.

Make this glow-stick your prayer: it is your promise to God to do something loving, kind or helpful for someone else. Make your promise, then crack your glow-stick to let the light break out. Let there be light!

Allow some time for people to make their prayers, then invite everyone to join the sticks up in a huge circle, either by laying them end-to-end on the floor, or by using the connectors supplied. A connected circle of sticks can be held in people's hands. You may like to turn out the lights at this point, too.

Let's take a moment to look at this circle of light, made up of our prayers which represent the light that shines in each of us.
God of all goodness, help us to do good.
May this light of your love encircle the world.
Amen.

Music

Shine, Jesus, shine

Conclusion

Shining Lord,
may you make your face shine upon us
and be gracious to us;
may you look kindly on us and give us peace.
Amen.

Give notices, announce the next all-age service and invite everyone to the feast.

Love in action

Theme	Showing who we are in what we do
Scripture	Matthew 11:2–11

Running order	Total: 50 minutes
Welcome	Lighting a votive candle each *(5 minutes)*
Introduction	Opening the theme
Activity	Sketch – Is there a doctor in the house? *(10 minutes)*
Music	My song is love unknown *(5 minutes)*
Storytelling	Dramatised reading of Matthew 11:2–11 *(5 minutes)*
Exploring	How do we know who people really are? *(15 minutes)*
Prayer action	Elastic heart – interactive thanksgiving *(5 minutes)*
Music	Wide, wide as the ocean *(5 minutes)*
Conclusion	Closing prayer and invitation

Resources

- Votive candles and matches
- A parcel wrapped in brown paper
- Toy animals, some with bandages, eye patches etc.
- Any *Doctor Who* prop or sound effect, such as a Sonic Screwdriver, a snatch of the theme tune or the distinctive sound of the TARDIS
- A scarf and a walking stick, to plant on volunteers
- Fur/animal skin for John
- Chains for John
- Dark robe for Disciple
- White robe for Jesus
- Copies of the heart puzzle *(see appendix)* and envelopes
- Pens and pencils
- Music and words
- A long piece of elastic *(at least 4 m)*, with the ends firmly knotted together

Leaders

Minimum: 5

- Leader/cast member
- Cast/Storytellers x 4

Optimum: 9

- Leader *(Introduction and Conclusion)*
- Three Storytellers *(John, Disciple and Jesus)*
- Music Leader
- Explorer
- Prayer Leader
- Cast x 5 *(may also be Storytellers)*

The Postman/ woman, wearing a navy jacket and a big bag

The Vet, wearing white or green

Doctor Who, wearing anything recognisable as the current Doctor

The Scruff/Doctor, wearing messy or unexpected clothes (such as a hippy, biker or goth outfit)

Injured person

Suggestions for additional music

- Tell out, my soul
- We have a gospel to proclaim
- Will you come and follow me

Service

Welcome Light a votive candle each.

Introduction Today we will be thinking about John the Baptist, God's messenger who was sent to prepare the way for the Messiah. John knew this was his purpose in life, but how did he know that Jesus was the One? How could he be sure that Jesus was the Son of God he had spent his life preparing for? Today we will be thinking about how we can know this, too. We will start with a sketch about a different kind of messenger who is looking for someone.

Activity

Postman *(Addressing the congregation)* Excuse me, I'm trying to deliver this parcel. It says here it's for the Doctor, but the address has been torn off. So I need to look for someone who might be a doctor. Here's someone now . . .

Vet walks on, surrounded by toy animals – many in bandages.

Postman Well, this person certainly looks kind, and they obviously know how to use bandages. Excuse me, are you the Doctor?

Vet Sorry – I do help the sick, but I'm a vet. I only look after animals.

Postman Oh. Never mind, here's someone else. Who's this?

Doctor Who walks on. Someone shouts, 'Doctor Who!'

Postman Doctor – who? So he's the Doctor I'm looking for! Excuse me, sir, I think this presentl is for you.

Doctor Who Present? I wouldn't even be in this dimension if the TARDIS hadn't malfunctioned! Sorry – I don't think it can be for me.

Postman Oh well – I thought, as your name was the Doctor – but never mind.

Scruffy person rushes on from the back and speaks to the people watching.

Scruff Can I have that scarf? And that walking stick? And I'll need that chair.

Taking these items to the front, the Scruff then helps a hobbling person on, sits them down and proceeds to bandage their leg with a makeshift splint.

Postman Well this person looks too much of a mess to be a proper doctor, and they've got no manners – fancy taking all your stuff like that! But they do seem to know what they are doing.

Injured person Thank you, that feels so much better.

Postman I wonder – are you the Doctor?

Scruff Look at this: what do you think?

Postman *(To the people)* What do you think? Is this the Doctor I've been looking for?

All YES!

Postman At last! *(Hands over parcel)* Then this is for you. Cheerio!

Music

My song is love unknown

Leader Today's Bible story begins with John the Baptist. He has been thrown into prison because of everything he had been saying about the coming of the Saviour. This is what happened.[1]

Storytelling

Jesus is unwrapping the leg of the injured person from the last scene and encouraging him/her to stand. The disciple is a little distance away, with John in chains.

John Go on – ask him. Is he the One?

Disciple *(To Jesus)* Are you the one who is to come, or are we to wait for another?

Jesus Go and tell John what you hear and see: the blind receive their sight, the lame walk, the lepers are cleansed, the deaf hear, the dead are raised, and the poor have good news brought to them. And blessed is anyone who takes no offence at me.

(To the crowd) What did you go out into the wilderness to look at? A reed shaken by the wind? What then did you go out to see? Someone dressed in soft robes?

1. After John's first question, the lines are taken directly from Matthew's Gospel (NRSV): you may prefer to use a different translation.

Look, those who wear soft robes are in royal palaces. What then did you go out to see? A prophet? Yes, I tell you, and more than a prophet.

(Pointing at John) This is the one about whom it is written,

> 'See, I am sending my messenger ahead of you,
> who will prepare your way before you.'

Truly I tell you, among those born of women no one has arisen greater than John the Baptist; yet the least in the kingdom of heaven is greater than he.

Exploring

In our sketch, the postman found who he was looking for not because of the Doctor's appearance or title, but because of what he/she actually *did*. Today's Bible story is all about actions speaking louder than words. John wants an answer: who is this Jesus? Is he the Messiah? Jesus says simply, 'Look at what I do: I heal the sick, raise the dead, bring good news to the poor.' He lets what he does explain who he is.

I wonder what our own actions say about us? In front of you, you will find a three-piece puzzle. Take the section labelled, 'Knowing ourselves' and on the back of it, write down anything you do which shows other people the best of you.

Allow a few minutes for everyone to do this. You may need to start people off by asking, 'Have you helped anyone? Done a kind thing? Sacrificed something for the sake of others?'

Now take the second section, 'Knowing others'. Do we judge other people by what they are or by what they do? On the back of this piece, write anything that other people have done for you which has shown you the best of them.

Allow a few minutes for everyone to do this. You may need to start people off by asking, 'Has anyone helped you? Done a kind thing? Sacrificed something for your sake?'

Now take the third section, 'Knowing God', and do the same thing. What has God done to show us the best of himself?

Allow a few minutes for everyone to do this.

God showed himself to us when he gave us his Son. Through Jesus and the things that he did, we know who God is: God is love. These pieces fit together to form a shape to remind us of this. What is it? (*Give everyone a moment to form the shape of a heart, then hold up your own fitted-together shape.*) This is what God is all about, and this is what the best part of each of us is all about, too. Love.

Prayer action

Take the big circle of elastic and invite volunteers to help you lay it out in the shape of a big cross on the floor.

In our prayers today, we will use this shape to help us understand who and what God is. God showed us himself in his Son, Jesus. Jesus loved us so much that he died for us on the cross. (*Then get everyone to move the elastic into the shape of a heart.*) This shows us what God is: God is love. And his love is so big and long and wide and stretchy that it includes us all. (*Invite everyone to step inside the heart shape, picking it up and stretching it out to reach round everyone.*)

Loving God,
thank you for our love for each other.
Thank you for your love for us,
which surrounds us and includes us,
whoever and wherever we are.
Amen.

Music

Wide, wide as the ocean

Conclusion

Love is the heart of the Gospel and we live out the Gospel most powerfully in our lives when we *show* people what love means, rather than merely *telling* them about it. I leave with you the command which St Francis of Assisi gave to his followers: 'Go – preach the Gospel. If necessary, use words.'

Let us pray:
Lord Jesus,
John knew you when he saw your love in action;
may we know you, too, through the love in our lives,
and may we share the good news of your love
in all that we say and do.
Amen.

Give notices, announce the next all-age service and invite everyone to the feast.

Here he is!

Theme	Recognising Jesus
Scripture	John 1:29–42

Running order	Total: 50 minutes
Welcome	Making footprints *(5 minutes)*
Introduction	Opening the theme
Activity	The line-up – 'Spot the minister!' *(5 minutes)*
Storytelling	Sketch – John and the disciples finding Jesus *(10 minutes)*
Music	I believe in Jesus *(5 minutes)*
Exploring	How can we recognise God? *(10 minutes)*
Music	Be still, for the presence of the Lord *(5 minutes)*
Prayer action	'Be still' – contemplative prayer *(5 minutes)*
Music	Make me a channel of your peace *(5 minutes)*
Conclusion	Footprints prayer

Resources

- A sheet of lining paper and felt-tip pens, in front of the altar
- Your minister or priest, plus four volunteers of the same gender
- Five silly or decorative (not scary!) masks
- Placards with numbers 1–5 on
- Music and words
- Copies of the show-and-teller *(see appendix)*
- Pens and pencils
- A recording of 'Be Still, for the presence of the Lord' or a musician to play it
- Some cushions or rugs for the floor

Leaders

Minimum: 5

- Leader / Cast member
- Cast x 4

Optimum: 10

- Leader *(Introduction and Conclusion)*
- Activity Leader
- Cast x 5 (all in modern dress)
  John the Baptist, wearing scruffy clothes
  Andrew, wearing jeans and a hoodie
  Disciple 1, as Andrew
  Jesus, wearing something white
  Simon Peter, wearing wellies
- Music Leader
- Explorer
- Prayer Leader

Suggestions for additional music

- God is the giver of love
- God is working his purpose out
- When I needed a neighbour

Service

Welcome

Invite people to come up to the altar and draw round their feet on the sheet of lining paper as a way of saying, 'Here I am, Lord'.

Introduction

Our Bible reading today is all about recognising Jesus, so we are going to begin today with a game to test our skills of recognition: it's called, 'Spot the minister!'

Activity

Bring on the masked line-up of four volunteers and your minister, each carrying a placard with a number. Line them up to face the congregation and invite guesses by asking questions, such as:

- What kind of shoes does the minister usually wear?
- Whose hands look like they shake other people's hands a lot after church?
- What colour clothes does the minister wear?

After lots of guessing, ask people to agree on which number they are going to pick, and reveal their choice. If they guess wrongly, unmask the real minister! Applaud your volunteers and ask them all to return to their seats as you introduce the following sketch:

Like the game we have just played, today's story is about recognition.

Bring on John, Andrew and Disciple 1 to stand still at the front, as if frozen in mid-conversation. Position Simon at the back of church. Jesus should also be at the back, ready to walk down the aisle and be spotted. Introduce the characters:

This is what happened when Jesus and some of his disciples met for the first time. This is Andrew and his friend, and they are talking to John the Baptist.

Storytelling

Sketch – John and the disciples finding Jesus.

Jesus begins to walk down the aisle and the scene at the front comes to life.

John — There he is! When I baptised him, I saw God send his Holy Spirit like a dove and the dove stayed on him. That shows he's the Son of God! *(John walks off.)*

Andrew *(To Disciple 1)* Come on – let's follow him and see where he goes!

Jesus Can I help you?

Andrew and Disciple 1 *(Overawed)* Er . . . um . . .

Jesus What are you looking for?

Andrew Teacher, where are you staying?

Disciple 1 *(Embarrassed)* Don't ask him that!

Jesus Come and see.

Jesus and Disciple 1 start to walk towards the altar.

Andrew Hang on – I'm just going to fetch my brother! He's down by the lake – I won't be long!

He runs to the back of the church where Simon Peter is sitting.

Simon, Simon! Come quick! I've found him!

Simon Who?

Andrew Jesus, of course! The Messiah! Come on!

They run back down towards Jesus and Andrew calls out.

Teacher! Wait! This is –

Jesus turns and looks at Simon, then interrupts.

Jesus Simon, son of John. You will be called Peter.
Andrew, Simon and Disciple 1 look amazed.
Well come on then – follow me!
Jesus leads the way off.

Music I believe in Jesus

Exploring In our line-up, we spotted the minister by how he/she looked – clothes and colours helped us to recognise him/her. In our story, John recognised Jesus because he had had a very clear sign: when God sent his Holy Spirit like a dove, it was the equivalent of a big neon sign saying, 'Here he is! This is the Son of God!' But our question is this: how can *we* recognise God in our lives today? How can we tell when he is at work if we can't recognise him by his physical appearance and if there aren't any heavenly signs?

To explore this question, we will use something which you may know as a 'fortune-teller'. This is a bit different:

we will use it to think about how God shows himself to us in our daily lives, so we'll call it a 'show-and-teller'. To begin with, we need to complete these sentences with some examples. On each panel, there is a sentence which begins like this one: 'Being kind is . . .' If you lift up that particular flap, you will find one way in which that sentence might end: 'Being kind is . . . sharing the last thing you have.' I could have added, '– especially when it's my last piece of chocolate and I don't want to!' Or I could have drawn a picture of people sharing something.

Take some time now to complete each sentence with words or a picture – ask for help if you're not sure what the words mean – and then fold up your show-and-teller ready to use.

Allow plenty of time for people to complete their show-and-tellers. Then demonstrate how to use them (see appendix).

Encourage people to move around the church and try this out on each other. Then call everyone back together.

Now, look at all the things which you have written or drawn to complete these sentences. They have one thing in common: they all give us a glimpse of God. Why? Open up your show-and-teller to find out.

All open up the show-and-tellers to reveal the message in the centre: God is Love.

God is love. Every time we show a little bit of that love by behaving in a way which is kind or friendly or charitable or generous, we reveal something of God to the rest of the world. And whenever we recognise love in others, we can say, like John and the disciples, 'Here is God! Here he is!'

Music

Be still, for the presence of the Lord

Prayer action

You may like to demonstrate these positions yourself, or ask for a volunteer!

In the Bible, God said, 'Be still, and know that I am God!' In our prayers today, we are going to settle into stillness as a way of recognising God's presence with us now. Many people kneel down to pray – but if you have bad knees, staying still in that position may be difficult. Some people pray standing up, with their arms like this: *(demonstrate palms-up, open gesture).* Some people sit cross-legged *(demonstrate the 'meditation' posture, with an open hand resting on each knee).* Some people even pray like this *(demonstrate prostrate position, arms extended in a cross position).* We may be more comfortable simply sitting to pray. Today, find a position for your prayers in which you can stay still. Rest quietly in God's presence now and know that he is here.

Play the tune of 'Be still, for the presence of the Lord' as people begin to settle into stillness. Pause for a moment when the music finishes.

Gracious Lord,
may this stillness be with us
in the heart of all our busyness.
May we know your presence beside us
and your peace within us
today and always.
Amen.

Music Make me a channel of your peace

Conclusion *Turn the sheet of lining paper with footprints on it so that the footprints are facing towards the door of the church, or heading down the aisle.*

Jesus,
send us out into the world with new eyes
to see you when we look for you,
to recognise you where we least expect you
and to love you wherever we find you.
Amen.

Give notices, announce the next all-age service and invite everyone to the feast.

Follow me!

Theme	Following Jesus
Scripture	Matthew 4:18–22

Running order	Total: 50 minutes
Welcome	Making footprints and lighting candles: singing the Taizé chant, 'The Lord is my light' *(10 minutes)*
Opening the theme	The people who walked in darkness have seen a great light
Activity/Storytelling	'Picture reveal' – the disciples leaving their fishing *(10 minutes)*
Music	Follow me *(5 minutes)*
Exploring	How do we follow Jesus? *(10 minutes)*
Music	Jesus Christ is waiting *(5 minutes)*
Prayer action	Fishing-net prayers – intercessions *(5 minutes)*
Music	I danced in the morning *(5 minutes)*
Conclusion	Footprints prayer

Resources

- A sheet of lining paper and felt-tip pens, in front of the altar
- On the altar, lit Paschal candle or other large candle
- Tea-lights, matches and tapers
- Music and words
- Picture and requisite technology for the 'Picture reveal' activity *(see appendix)*
- Props:
  - A table which is covered in books
  - Children's toys, tippee cups, etc.
  - Gardening gloves and a spade
  - A bag each
- Lots of small, fish-shaped pieces of paper *(see appendix)*
- Pens and pencils
- Lots of short lengths of wool or string
- A piece of fishing net or length of garden netting

Leaders

Minimum: 4

- Leader/Jesus
- Cast x 3

Optimum: 9

- Leader *(Introduction and Conclusion)*
- Activity Leader/Storyteller
- Cast x 4 (all in modern dress)
  Teacher, wearing smart clothes
  Parent, wearing casual clothes
  Gardener, wearing work gear
  Jesus, wearing something white
- Music Leader(s)
- Explorer
- Prayer Leader

Suggestions for additional music

- From heaven you came
- Will you come and follow me

Service

Welcome

Invite people to come up to the altar and draw round their feet on the sheet of lining paper as a way of saying, 'Here I am, Lord'. Then each person lights a tea-light on the altar as the Music Leader begins to lead the singing of the Taizé chant, 'The Lord is my light'. Encourage people to join in and let the music swell, then fade.

Introduction

Our opening song reminds us that Jesus is the Light of the world. Today we will be thinking about what it might mean for us to follow the light of Jesus in our lives.

Activity/Storytelling

Begin with your covered-up picture and gradually reveal it one detail at a time. At each stage, invite people to guess what is happening in the picture. The accuracy of the guesses is not as important as the process of speculation which engages everyone in the puzzle of working out the story. Finally reveal the complete picture and explain what is happening:

This is today's Bible story. It takes place by Lake Galilee and these men are professional fishermen – Simon Peter and his brother Andrew, James and his brother John. This is Jesus who has just turned up and said to the fishermen, 'Follow me, and I will make you fish for people'. They have dropped everything – their precious, half-mended nets and their boat, all the tools of their trade – and are following Jesus. And this is Zebedee, father of James and John, who is left behind wondering what on earth is going on!

Music

Follow me

Exploring

When Jesus called his disciples to follow him, he didn't wait for them to come and meet him in a holy place: he went to the place where they worked and called them when they were up to their elbows in fish and soggy nets. And he asked them to do a job: they were fishermen, so he said he wanted them to 'fish for people' – in other words, to gather people together and bring them to God, like fish in a net. How might he call any of us, today? What job might he ask us to do, and how might we answer him? Here is a short sketch to help us think about these questions.

At the front, position the teacher behind a table which is covered in books; then the parent, kneeling on the floor surrounded by children's toys, tippee cups etc.; then the gardener, with gardening gloves and a spade, miming digging. Jesus comes towards them down the aisle.

Jesus *(To the teacher)* Come with me! I've got a job for you.

Teacher What is it?

Jesus I need you to teach people about God's love.

Teacher Oh – I'm really busy – I've got all these books to mark, and then I've got a lesson to plan for tomorrow and then –

Jesus moves on to the parent as the teacher starts to pack a bag.

Jesus Come with me! I've got a job for you.

Parent What is it?

Jesus I need you to show people how God loves them like a mother and a father.

Parent I'd love to! Let me just put all these toys in a bag – oh, and I'll need to make us a packed tea, and I'll have to pack clean socks and pants, and my daughter won't go anywhere without her blankie, and –

Jesus moves on to the gardener as the parent starts to pack a bag.

Jesus Come with me! I've got a job for you.

Gardener What is it?

Jesus I need you to help grow God's love in the world.

Gardener *(Drops spade immediately and takes off gardening gloves)* OK – let's go.

Jesus and the gardener walk briskly off together as the teacher and the parent come forward with bags packed.

Parent Ready!

Teacher Where's he gone?

Looking rather lost, they wander off in the opposite direction.

Explorer

Now, I need our actors to come back on so that we can talk about the sketch they have just shown us. *(Characters return to their starting positions.)* I also need some helpers who are good at running about. *(Invite your volunteers to the front.)* This is my question for you: how did each of these people react when Jesus asked them to follow him? First of all, run and stand by the person who didn't come when Jesus asked them to because they were too busy. *(They run to a character – it doesn't matter if they don't all choose the same one.)* Now find the person who dropped everything and came straight away. *(They run to a character.)* Now find the person who didn't want to come until they had got everything ready first. *(They run to a character.)* Now think about the fishermen in our story: what did they do when Jesus asked them to follow him? Which person in our play behaved most like the fishermen who became disciples? *(They run to a character. Thank your volunteers and ask them to sit down.)*

The last question is one for us all to think about. If Jesus asked us to follow him, now, which person in our play would we resemble? Would we be like the teacher, too busy to think about anything else except all the jobs we have to do? Would we be like the parent, keen to go but worrying about being completely ready and prepared for every eventuality? Or would we be like the gardener – and like the fishermen in our story – who dropped everything and went? I wonder if Jesus is calling us today? I wonder how we will answer?

Music

Jesus Christ is waiting

Prayer action

Jesus told his disciples that they would fish for people, and in our prayers today we are going to do that, too. When we pray for particular people and situations, we can trust that they are already surrounded by God's love and care, like fish in the sea. Our prayers are like a fishing net, scooping up particular, pressing needs and bringing them before God. Today, think about anyone you know who particularly needs God's love and care at the moment. *(Pause.)* Write that person's name on a little fish and add it to this net which gathers up all our prayers together.

Allow enough time for everyone to write and attach their fish-prayers.

Heavenly Father,
in our net of prayer
we offer you this catch.
We name before you
all those we remember especially today,
trusting that your love embraces them
and us
and all those we have forgotten.
Amen.

Music I danced in the morning

Conclusion *Turn the sheet of lining paper with footprints on it so that the footprints are facing towards the door of the church, or heading down the aisle. Then carry the Paschal candle and walk down the aisle. As you walk, say:*

Lord Jesus,
call us to follow you.
May we be ready to follow your light
wherever it may lead us.
Amen.

Give notices, announce the next all-age service and invite everyone to the feast.

Salt and light

Theme	What God wants us to be
Scripture	Matthew 5:13–20

Running order	Total: 50 minutes
Welcome	Fingerprints *(5 minutes)*
Introduction	Opening the theme
Storytelling	Reading Matthew 5:13–20 *(2 minutes)*
Activity	Tasting and seeing – losing the salt and hiding the light *(10 minutes)*
Music	Jesus bids us shine *(5 minutes)*
Exploring	Brainstorm – how can we be salt and light? *(13 minutes)*
Music	This little light of mine *(5 minutes)*
Prayer action	Salt-dough candle-holders – creative prayer *(10 minutes)*
Conclusion	Fingerprints

Resources

- Double quantities of salt dough *(see appendix for Crib Service)*, the first rolled out on a large tray or piece of board to form a slab the size of a large paving stone. It should be thick enough to accommodate handprints. In the middle, press the imprint of a small cross. Place the second lot of dough in a bowl for the prayer action
- Music and words
- A loaf of home-made bread, sliced and buttered with salted butter
- A loaf of bread made using the same recipe but without salt, sliced and buttered with unsalted butter
- Two large plates for the bread
- A small dome tent, erected in a suitable corner, perhaps covered with a cloth to make it darker inside
- Inside the tent, several torches and electric lanterns, switched on and hidden under boxes or baskets.
- Two 'brainstorm boards': a flip chart or whiteboard with the headings: 'You are the salt' and 'You are the light'
- Pens for the brainstorm boards
- Thin votive candles
- One ready-made candle-holder: a simple ball of dough (or something more deliberately shaped) into which you have pressed a candle
- Matches
- Tables to work at
- Wet wipes for hands

Leaders

Minimum: 1

- Leader

Optimum: 6+

- Leader *(Introduction and Conclusion)*
- Storyteller
- Activity Leader(s)
- Music Leader
- Explorer
- Prayer Leader(s)

Suggestions for additional music

- Brother, sister, let me serve you
- Here I am

Service

Welcome

In front of the altar, place your rolled-out slab of dough on a board or tray. As people arrive, invite them to make a handprint or fingerprint in the dough, as a way of saying, 'Here I am, Lord'.

Introduction

Imagine a famous leader came here, today – perhaps the Queen, or the president of the United States. Imagine sitting in respectful silence and waiting for that person to speak. Then, when they do, they look you straight in the eye and say, 'You – you're amazing. You could make such a difference.' Wow! Imagine how that would feel. Jesus said something similar to the enthusiastic crowds in Galilee who would hang on his every word when he began his preaching and teaching. He looked them in the eye and spoke directly to them, and his words speak to us, today. This is what he said:

Storytelling

Read Matthew 5:13–20

Activity

Jesus compares us to two things which we may take for granted – salt and light. Why are these things special? Let's see what life is like without them.

Show plates of bread and butter.

Here we have two plates of bread and butter – one made with an ordinary amount of salt, and the other containing no salt at all. Take some time to sample and compare the two plates of bread and butter, and decide which one you prefer.

Introduce the covered tent.

Here is a dark place. If you would like to, go in and see what you can find there to brighten it up. Let's get as much light in there as possible!

Allow plenty of time for people to taste the bread and butter and explore the tent.

Music

Jesus bids us shine

Exploring

Stand in front of the first brainstorm board, 'You are the salt', pen in hand.

So what difference do salt and light make? First of all, what did you think of our bread and butter?

Invite responses.

Salt is a precious resource – more precious than we realise, until we have to do without it. Never mind E-numbers and monosodium glutamate: a little salt brings out the natural flavours of food. Before fridges and freezers existed, salt preserved food so that people could have meat and fish to eat even when no fresh stocks were available. In medieval times, salt was heavily taxed so that only the rich could afford it. Kings even displayed the salt on their tables in gold caskets because it was so precious.

So I wonder what Jesus meant when he told his listeners that they were 'the salt of the earth', and that they must not lose their saltiness?

Invite responses and add them to the brainstorm board.

What might it mean for us to be the salt of the earth?

Invite responses and add them to the brainstorm board. Then turn to the second board: 'You are the light'.

What about light? What was it like in that dark place?

Invite responses.

What did you do to make it as light as possible?

Invite responses.

Jesus said that no one lights a lamp and then hides it under a basket; they put it on a lamp stand. Light is no good to us if it is hidden: it needs to be able to shine clearly to make a difference to the darkness. I wonder what Jesus meant when he told his listeners that they were 'the light of the world'?

Invite responses and add them to the brainstorm board.

What is our light? What might it mean for us to be the light of the world?

Invite responses and add them to the brainstorm board.

Music

This little light of mine

Prayer action

For our prayers today, we are going to make something which will remind us that Jesus wants us to be the salt of the earth and the light of the world. This is salt dough – with it we can make a simple holder for a candle, like this. *(Show the one you made earlier.)* The salt will preserve the dough so that, once it has hardened, you could paint it and keep it as a holder for your candle. Take a candle now and make a holder for it, before we come together in prayer.

Allow enough time for everyone to complete their candle holders, then gather people together. As you light your own candle, say:

Jesus, you call us to be the light of the world.
May this light spread among us now.

Pass the light from candle to candle.

May we carry your light into our homes
and into the world.
Amen.

Conclusion

Hold up the board with the dough imprinted with the cross, handprints and fingerprints.

Each of us is unique, like our fingerprints. We are all the salt of the earth – and God loves us. Let us pray:

Lord, show me how I can be salt and light in the world. You know I am special – show me how I can make a difference.
Amen.

Blow out candles, give notices, announce the next all-age service and invite everyone to the feast.

One for All

Time to grow

Theme	How God helps us grow
Scripture	1 Corinthians 3:1–9

Running order	Total: 50 minutes
Welcome	Preparing the soil *(5 minutes)*
Introduction	Opening the theme
Activity	Match the baby photos *(10 minutes)*
Storytelling	*Zagazoo* by Quentin Blake *(5 minutes)*
Music	O, how good is the Lord *(5 minutes)*
Exploring	How do we grow? *(10 minutes)*
Music	One more step along the world I go *(5 minutes)*
Prayer action	Planting seeds – active offertory prayer *(5 minutes)*
Conclusion	Watering what has been planted *(5 minutes)*

Resources

- Lots of small plant pots or plastic/polystyrene cups
- A sack of soil or potting compost
- A couple of small watering cans

Place these outside or at the back of the church. Then place the following on a table by the altar:

- Sticky labels and pens
- Several packets of sunflower seeds (in the summer months) or poppy seeds (at any other time of year)

You will also need:

- Music and words
- Two photographs of each of your leaders (or of well-known people in your church): one when they were a baby and one as they are now
- A long table
- A copy of *Zagazoo* by Quentin Blake *(see appendix)*
- Two boards or a flip chart with the following pictures *(see appendix)*:
  - A growing plant next to some of the baby photos
  - A signpost pointing two ways
- Three individual signs, ready to add to the above pictures: *God gives the growth*, *We get to choose* and *Choose life*
- Blu-tack

Leaders

Minimum: 1

- Leader

Optimum: 6+

- Leader *(Introduction and Conclusion)*
- Activity Leader
- Storyteller
- Music Leader
- Explorer
- Prayer Leader(s)

Suggestions for additional music

- The Spirit lives to set us free
- I heard the voice of Jesus say

Service

Welcome

Greet people at the church door – outside it if weather permits. Invite everyone to choose a pot and fill it with potting compost, then take it to the altar and label it.

Introduction

Wherever we look around us there is always something growing, whether it is the trees in the park or the weeds between the cracks in a paving stone. The natural world never stays the same. In today's service, we will be thinking about how we are growing and changing, too, throughout our lives.

Activity

We will begin today by looking at how some of us have changed physically over the years. Here is a collection of beautiful babies *(indicate the baby photos)* and here are photographs of what these babies look like now *(indicate the grown-up photos).* You may recognise some of these people – can you match them up with the right baby photo?

Allow plenty of time for people to mix and match the photos, spreading them out in pairs along the table. When the guessing is complete, reveal the correct pairs and invite the owners to come forward and collect their photos. Keep a few to add to the first picture in the Activity.

Storytelling

Today's story is about growing and changing, too. It is a children's book by Quentin Blake which has something to say to us all. It is called *Zagazoo.*

Read the story, showing and describing as many of the vivid pictures as possible.

Music

O, how good is the Lord

Exploring

Display the first pictures: the growing plant and the baby photos.

What did the sweet little baby in the story change into?

Invite responses.

And what did his parents change into at the very end?

Invite responses.

Throughout our lives, we are all growing and changing. It is a process which continues whether we want it to or not. Some of us may still feel like a bad-tempered dragon at times, or a clumsy elephant! This growing and changing is part of God's plan for us, however old we are. In the Bible, St Paul explains it like this: we are each like new seeds that have been planted and watered, but it is 'only God who gives the growth'. Paul was talking about the lives of people in a new church, but what he says is true of all our lives. We are each 'God's field, God's building' – in other words, God is continually growing us, building us up, wanting us to change and become better people. Paul sums that up for us when he says, 'God gives the growth'.

Stick the 'God gives the growth' sign above the first picture.

Think back to *Zagazoo* and the creatures which the baby turned into. What were they like? Which ones would be hard to live with?

Invite responses and put up the picture of a signpost.

Although we cannot help growing and changing, we can influence what we become. We get to choose. *(Stick the 'We get to choose' sign above the signpost.)* As we grow older, we get to choose between good ways of living which make life better for us and the people around us, and bad ways of living which in the end make us and those we love unhappy. The Bible has lots to say about bad ways of living: killing, stealing, lying, cheating others and bearing grudges are all bad because they make life worse for everyone. Their opposite is love, because any actions which are truly based on love tend to make life better: they are life-enhancing, life-affirming and life-giving.

So as we grow, we are faced with choices. When we can choose which path to take, which way to live, let's choose love, because it is the best way – it is God's way, the life-giving way. The Bible reading puts it very plainly: 'Choose life'.[1] *(Stick the 'Choose life' sign on one side of the signpost.)*

Music

One more step along the world I go

Prayer action

Show some poppy seeds in your hand. If using sunflower seeds instead, adapt the words before the Prayer action and the Conclusion as necessary.

In our prayers today, we are going to use these seeds. A seed is one of God's miracles. Tiny and hard, it sits in the dark soil and it looks to us as if nothing is happening. Then it sprouts and grows, and something beautiful – like a poppy with big, bright petals – can come out of it. That flower produces a seed head which holds hundreds more seeds – enough to start growing a whole field of poppies. Seeds remind us that 'God gives the growth': our lives can have the same capacity for amazing growth and change, as well as periods of waiting in the dark. Today, these poppy seeds will be a sign of our prayer. We will plant them and offer them to God as a prayer for new life and growth for us all. You may like to offer your prayer for yourself, or for someone you know who is facing a lot of change in their lives at the moment.

Invite everyone to come up to the altar to claim their plant pot filled with soil and plant some seeds in it. Then gather everyone together in prayer:

Lord of all growth and change,
may you bless the dark before the growing,
bless the sprouting and greening,
bless the rain and shine,
bless new growth and strength,
bless the flowering,
bless the fruits of maturity,
bless the fading and dying,
bless the dark before new life begins.
Amen.

1. Deuteronomy 30:19.

Conclusion

Invite everyone outside to water their seeds.

When you get home, dig over a tiny corner of your garden then empty your pot of soil and seeds into it. Poppies like to start off in the cold and dark, then by the summer they are ready to burst into flower. Keep the soil well watered and enjoy watching your plants grow!

Let us pray:
Nurturing God,
look after us like these newly-planted,
freshly-watered seeds,
for you alone give the growth.
Let us grow strong in your love.
Amen.

Give notices, announce the next all-age service and invite everyone to the feast.

Seeing and believing

Theme	How we can believe in God
Scripture	John 20:19–31

Running order	Total: 50 minutes
Welcome	Adding leaves to the living prayer tree *(5 minutes)*
Introduction	Opening the theme
Storytelling	Dialogue – Jesus and Thomas *(5 minutes)*
Exploring 1	Hot-seating Thomas *(10 minutes)*
Music	We have a gospel to proclaim *(5 minutes)*
Activity/Exploring 2	'How can we believe?' Hands-on investigation into knowing and believing *(15 minutes)*
Music	Jesus, stand among us *(5 minutes)*
Prayer action	Christ be with me – lighting candles *(5 minutes)*
Conclusion	Closing prayer and invitation

Resources

- A living 'prayer tree': some budding branches in a large pot or vase, filled with water and pebbles to weigh it down *(see appendix)*
- Prayer leaves *(see appendix)*
- Two tables, labelled 'Exhibit A' and 'Exhibit B', with the following:
  - A: Bottles and jars of saltwater
  - B: Information about the sea, for example: books about the ocean and marine life, a tide timetable, pictures of surfers, a video clip from *The Blue Planet*
- Music and words
- A large heart-shape in red card
- A Bible
- Lit candles all around the church, on windowsills and on side tables, each with a few unlit tea-lights clustered around it

Leaders

Minimum: 2

- Leader
- Storyteller (Thomas)

Optimum: 7 or 12

- Leader
- Storytellers x 1 or x 6 (Narrator, Jesus, Thomas, three disciples)
- Explorers x 2
- Music Leader
- Activity Leader
- Prayer Leader

Suggestions for additional music

- I believe in Jesus
- Immortal, invisible, God only wise
- Low in the grave he lay

Service

Welcome

Invite people to add prayer leaves to the living prayer tree as they arrive.

Introduction

Our service today takes us back to the time when Jesus had just risen from the dead. For his disciples, who had not even had time to come to terms with his death, the news that he was alive tested their faith to the limit. Today we will find out what happened to them in the evening of that first Easter Day. They are a frightened bunch: if the religious leaders in Jerusalem could have someone as popular as Jesus killed, then what might they do to his friends? The scene is a safe house where the disciples are in hiding, behind locked doors.

Storytelling

Read John 20:19–29 with one voice, or with a Narrator, Jesus, Thomas and three disciples who say together, 'We have seen the Lord.'

Exploring 1

Explorer: Let's ask Thomas a bit more about this story. Thomas, when Jesus first appeared to your friends, you weren't there. How did you feel when they told you what you'd missed?

Thomas: I'm ashamed to say so now, but I thought they were having delusions. Grief does that, you know – and we were all so sad, and so scared, I wouldn't have been surprised if some of us had started seeing things. So I tried to be kind when they told me. I said, 'Well, show me the evidence and then I'll know for sure.' They say seeing is believing, but I wanted to touch him and know whether he was as real as the man who washed my feet before supper last week. I saw the soldiers cut his side to check that he was really dead: I wanted to touch the hole so I'd know it was him.

Explorer: And how did you feel when Jesus appeared to you?

Thomas: Thinking about it now, I wonder why I wasn't scared out of my wits when he appeared like that. But he said, 'Peace be with you,' and held out his hands to me, and

I just felt calm and loved and certain that everything would be all right. I held his hands and they were warm. He let me touch the wounds left by the nails, and showed me the hole in his side and let me touch that, too. There's no doubt in my mind. Jesus really is alive! I know, because I've had proof.

Music

We have a gospel to proclaim

Activity/Exploring 2

We can all sympathise with Thomas, who is often called 'Doubting Thomas'. Believing is so much easier if we have real, physical proof in front of us that we can see and hear and touch. How can we believe in God, without that kind of proof?

Today we have an activity which may help us think about how we believe in God. I want you to imagine that you are a visitor from another planet – a hot, dry planet. You have never seen the sea and you don't know anything about it. If I showed you this to explain what the sea was, what would you discover?

All gather round the bottles and jars of water on 'Exhibit A' table. Encourage people to explore what they find there.

What would the evidence here tell you about the sea? *(Invite responses.)* Because you can see and taste and feel this seawater, you know for sure that the sea is salty and wet. 'Exhibit A' may not tell us about waves and sharks and coral and currents, but it shows us the essential things about the sea.

All gather round the material on 'Exhibit B' table.

Now what else can we learn about the sea from the things on this table?

Encourage people to look through the materials, then invite responses.

If we want to know more about the sea, we need the help of 'Exhibit B': the work of witnesses and experts. We need the books they have written about tides, the photographs they have taken of whales, the amazing films they have made of the tiny creatures which live in the deepest, darkest parts of the ocean which we could never see for ourselves.

Invite everyone to sit down again. Stand between the two tables.

So if we had never seen the sea and were trying to understand it, we would be helped first of all by our direct, physical experience of seawater, and secondly by the evidence of experts. The experience of trying to understand the sea when you have never seen it is rather like faith. We have never met God, and he is beyond our understanding, but we know that God is good and God is love, so whatever loving-kindness we experience in our lives gives us a taste of God. Our direct experience shows us the essential thing about God – he is love. (*Stand your heart-shape on the 'Exhibit A' table.)*

Then, if we want to know more about God, we need to look at Jesus. If we want to know all about Jesus, then we need the help of witnesses and experts – in other words, the people who wrote the Gospels. *(Stand the Bible on the 'Exhibit B' table.)* The Gospels give us the best information we can have about Jesus, because they record the detailed accounts of his life which were passed on by those who had been closest to him. We may not be able to see and touch Jesus like Thomas did, but the Gospels show us the reality of Jesus so that we might know and believe. Today's Gospel reading ends with these words:

> Now Jesus did many other signs in the presence of his disciples, which are not written in this book. But these are written so that you may come to believe that Jesus is the Messiah, the Son of God, and that through believing you may have life in his name.

So if, like Thomas, you need help with believing, remember that we all have two kinds of proof to rely on *(indicate the Bible and the heart)*: the evidence of

Christ's witnesses in the Gospels, and our own direct experience of God's love, shown in and through the goodness and love we experience in our lives.

Music

Jesus, stand among us

Prayer action

Jesus is always with us, wherever we are. As we prepare to pray together today, we will light candles all around the church to remind us that Jesus' love surrounds us. Can you look around and find a lit candle, then see if there is another one nearby for you to light?

Allow enough time for everyone to find and light a candle, then return to their seats. Turn the lights off.

Let us pray:
Jesus, as your light fills this church, we pray for your presence to fill our lives.
Christ be with me, Christ within me,
Christ behind me, Christ before me,
Christ beside me, Christ to win me,
Christ to comfort and restore me;
Christ beneath me, Christ above me,
Christ in quiet, Christ in danger,
Christ in hearts of all that love me,
Christ in mouth of friend and stranger.[1]
Amen.

Conclusion

As we go out into the world, may the Lord be always before us;
may he be at our right hand so that we shall not fall.[2]
Amen.

Give notices, announce the next all-age service and invite everyone to the feast.

1. Ascribed to St Patrick (372-466), trans. Cecil Frances Alexander (1818-1895).
2. From Psalm 16:7.

Christ in me and you

Theme	We are not alone
Scripture	John 14:15–21

Running order	Total: 50 minutes
Welcome	Adding leaves to the living prayer tree *(5 minutes)*
Introduction	Opening the theme
Storytelling	'We are not alone.' Reading and explaining Christ's promise *(5 minutes)*
Music	Such love *(5 minutes)*
Exploring	'Where is Jesus now?' Visual exploration – the web of love *(10 minutes)*
Activity	Collage – all sorts of people *(15 minutes)*
Music	When I needed a neighbour *(5 minutes)*
Prayer action	Prayer flags – creative intercessions *(5 minutes)*
Conclusion	Closing prayer and invitation

Resources

- A living 'prayer tree': some budding branches in a large pot or vase, filled with water and pebbles to weigh it down *(see appendix for Seeing and believing)*
- Prayer leaves *(see appendix for Seeing and believing)*
- Gold envelope containing a card with the Scripture reading
- Music and words
- A simple, large model of a spider's web *(see appendix)*
- Three cardboard signs with strings so they can be hung around a person's neck, reading 'Father', 'Son' and 'Holy Spirit'
- A large piece of sugar paper with a spider's web drawn on it; 'GOD' in big, bright letters in the middle
- Lots of newspapers and magazines
- Scissors and glue-sticks
- Lots of strips or squares of fabric for prayer flags
- Some fabric pens or felt-tip pens which can write on fabric flags
- A long string or piece of tape to which you can attach the flags
- Pins or staples (These are to fix the prayers temporarily, during the service. Afterwards, and before you hang the prayer flags outside, they will need to be sewn onto the string)

Leaders

Minimum: 1

- Leader

Optimum: 6

- Leader *(Introduction and Conclusion)*
- Storyteller
- Explorer
- Activity Leader
- Music Leader
- Prayer Leader

Suggestions for additional music

- Do not be afraid
- Love divine, all loves excelling

Service

Welcome

Invite people to add prayer leaves to the living prayer tree as they arrive.

Introduction

Between Jesus' resurrection and the day when he went back up to heaven, there were just forty days. He appeared to his friends repeatedly in that time, and talked to them a little about what would happen next. They must also have remembered the promises he gave them before he was arrested and killed: it is one of those promises which we will hear today.

Storytelling

Take the promise out of a gold envelope.

Jesus made this promise to his friends, and to all of us who do things his way – and his way is love. This is what he promised:

Read John 14:15–21.

Jesus' promise to us is this: we are not alone. Love is what joins us together with God, because love is what God is all about.

Music

Such love

Exploring

We are going to think about Jesus' promise that we are not alone. He said, 'I will not leave you orphaned . . . you will know that I am in my Father, and you in me, and I in you.' What did he mean? Where is Jesus now?

Let's begin our exploration in a surprising place. Come into this spider's web . . .

Invite three volunteers to come and stand in the hoop at the centre of the web, holding the hoop up around waist height. Each holds two of the strings where they meet the hoop; one person holds two strings in each hand.

These three people together make our spider, poised in the centre of her web with a foot on each strand. What happens when a fly gets caught in the web?

Invite another volunteer to be a fly and tug on one of the strands.

The spider knows exactly where the fly has landed, because the thread vibrates under her foot. She is connected like this to every bit of her web, so that wherever a fly lands, she feels it.

Now let's use this spider's web to think about God.

Give your three volunteers in the centre a sign each: Father, Son and Holy Spirit.

When Jesus went back up into heaven – on the day we call the Ascension – then God the Son took his place again with God the Father and God the Holy Spirit. These are the three persons of the one God, the God who is at the centre of everything. Now the spider spins her web from very strong, flexible silk which is created by her own body. This web has God at the centre and it represents love, that powerful stuff which is the very essence of God. Love is the unbreakable silver thread which joins God the Father, God the Son and God the Holy Spirit with all of creation: it is as if God's web of love spreads out and catches us all in it. And unlike the spider's web, this is a web which brings life. Each of us is eternally connected to God at the centre, however far from him we may sometimes feel. That kind of connectedness is what Jesus was describing when he said, 'You will know that I am in my Father, and you in me, and I in you.' This is his wonderful promise: we will never be alone again.

Activity

This image of the web of love reminds us that we are not only connected by love to God, but to each other, too. Love is the thing which holds us all together, because however different we may seem, we all have that God-given capacity to love and be loved. Today we are going to create a collage to remind us of this fact. Here is a picture of God's web of love, but we need people in it. Can you cut out pictures of as many different sorts of people as you can, and add them to the web?

Allow plenty of time for people to complete the collage. Display the finished result.

Music When I needed a neighbour

Prayer action This collage represents the variety of people in this world, and it reminds us of the fact that we are all loved by God. Today we are going to remember the variety of people in our local community, and we are going to spread our prayers amongst them by making prayer flags. This idea comes from Tibet: prayer flags are used not to waft prayers heavenwards, but to spread their love, peace and goodwill into the surrounding community, like seeds on the wind. Take a flag and call to mind someone who particularly needs God's blessing: a friend or a neighbour, maybe even someone you don't really like or someone who has no one else to pray for them. On your flag, write that person's first name. You could write lots of names. Then attach your flag here as a sign of your prayer.

Allow enough time for everyone to complete at least one flag and attach it to the string. Then fix or hold the string up outside the church. Gather around the finished flags to offer them to God.

Father of all,
we leave these flags fluttering in the wind
as a sign that your Spirit is moving in the world.
We pray for the people named here
and for all in our community.
Lord, in your mercy, hear our prayer.
Amen.

Go back inside the church for the closing prayer.

Conclusion God of love,
in you we live and move and have our being.[1]
We thank you that through your Son
we are connected to you for ever.
Amen.

Give notices, announce the next all-age service and invite everyone to the feast.

1. Acts 17:28.

One for All

Sitting down with Jesus

Theme	Jesus keeps company with those who need him
Scripture	Matthew 9:9–13

Running order	Total: 50 minutes
Welcome	Tea-light heart *(5 minutes)*
Introduction	Opening the theme
Storytelling	Sketch – The best doctor in the world *(10 minutes)*
Music	O Lord, all the world belongs to you *(5 minutes)*
Exploring	Whose company did Jesus keep? Musical reflection – 'Sit down' by James *(10 minutes)*
Activity	Musical chairs (with an extra chair added) *(10 minutes)*
Prayer action	The empty chair – contemplative prayer *(5 minutes)*
Music	One more step along the world I go *(5 minutes)*
Conclusion	Closing prayer and invitation

Resources

- Tea-lights, matches and tapers
- An upright cross
- A piece of board for the tea-lights to stand on
- A flask of tea for ***Patient 2***
- Music and words
- A recording of 'Sit Down' by James, plus the words *(see appendix)*
- Equipment for playing the song
- A few chairs (if your church has pews)

Leaders

Minimum: 6

- Leader
- Cast x 5

Optimum: 11

- Leader *(Introduction and Conclusion)*
- Cast x 5 (may be male or female)
  Officials 1 and 2, wearing smart, formal clothes
  The Best Doctor, wearing casual clothes and a stethoscope (or carrying a first aid box)
  Patients 1 and 2, wearing scruffy clothes/pyjamas and something to indicate illness – bandages, pale make-up
- Storyteller
- Explorer
- Activity Leader
- Music Leader
- Prayer Leader

Suggestions for additional music

- What a friend we have in Jesus
- Just as I am, without one plea

Service

Welcome In front of the altar, place a cross in the middle of a large heart-shape laid out in unlit tea-lights. As people arrive, invite them to light a candle as a sign of their prayer.

Introduction Today our story is being acted out for us: here come our actors. *(Continue talking as the actors take their places.)* Here are two important-looking people; and – oh dear – this pair don't look very well at all. I hope whatever they've got isn't catching. Let's see what story they have to tell.

Storytelling *The two officials stand at the front, looking excitedly towards the back of church. They are ignoring the scruffy, ill-looking people who are sitting a little way away from them.*

Official 1 He's coming! He's really coming!

Official 2 Who is?

Official 1 The best doctor in the world! He's so famous – I've heard he can cure anyone. He's done amazing things in hospitals all over the world. He's a megastar!

Official 2 What – he's coming here, to our town? I must get my best jacket.

Official 1 We're having a banquet in his honour – with the Mayor!

The Best Doctor walks on from the side, taking the officials by surprise.

Official 1 Oh! Professor – Doctor – Sir – we thought you'd be arriving by private jet.

The Best Doctor I took the bus. Excuse me, please.

He goes over to the ill-looking people.

Hello, there.

He shakes Patient 1's hand, then sits down next to him/her.

How are you?

Patient 1 Not so good.

The Best Doctor Where does it hurt?

Patient 1 shows him.

I think I can help.

Patient 2 *(Holding a flask of tea)* What about me?

The Best Doctor — Hello! *(Shaking Patient 2's hand)* – I can help you, too. Any chance of a cup of tea?

Patient 2 pours a cupful from the flask; the Best Doctor takes a sip.

Mmm – smashing!

Official 1 — Er – excuse me, Sir, but did you know there is a reception for you at the town hall?

Official 2 — Would you like to take tea with the Mayor?

The Best Doctor — Is the Mayor ill?

Official 1 — No . . .

The Best Doctor — Then my place is here. I came to make people better, so I'll stay here with those who need me.

Official 2 — But –

The Best Doctor — I'm a doctor – my place is with sick people, not healthy ones.

Officials 1 and 2 — *(Huffily)* Well!

Applaud the cast and ask them to sit down.

Storyteller — Jesus compared himself to a doctor like the one in our story. The important religious leaders thought that Jesus should stick with them. They didn't like it when instead, he went to dinner with a very different bunch of people. Jesus mixed with people who were hated for their dishonest money-making; people who were despised because they had made bad choices; people who lived chaotic, messed-up lives. He sat down and ate with those whom the good, religious people rejected and ignored. When they complained, he said, 'Those who are healthy have no need of a doctor. I have come to call not the righteous but sinners.' In other words, like the doctor in our story, he knew he had to be where people needed him – and that was with those whose brokenness needed mending.

Music — O Lord, all the world belongs to you

Exploring — Today we are going to think about the company Jesus kept – the people at whose tables he sat down and shared food. In a TV retelling of the Easter story, Jesus sang a modern pop song as an invitation to his followers. The chorus sounded like an invitation to *all* of us to sit down with him, whoever and whatever we are. We are going to listen to that song now. Follow the words and as you do so, think of the people Jesus sat down to dinner with.

Play 'Sit down' by James and display the words of the chorus:

Those who feel the breath of sadness,
Sit down next to me.
Those who find they're touched by madness,
Sit down next to me.
Those who find themselves ridiculous,
Sit down next to me.
In love, in fear, in hate, in tears . . .
Oh sit down,
Sit down next to me.[1]

Jesus didn't say, 'Come to me if you have a perfect life,' or, 'You can only come to me if you are very good and holy.' When Jesus sat down to dinner with unpopular people, his actions seemed to say, 'Come to me if you are sad. Sit down next to me if you feel as if you're going crazy. If you look in the mirror and don't like what you see, come to me.' As he told the Pharisees, it is broken people who need mending, not whole and perfect ones. Jesus says to us, now, 'Whatever state you're in, I'm here for you: "In love, in fear, in hate, in tears, sit down next to me."'

Activity

Place two chairs at the front.

Now it is time to get you moving about, and as our service today is about sitting down, what could be more appropriate than a game of musical chairs?

Choose three volunteers and start the music – use James' 'Sit down' again. As the music plays, add an extra chair. When the music stops, all sit down. Don't comment – just start the music again. This time, add a fourth chair, then stop the music.

Look – there's a spare chair! Room for one more to join in: who would like to come and play?

Bring another volunteer forward and start the game again. Keep adding chairs and inviting more people to join in until you run out of room or energy!

1. James, 'Sit Down', © 1998 Fontana/Mercury.

What was different about that game of musical chairs?

Invite answers.

This game demonstrates what Jesus' love is like: no one is ever 'out' and there is always more room for someone else to sit down next to him.

Prayer action

Place a single empty chair at the front.

In our prayers today, we remember Jesus sitting down next to those who needed him most. Here is an empty chair. Take a moment to think of someone you know who is finding life hard at the moment. Imagine that person sitting here in this chair. *(Pause, then place a second chair beside the first.)* Now here is another chair. If Jesus were physically here, today, he would sit down beside this person. He isn't – but we are. In a moment of quiet, let's pray for whoever we are thinking of in this chair, and pray for ourselves: how might we sit down next to this person? What could we do to keep them company?

Keep silence for a short time.

Let us pray:
Brother Christ,
you came as one of us and sat down next to those who needed you most.
Be with us now as we try to follow your example
and keep us company, now and always.
Amen.

Music

One more step along the world I go

Conclusion

Lord, you opened your arms to the world.
In love, in fear, in hate, in tears,
in whatever joy or pain we find ourselves,
may we sit down next to you.
Amen.

Give notices, announce the next all-age service and invite everyone to the feast.

Travelling light

Theme	What we need in order to be disciples
Scripture	Matthew 9:35–10:1, 10:5–14

Running order	Total: 50 minutes
Welcome	Bubble-blowing prayers *(5 minutes)*
Introduction	Opening the theme
Storytelling	Reading Matthew 9:35–10:1, 10:5–14 *(5 minutes)*
Exploring	'What do we need in order to be disciples?' Off-loading the baggage *(15 minutes)*
Music	Come on, let's get up and go *(5 minutes)*
Activity	Charades *(10 minutes)*
Prayer action	Barefoot – contemplative prayer *(5 minutes)*
Music	Make me a channel of your peace *(5 minutes)*
Conclusion	Closing prayer and invitation

Resources

- Several pots of bubble mixture
- The Disciple's baggage:
  - A money belt or 'bum bag'
  - A very large backpack, stuffed full of light things such as plastic bags, to make it look bulky and heavy
  - A smaller backpack, similarly stuffed
  - A carrier bag bulging with hymn books, files and Bibles
  - A big walking stick like a staff, or a modern walking pole
- A list of emotions for people to act out
- *Optional:* Some different textures on the floor for people to walk on during the barefoot prayers: for example, a sheepskin rug, a sheet of bubble wrap, some sand, some pebbles, some scattered copper coins

Leaders

Minimum: 2

- Leader
- Disciple

Optimum: 7

- Leader *(Introduction and Conclusion)*
- Disciple (male or female), wearing trousers, a t-shirt, walking boots, big socks and a coat, with another coat tied around the waist
- Storyteller
- Explorer
- Music Leader
- Activity Leader
- Prayer Leader

Suggestions for additional music

- Forth in the peace of Christ we go
- All that I am, all that I do

Service

Welcome

As people arrive, invite them to blow bubbles as a sign of their prayer.

Introduction

Today we will be hearing the story of –

The very heavily-laden disciple staggers in.

Hello – who on earth is this?

Disciple: I'm off to spread the good news about Jesus.

Leader: Like that? Do you really need all that stuff? Let's see what instructions Jesus gave his first disciples when they went off to do his work.

The disciple digs out one of many Bibles and hands it to the Storyteller.

Storytelling

This is the bit where Jesus told his disciples what they would need in order to do his work.

Read Matthew 9:35–10:1, 10:5–14

Exploring

The Explorer brings the disciple forward.

Now – you heard what Jesus said. Let's see what you can do without. 'Take no gold, or silver, or copper in your belts' – so you can take off your money belt.

The disciple takes off the big belt.

'No bag for your journey' – that means you don't need this enormous rucksack, or your day sack.

The disciple heaves both bags to the floor.

'Nor two tunics, nor sandals, nor a staff' – so you can give me your coats, and your walking boots, and your big walking stick.

The disciple hands over the spare coat he/she is carrying and the stick, then takes off his/her coat, walking boots and socks. The disciple is left standing in a t-shirt and trousers with bare feet.

Now how does that feel?

Disciple: That's so much better! I can see where I'm going and my back doesn't hurt any more, and now I'm not always going to be worried about whether my stuff is safe and where I'm going to keep it. I've got so much more energy to do God's work! But I am a bit worried. How am I going to manage? What will I eat? Where will I sleep? And I'm not sure about having bare feet – there might be sharp stones in my way.

Explorer

Jesus told his disciples to go out into the world like this to do his work. He told them to trust in God and in the kindness of other people – they were to accept whatever they were offered because, he said, 'labourers deserve their food'. They had to be open to offers of hospitality, but that also meant they took the risk of being turned away or even attacked. He asked them to do no more than he was doing himself: from the moment Jesus was born, he was vulnerable. As a baby, Herod wanted him dead. When Jesus began his ministry, he laid himself open to his followers and also to those who wanted to kill him. Jesus could have asked God to protect him and keep him safe, but he loved us so much that he risked everything for us.

Let's think for a moment about this barefoot disciple, travelling light as Jesus instructed.

The disciple comes forward.

Then let's remember this disciple as he/she was at first, weighed down with baggage.

The Explorer puts on some of the baggage.

I wonder which disciple reminds us of ourselves – the one with all the baggage, or the one who is travelling light? Are we surrounded by stuff we feel we need for our own comfort and security, or are we open to new people and experiences? Do we hang back from doing God's work because we feel we are not fully equipped?

The Explorer puts on the rest of the baggage.

I wonder which disciple our church is like? Are our hands free to spread the good news about Jesus? Or are we carrying a load of unnecessary luggage? Let's take a moment to think about these questions, either on our own or with the people sitting around us.

Allow some time for discussion. Before moving on, you may like to invite people to share some of the things which have been said.

Music Come on, let's get up and go

Activity St Francis of Assisi took Jesus at his word when it came to travelling light. He gave up all his family's wealth and vowed to live in poverty with the poorest people of his day. He is said to have given his followers this instruction: 'Go – preach the good news about Jesus Christ. If necessary, use words.' He reminds us that sometimes, even words are unnecessary baggage. Often the most powerful witness is what we do, rather than what we say. Our activity today reminds us that we can do without words.

Invite everyone to form themselves into teams of 4–6 people.

Here is a list of emotions, such as 'happiness' and 'fear': take it in turns to act out each one, demonstrating it without using words. When your team guesses correctly, the next person can come up and hear which emotion they have got to act out, and so on, until your team reaches the end of the list.

Invite the first volunteers to come up and hear which emotion they have got to act out for their teams. The charades continue until each team has gone through the list, or until one team finishes first and is pronounced the winner. You may like to restate the point about actions speaking louder than words.

Prayer action Think of your bare feet and wiggle your toes. Our bare feet don't see the light of day much. Right now yours are probably wrapped up in cosy socks and encased in good, solid shoes. They can't feel whether the ground they are standing on is cold or warm, rough or smooth. Sometimes, we can go through life a bit like this, wrapped up in our own concerns and not really making contact with the world – or the people – around us. For our prayers today, you are all invited to take off your shoes and socks and walk barefoot around the church, feeling the different sensations in your feet. It is a way of reminding ourselves, in God's presence, that we need to make direct contact with the world and other people, just as Jesus did, if we are to lead the full lives which God wants for us.

Allow plenty of time for people to move around the church, then call for a moment of stillness and quiet.

Living Lord,
you came and lived among us –
you met the fullness of life head-on,
felt the best and the worst of it,
touched people in all their extraordinary variety.
May we have the courage to walk in your footsteps
as if walking barefoot.
Amen.

Music Make me a channel of your peace

Conclusion Gracious Lord,
as we go out into the world,
may we travel light and tread softly;
may our actions speak loudly of your love.
Amen.

Give notices, announce the next all-age service and invite everyone to the feast.

Lightening the load

Theme	Jesus' yoke is easy and his burden is light
Scripture	Matthew 11:28–30

Running order	Total: 50 minutes
Welcome	Bubble-blowing prayers *(5 minutes)*
Introduction	Opening the theme
Storytelling	Sketch – The overburdened worker; reading Matthew 11:28–30 *(10 minutes)*
Exploring	How does Jesus lighten our load? Visual exploration *(10 minutes)*
Activity	Naming our burden *(10 minutes)*
Music	We will lay our burden down *(5 minutes)*
Prayer action	Laying down our burdens – active offertory prayer *(5 minutes)*
Music	I danced in the morning *(5 minutes)*
Conclusion	Closing prayer and invitation

Resources

- Pots of bubble mixture
- Three parcels of different shapes and sizes, wrapped in brown paper
- Fourth parcel wrapped in birthday paper
- A fifth, breakable parcel – for example, a packet of long bread sticks, taken out of their cardboard outer packet and loosely wrapped in brown paper
- A big, empty cardboard box marked with a large cross
- Picture of oxen ploughing *(see appendix)*
- A second large cardboard box, nearly full of books and wrapped in plain paper. Cut some slits into the top
- Lots of slips of paper (e.g. the squares from a telephone memo pad)
- Music and words
- *Optional* – a long piece of rope with which to drag the heavy box
- Tea-lights, matches and tapers

Leaders

Minimum: 4

- Leader/Storyteller
- Cast x 3

Optimum: 9+

- Leader *(Introduction and Conclusion)*
- Storyteller
- Cast x 3

  Manager, formally dressed

  Worker, wearing something which looks like a uniform

  Jesus, wearing white
- Explorer
- Music Leader
- Activity Leader
- Prayer Leader(s)

Suggestions for additional music

- Forth in thy name, O Lord, I go
- Give thanks

Service

Welcome

As people arrive, invite them to blow bubbles as a sign of their prayer.

Introduction

Today's service is for all those of us who have ever felt overwhelmed. It's for those times when we remember the line which has been printed on everything from t-shirts to fridge magnets: 'I try to take each day as it comes – but sometimes they gang up on me'. Our story today begins with someone who is about to have that kind of day.

Storytelling

Manager — We have a new member of our workforce today. Welcome. Now, your first job is to take this parcel down to the ground floor.

Hands over the first parcel and goes off, then rushes back with two more parcels.

Oh – message from the Accounts department – could you deliver these to the fifth floor?

Hands over the parcels and goes off.

Worker — I've just remembered – I need to send my mum this present because I forgot her birthday. I'd better take it with me.

Picks up the birthday present.

Manager — *(Returning with the breakable parcel)* Change of plan! You need to get this to the boss on the first floor, urgently.

Manager leaves.

Worker — This is crazy! *(Throws the parcel to the ground in a fit of temper)* Oh no! I think I've broken it. I'll have to see if I can mend it before I deliver it.

Manager returns.

Manager — Still here? The boss is in a meeting on the seventh floor, so you'd better get up there, fast. By the way – the lift's broken.

Manager leaves.

Worker — Help!

Jesus Let me help. Give me all of that – I'll carry it for you.

Jesus puts all the parcels in his box.

Better?

Worker Much – but what do you want from me?

Jesus Come with me.

Worker That's it?

Jesus Come and work for me – this way.

Worker Coming!

They walk off together, Jesus carrying the box of parcels.

Storyteller We all feel a bit like the worker in our sketch, sometimes. We get overloaded and life feels overwhelming. In today's Bible story, Jesus speaks to all of us who find ourselves in this sort of state.

Read Matthew 11:28–30

Exploring

Jesus promises rest to all of us who are carrying heavy burdens. I wonder what sort of burdens they might be? Let's look at all the things the person in our sketch was struggling with.

Get the box and take out the work packages.

First there were all those conflicting demands – different things which needed doing in different places, all at the same time. Some of us may have busy, demanding lives which feel a bit like that.

Take out the birthday present.

Then there was the forgotten birthday present which still needed posting. Sometimes we can feel as if we are still living with our past mistakes, and they drag us down.

Take out the broken parcel.

Then there was the parcel which got broken in that fit of anger, which became yet another burden because it had to be fixed before it could be off-loaded. Sometimes we do things which are wrong, and the regret weighs heavy on our hearts.

All these different burdens can be lifted off our shoulders by Jesus. Remember how he helped in the sketch: he didn't leave all the burdens behind or say they didn't matter, but he helped by carrying them for the worker who was struggling under their weight.

Show the cross on the box.

Jesus died for us so that whatever we have done or failed to do, all our sins might be forgiven. He gives us rest for our souls because when we come to him, we find the peace which is ours when we say sorry and know that we are forgiven.

But that's not all. In the sketch, what did Jesus tell the overloaded worker to do? *(Invite contributions.)* He didn't say, 'Now off you go and don't worry about any of this' – he gave the worker a new direction: 'Come to me.' In today's Bible reading, he doesn't say, 'Leave all your burdens with me and then go off and do nothing' – he says, 'Take my yoke upon you and learn from me.'

Show the picture of oxen ploughing.

A yoke is a collar worn by a working animal like a donkey or an ox. The yoke is tied to a plough or a cart which the animal then has to pull along. So when Jesus says, 'Take my yoke upon you,' he expects us to work, but he calls us to do *his* work. He is like a kind farmer who gives his donkey a comfortable yoke to wear and a light load to pull. Jesus promises us that if we follow him, he will never burden us with more than we can bear. He promises us that he will work with us, like the farmer who works with his animals to plough a field because they could not do the job alone, without his guidance. With Jesus, there is still work for us to do, but we have the peace of mind which comes from knowing that we are in safe hands and are being guided on the right path.

Activity

The first step to finding the restfulness and peace which Jesus promises is to lay down our burdens in his presence. Here is a very heavy box which we are going to use today to represent all those things which weigh heavy on our hearts and minds. Let's take some time now to think what our own particular burdens might be. Write or draw them on some of these little pieces of paper, then add them to this heavy weight.

Allow plenty of time for people to write down their burdens and add them to the box. As they do so, you might ask your musicians to play through the tune for the following hymn a few times.

Music We will lay our burden down

Prayer action Our prayers today will follow the actions described by our last hymn. We will lay our burden down, then we will light a candle as a sign of God's love in the world. First, let's bring forward the weight which represents all our burdens: we name them before God and leave them in his hands.

The heavy box is brought forward, carried by several people or tied with a rope and dragged forward.

Please come forward and light a candle as a sign of your prayer.

When all the candles have been lit, gather everyone together.

We come to you, Jesus.
We lay our burdens down so that our hands are free
to carry the light of your love into the world.
Amen.

Music I danced in the morning

Conclusion Gentle Lord,
take our burdens from us
so that we may walk in your footsteps with a light heart.
Amen.

Give notices, announce the next all-age service and invite everyone to the feast.

Freedom food

Theme	Passover; pilgrims and settlers
Scripture	Exodus 12:1–14

Running order	Total: 50 minutes
Welcome	Flame flags *(5 minutes)*
Introduction	Opening the theme
Storytelling	The Passover meal – interactive story with food *(10 minutes)*
Music	As we are gathered *(5 minutes)*
Activity	Settlers or pilgrims? Exploring the house and the tent *(10 minutes)*
Exploring	How do we follow the Way? Packing up the house and the tent *(10 minutes)*
Music	All who would valiant be *(5 minutes)*
Prayer action	Leavened and unleavened bread – sensory reflective prayer *(5 minutes)*
Conclusion	Closing prayer and invitation

Resources

- Short lengths of bamboo pole or similar for the flame flags *(see appendix for Together in unity)*
- Red, yellow and orange paper, cut into rough strips
- Pens
- Sellotape
- At the front of church, a small table laid with the Passover food (see below)
- On either side of the table, two columns to represent the doorposts *(see appendix)*
- Roast lamb, cut into small pieces
- Pieces of unleavened bread: matzo if you can find it, or other flatbread
- Romaine lettuce, or other bitter lettuce/herbs such as rocket or parsley
- A dish of red liquid (e.g. red food colouring or undiluted Ribena)
- Music and words
- Two separate areas in church, set up as follows:

  Pilgrims: A simple dome tent; a sleeping bag; a folding table and chair; other lightweight and portable camping equipment. Leave all tent bags etc in a pile to one side

  Settlers: A floor rug; a large, heavy table and set of chairs. Lay the table with lots of non-breakable crockery and other items such as napkins, plastic flowers, etc. Leave the boxes you packed all this in to one side
- A plate of ordinary bread, broken into small pieces
- A plate of flatbread pieces (the remains of the Passover meal)

Leaders

Minimum: 1

- Leader

Optimum: 6

- Leader *(Introduction and Conclusion)*
- Storyteller
- Activity Leader
- Explorer
- Music Leader
- Prayer Leader

Suggestions for additional music

- Blessèd are those
- In bread we bring you, Lord

Service

Welcome

As people arrive, invite them to write their prayer on a paper flame and attach it to a flag.

Introduction

Today's story is all about one of the most important meals in the Bible: the Jewish Passover meal. Jews still celebrate it today and we remember it because the bread Jesus broke at the Last Supper was the special bread eaten at Passover.

Storytelling

Sit at the table which is between the doorposts. Invite people to gather round you; if your congregation is large, gather the children round.

God's people were slaves in Egypt. God called Moses to set them free, and nine times Moses had asked Pharaoh to release his people. Each time Pharaoh refused, God sent a terrible plague on the Egyptian people, but still Pharaoh would not let Moses and his people go. So God told Moses to prepare for the worst plague of all. God said, 'Tell all my people to find a perfect lamb, one for each family. You must kill the lamb and roast it.

Place the pieces of roast lamb on the table.

You must eat it with unleavened bread.

Place the bread on the table.

You must eat it with bitter herbs.

Place the lettuce on the table.

Eat your meal with your shoes and coat on, ready to leave your homes, and eat it quickly.' God said, 'Most important of all, you must mark your doorway with some of the lamb's blood.

Make a mark with the red liquid on the two doorposts.

Tonight I will send my deadliest plague to Egypt: I will kill all Egyptian firstborn children and animals. When

I see the lamb's blood on your houses, I will pass over you and your children will be safe. From this day forward, you will celebrate this day as the festival of Passover.'

That night, God passed over Egypt and killed all the firstborn children. Pharaoh finally told Moses to take his people and go. The Israelites left at daybreak, taking with them everything they could carry. They left Egypt and slavery behind them: they were free at last!

This is the food which they shared on the eve of their freedom, the first Passover. Let's share some of it now.

Encourage people to eat the lamb, bread and lettuce. Allow time for everyone to sample some of the food, passing plates around church if necessary.

What's different about this bread? *(Invite comments.)* Bread was a staple food for the Israelites in Egypt. Every morning at dawn, women would get up to prepare that day's bread: they mixed flour, water, salt and yeast and left the dough to rise, then baked it over the fire. The day they escaped from Egypt was different. They were packed and ready to leave in a hurry, so there was no time to wait for dough to rise. The bread was made without yeast, then baked quickly to make round, flat loaves. This kind of bread was also useful if you were going on a long journey, because it kept well. The Israelites had no idea how long their journey out of Egypt would be: all they knew was that ahead of them lay miles and miles of sandy, stony wilderness. They would need some bread for such a journey.

So this flat Passover bread is bread for travellers, bread for refugees who have to escape in a hurry – bread for pilgrims who are looking for the land of their own which God had promised them.

Music As we are gathered

Activity When God's people left Egypt, they became pilgrims on their way to the promised land. Today we are going to think about pilgrims who are always on the move, travelling as a group: they are represented by this temporary tent here. We are also going to think about the opposite of the pilgrim: the settler, who stays in one place and becomes part of a rooted community. The settler is represented by this permanent house here. Take some time now to explore these two different living spaces and as you do so, think about pilgrims and settlers. Which area do you like best? Would you feel more at home as a pilgrim or a settler, or a bit of both? Think about our church, too. Is this church like a pilgrim or a settler?

Allow some time for people to explore the areas, think and discuss. Then invite some responses to the above questions, encouraging people to explain their answers.

Exploring

Jesus does not tell us *where* to live. Some of us may be settled in a rooted community, and others of us may have to move more frequently from place to place. But he does tell us *how* we should live: he calls us to be pilgrims in our hearts, always ready to grow and change in response to God's call. He said, 'I am the way, and the truth, and the life.' He is the way, not the destination; when he calls his disciples – and us – he says, 'Follow me,' not, 'Stay put with me.' But how do we follow the way? It's not always easy. To help us explore this question today, I need some volunteers to be pilgrims and settlers.

Pick your volunteers and ask them to stand in their own area.

Here's the challenge: I am going to call all of you to follow me out of the church, but you have to pack up everything you have and bring it with you. I wonder who will be first? On your marks, get set – follow me!

Move to the back of the church and watch as the two teams race to pack everything up. The first through the church doors is the winner. If you have chosen big enough furniture for the settlers, the pilgrims should win!

How easy was it for the pilgrims and the settlers to get moving? What held the settlers back? *(Invite responses.)* If Jesus called us today to follow him and do his work in the world, I wonder what might hold us back? Here is a question for us all to take away and think about, individually and as a church: whenever Jesus calls us, are we ready to follow him?

Music

All who would valiant be

Prayer action

As a focus for our prayers today, we will use the unleavened bread which God's people ate in a hurry on the night they escaped from Egypt. We will also use the soft, fluffy bread eaten by those who are comfortably settled in one place, where there is plenty of time to make bread and let it rise.

Our Father in heaven,
give us this day our daily bread.

Share the leavened bread.

We give thanks for this well-risen bread
and for the comforts of being settlers.

Share the unleavened bread.

We receive this unleavened bread
as a reminder of our call to be pilgrims.
Lord, show us the way.
Amen.

Conclusion

Pilgrim Lord,
send us out into the world
to follow your way.
Amen.

Give notices, announce the next all-age service and invite everyone to the feast.

Show and tell

Theme	Putting our faith into practice
Scripture	Matthew 21:28–32

Running order	Total: 50 minutes
Welcome	Flame flags *(5 minutes)*
Introduction	Opening the theme
Storytelling 1	Retelling Matthew 21:28–32 *(3 minutes)*
Music	Father, we love you *(5 minutes)*
Storytelling 2	*Truelove* by Babette Cole *(7 minutes)*
Activity	Stations – Exploring different ways of loving our neighbour *(10 minutes)*
Exploring	How can we put our faith into practice? Responses and written reflection *(10 minutes)*
Music	Heaven shall not wait *(5 minutes)*
Prayer action	'I love you' – signed prayer *(5 minutes)*
Conclusion	Closing prayer and invitation

Resources

- Short lengths of bamboo pole or similar for the flame flags *(see appendix for Together in unity)*
- Red, yellow and orange paper, cut into rough strips
- Pens
- Sellotape
- Music and words
- A copy of *Truelove* by Babette Cole *(see appendix)*
- Three stations around the church *(see appendix)*
- Heart-shaped pieces of red paper *(see appendix)*

Leaders

Minimum: 1

- Leader

Optimum: 7

- Leader *(Introduction and Conclusion)*
- Storytellers x 2
- Music Leader
- Activity Leader
- Explorer
- Prayer Leader

Suggestions for additional music

- Jesus put this song into our hearts
- We have a dream

Service

Welcome

As people arrive, invite them to write their prayer on a paper flame and attach it to a flag.

Introduction

Our service today is about how actions speak louder than words. A hug tells someone clearly that we love them; a box of chocolates can say 'Thank you'. We may tell God that we love him, but today we will be thinking about what we do to show that love.

Storytelling 1

Our story today was told by Jesus in the temple in Jerusalem. For Jewish people in Jesus' time, the temple was the holiest place on earth and Jews from many countries made regular pilgrimages there. The chief priests were the most important people in the temple. They were in charge of all the religious laws, sacrifices and worship. Jesus told them this story, in front of all the crowds in the temple courtyard.

Jesus said, 'What do you say to this? A man owned a vineyard and he had two sons. He said to the first son, "Go and pick grapes for me today."

The first son said, 'No, I won't – but later on he changed his mind. He went to the vineyard and started picking grapes for his father.

Meanwhile, the man called his second son and said, "Will you go and work for me in the vineyard today?"

The second son said, "Yes – of course, father." But then he sat in the shade instead and never went near the vineyard.'

Jesus said, 'What do you think? Which son did what his father wanted?'

The chief priests answered, 'The first one did.'

Then Jesus said to the chief priests, 'You think you are so much better than all the sinners you despise – but all those dishonest, messed-up, wayward people are going to get into God's kingdom ahead of you. They believed that God sent John the Baptist before me, but you refused to believe. They are getting on with the business of believing, while you just talk about it.'

Music Father, we love you

Storytelling 2

What an accusation Jesus made! He publicly criticised the chief priests and said they should 'walk it like they talk it' – in other words, they spent a lot of time talking about God's will without actually putting their faith into practice. He compared them to the son who said he would work in his father's vineyard, and then didn't lift a finger. Today we will be thinking about putting our faith into practice: to help us, we have another story. This story is about love and how actions speak louder than words.

Gather as many people round you as possible and read Truelove *by Babette Cole, showing the pictures and describing them as necessary.*

Activity

Truelove is a wonderful story about showing someone you love them in what you do, rather than what you say. What did Truelove the dog do to show he loved his family? How did he and the stray dogs behave kindly to each other?

Invite responses.

And what did the family do in the end to show that they loved Truelove?

Invite responses.

When Jesus' friends asked him the most important rules for doing things God's way, Jesus replied: 'Love God with all your heart and soul, mind and strength' and 'Love other people as you love yourself'. So it is not enough to say we believe in God: we have to demonstrate this belief by behaving in a kind and loving way. Around the church are three stations: one helps us to consider what Jesus did to show his love for us, and the other two help us to think about how we can show God's love in our lives. Take some time now to visit each station and explore what you find there.

Allow plenty of time for people to visit the stations.

Exploring

What about the first station? What did that tell us about God's love for us?

Invite responses and try to value all contributions.

John's Gospel tells us, 'God so loved the world that he gave his only Son, so that everyone who believes in him may not perish but may have eternal life'. God did not remain aloof in heaven, thinking loving thoughts about us: he sent his beloved Son to show us his love in his life and work, his body and his blood.

What did the other stations show us about how we love each other and God?

Invite responses to these stations: people may like to respond to the objects and question, or explain what they drew or wrote, and why. Allow plenty of time for this discussion, then draw it to a close by producing the heart-shaped pieces of paper.

Here we have a symbol of love: take one each and we will use these hearts as a focus for our own thoughts. *(Hand round the hearts and the pens.)* Let's take some time now to think about our own lives. First of all, try and think of an act of kindness which has shown you how much someone cares about you. Whatever that action was, write it down on one side of this heart.

Allow some time for people to think and write.

Now we need to ask ourselves, 'What kind and loving thing could I do for someone else today?' Take some time to think what that good deed might be, and write it as your intention on the other side of your heart.

Allow some time for people to think and write.

Let's keep these hearts as a sign of the love we have received, and a reminder that however much we tell people about God's love, we are not doing things God's way unless we also show that love in the way we treat others.

Music

Heaven shall not wait

Prayer action

Today we are going to pray with actions, not words: we are going to use sign language to tell God that we love him. There are two versions of this sign, American and British: use whichever one you like best. One is a simple sign which is made like this:

I *(show a closed fist, palm facing forward, with the little finger extended)*
love you *(extend the thumb and forefinger to make an 'L' shape).*

Your hand makes the letters 'I', 'L' and 'Y' all together.

Indicate where these letters are: the little finger is the 'I'; the thumb and forefinger are the 'L' and the forefinger and little finger, together with the hand, suggest a 'Y'.

Alternatively, there is a simple action:

I *(point at yourself)*
love *(cross your hands over your heart)*
you *(point and look upwards).*

You could repeat the sign several times or remain still with your hands in that position. Let us rest in God's presence now and call to mind all the love he has shown us, and all the love we have received in our lives. All love is from God, because God is love. Let us pray.

In a time of quiet, everyone signs 'I love you'.

Amen.

Conclusion

God of love,
show us how to put our faith into practice;
may we live out your love in our lives,
in Jesus' name,
Amen.

Give notices, announce the next all-age service and invite everyone to the feast.

All you need is love

Theme	The greatest commandments
Scripture	Matthew 22:34–40

Running order	Total: 50 minutes
Welcome	Natural treasures *(5 minutes)*
Introduction	Opening the theme
Storytelling	Dramatised reading of Matthew 22:34–40 *(2 minutes)*
Music	A new commandment *(5 minutes)*
Exploring/Activity 1	'What hangs on these commandments?' Making a mobile and deciding what comes from love and what doesn't *(10 minutes)*
Music	God's love *(5 minutes)*
Exploring/Activity 2	'What hangs on these commandments?' Completing the mobile and exploring how to demonstrate love in our own lives *(13 minutes)*
Prayer action	Glow-stick heart – active prayer and Taizé chant: Ubi caritas *(10 minutes)*
Conclusion	Closing prayer and invitation

Resources

- Natural treasures such as shells, polished stones, feathers, flowers and leaves, attractively displayed – perhaps on a velvet cloth, or in a collection of little jewellery boxes
- Music and words
- Circlet, hearts and boxes with text and pictures *(see appendix)*
- Glue sticks
- Pens and pencils
- Sellotape
- Cotton thread
- An empty bin
- *Optional*: a recording of 'All You Need Is Love' by the Beatles, plus equipment to play it on
- Lots of tubes of glow-sticks *(see appendix for Living in the light)*

Leaders

Minimum: 2

- Leader / ***Lawyer***
- ***Jesus***

Optimum: 7

- Leader *(Introduction and Conclusion)*
- Cast x 2
  Jesus, wearing white
  Lawyer, wearing black robes
- Explorer / Activity Leaders x 2
- Music Leader
- Prayer Leader

Suggestions for additional music

- Let there be love
- Love is his word

Service

Welcome

As people arrive, invite them to spend some time in quiet contemplation of the natural treasures you have displayed.

Introduction

Life can be confusing sometimes. We get busy or mixed up and can lose sight of what is really important. Our service today focuses on what Jesus said was more important than anything else. The religious leaders – the Pharisees – were badgering him with questions again. He had challenged their authority and they didn't like it one bit, so they kept testing him to try and catch him out. This is what they asked him.[1]

Storytelling

Lawyer: Teacher, which commandment in the law is the greatest?

Jesus: 'You shall love the Lord your God with all your heart, and with all your soul, and with all your mind.' This is the greatest and first commandment. And a second is like it: 'You shall love your neighbour as yourself.' On these two commandments hang all the law and the prophets.

Music

A new commandment

Exploring/Activity 1

In our story today, Jesus makes faith sound beautifully simple. It all comes down to one thing: love. The most important thing of all is to love God completely, and to love other people as we love ourselves. Jesus says, 'On these two commandments hang all the law and the prophets.' In other words, everything God requires of us is all about love: all the laws he laid down, and all the important communications he made through his spokespeople, the prophets.

Today we are going to explore what this might mean for us.

Show the circlet.

1. The following lines are taken directly from Matthew's Gospel (NRSV): you may prefer to use a different translation.

Here we have a circle which, like God's love, has no beginning and no end. The words on it form a never-ending description of what God wants us to be doing: 'Loving God loving people loving God loving people loving God . . .' This love is never-ending and from this circle we can hang lots of loving words and actions, like a mobile. Here's one: 'Don't steal.' If we are really trying to love other people, then we won't steal from them – so that belongs here, because it comes from love.

Stick it onto a heart and attach it to the circlet.

Here's another one: 'Don't get your own back on someone who has hurt you.' If we are really trying to love other people, and ourselves, we won't make things worse for everyone by getting our own back, and then being frightened that they will hurt us again in return. God wants to free us from that sort of pain, so that's why this instruction, too, is all about love.

Stick it onto a heart and attach it to the circlet.

Here's something different. 'Turn your back on people who don't agree with you.' That sounds closer to hate than love: it is certainly no way to love other people, so that one doesn't belong here.

Screw up the piece of paper and throw it in the bin.

Take some time now to look at all the words and pictures we have here, and decide where they belong: are they all about love? If so, add them to the mobile. If they are not, throw them in the bin.

Allow plenty of time for people to read, think, make decisions and add things to the mobile. You may then like to ask for contributions and talk about why people made particular choices (this includes the scrunched-up papers in the bin).

Music God's love

Exploring/Activity 2 There is a kind of dark stone called a touchstone. If you want to know whether some metal contains gold, you rub it with the touchstone. You can tell the quality of the gold by the colour of the mark the touchstone makes.

When Jesus said that the two greatest commandments were all about love, he gave us a kind of touchstone which we can use in our lives. There are all kinds of believers and leaders in the Church and the world, and they don't all agree with one another. In order to decide who we should listen to, we need to ask ourselves this: 'Are they talking about love or something else?' Love is the touchstone which helps us decide who is genuinely leading us in a Godward direction *(indicate the 'Love' mobile)* and who is leading us towards hatred *(indicate the bin).*

Love is also the touchstone which we can apply to our own lives. Let's take some time now to think about how our actions might show that we love God, and that we love the people around us as much as we love ourselves. What good deeds and kind things could we do to demonstrate our love?

Ask for a few suggestions, then show the blank boxes.

In these boxes, we'll write or draw anything which shows love. Let's stick them onto the hearts and fill this 'Love' mobile with as many good things as possible.

Allow plenty of time for people to add things to the mobile. You might like to play 'All You Need is Love' by the Beatles as they do so. When the mobile is full, invite people to share some of their contributions.

Prayer action

Gather everyone together in a large, clear area; turn off the lights.

For our prayers today we will join together in making a great big symbol of love, to remind us of God's love for us and the love which we should show in our lives. Take one of these glow-sticks and crack it to make it glow. Then let's join them all together to make the shape of a heart, as we pray that we might live our lives more lovingly.

People crack their glow-sticks and lay them end-to-end on the floor to make the shape of a large heart.

As we gather around this radiant sign of love, let's pray with music. The words of the chorus are:

Ubi caritas et amor.
Ubi caritas Deus ibi est.

These words mean, 'Where there is charity and love, there is God.'[2]

As people stand around the heart, they sing together the Taizé chant, 'Ubi caritas'. Pause for a moment before saying the closing words.

'Let us love one another
as God has loved us,'[3]
in Jesus' name,
Amen.

Conclusion

Let's each take our own glow-stick home, as a reminder that we should carry this love out into the world.

Everyone takes a glow-stick from the heart on the floor.

Let us pray.
God of love,
show us how the love we have sung about here
may be lived out in our lives,
in your name.
Amen.

Give notices, announce the next all-age service and invite everyone to the feast.

2. Translation taken from *Anglican Hymns Old & New*, Kevin Mayhew 2008.
3. From 'Ubi caritas', ©Ateliers et Presses de Taizé.

In the right direction

Theme	Avoiding false prophets and being led astray
Scripture	Matthew 24:1–14

Running order	Total: 50 minutes
Welcome	Holding crosses *(5 minutes)*
Introduction	Opening the theme
Activity 1	Obstacle course demonstration – true and false guides *(7 minutes)*
Storytelling	Retelling Matthew 24:1–14 – Jesus warns of false prophets *(3 minutes)*
Music	You are the King of Glory *(5 minutes)*
Exploring	Who are the true and false guides? Discussion with visual aids *(10 minutes)*
Activity 2	Following the right way – being led through the obstacle course *(10 minutes)*
Music	Dear Lord and Father of mankind *(5 minutes)*
Prayer action	Still, small voice – listening prayer *(5 minutes)*
Conclusion	Closing prayer and invitation

Resources

- Holding crosses *(see appendix for An open invitation)*. You may like to spread these out on a rug, with cushions for people to sit on
- Church layout: Ideally, you should move seating into long rows against the walls on either side of the church, leaving the whole central area free for the obstacle course
- The obstacle course should consist of large, moveable objects that will not hurt anyone who trips over them, such as empty cardboard boxes, large bean bags and floor cushions
- Lots of blindfolds
- Large cross made of lining paper, with the top cut into the shape of an arrow
- Music and words

Leaders

Minimum: 1

- Leader

Optimum: 7

- Leader *(Introduction and Conclusion)*
- Activity Leaders x 2
- Storyteller
- Explorer
- Music Leader
- Prayer Leader

Suggestions for additional music

- Great is the darkness
- Lord of all hopefulness

Service

Welcome

As people arrive, invite them to spend some quiet time handling the holding crosses.

Introduction

Today we will be thinking about finding the right direction in life – and about what can trip us up or lead us in the wrong direction. We will begin with a challenge for some willing volunteers.

Activity 1

Invite a minimum of three volunteers to come forward. Introduce them as a follower and his/her guides. The follower is blindfolded and positioned towards the back of church, on the far side of the obstacles. You and the other guides stand opposite him/her at the front of church. The aim is for you – the Leader – to call out directions to lead the follower safely through the obstacles to the other side. Do this once as a demonstration, then move some of the obstacles around.

Now, we are going to make this more challenging. This time, I will still be calling out the right directions, but these other guides will be calling out the wrong directions. The follower needs to concentrate on listening to my voice, not theirs.

Do it again, this time with the other guides calling out wrong directions.

Storytelling

In our activity, one guide told the follower the right way to go, but all the others were trying to make him/her wander in the wrong direction. Shortly before he died, Jesus told his friends about the dangers of trusting the wrong guides in life. He said that the future would hold some terrible things: wars, famines and earthquakes; hate and betrayal. He said that many people's love would grow cold in the face of all this. Then Jesus gave his friends a clear warning: 'Beware that no one leads you astray. For many will come in my name, saying, "I am the Messiah!" and they will lead many astray . . . And many false prophets will arise and lead many astray.'

The 'false prophets' Jesus talked about are like the false guides in our activity: they call the follower in the wrong direction and lead him/her astray. But Jesus is the true guide: his is the only voice we should listen to when it comes to deciding which way to go in life, because he will always lead us in the right direction and bring us closer to God.

Music You are the King of Glory

Exploring Let's think about Jesus' warning with the help of some of the things we used in our activity. If the guide who gave the right directions is like Jesus, then what are all these obstacles in the way? And what about those false guides? Who are the false guides we need to watch out for in our lives today? These are the questions we are going to be thinking about together.

Let's start with the obstacles. These make it harder for us to follow Jesus – they trip us up and make things difficult for us and our faith. I wonder what obstacles we might encounter in life? Let's think about that question or discuss it amongst ourselves for a short time. Come up and explore these obstacles if that would help.

Allow some time for thinking and discussion, then invite responses. You might like to suggest that some of the following could be obstacles:

- Bad things which happen to us
- World events like the wars and earthquakes Jesus mentioned
- Crime

Now let's think about the false guides. These are a bit like a car's faulty satnav system that tells you to drive down a road which – to begin with – looks fine. So you follow the satnav's directions, only to find that the road leads off the edge of a cliff. What kind of influences in our lives might lead us astray, like a faulty satnav system? Let's think about that question and discuss it amongst ourselves.

Allow some time for thinking and discussion, then invite responses. You might like to suggest that some of the following could be false guides, depending on the age-range of your congregation:

- Friends who don't have our best interests at heart
- Bullies
- Consumerism: the call to focus on getting and spending money
- Things we may become addicted to, like alcohol or drugs

Activity 2

We have thought about the obstacles and the false guides, and we know that we must listen to Jesus, who is our true guide. Bearing all those things in mind, I'd like to invite you all to try our obstacle course in pairs, if you would like to. One person should be the guide and the other, the follower. Followers, you need to tie your blindfold on, then disregard the instructions you hear from all the other guides around you. Just follow the voice you trust to guide you through the obstacle course.

Encourage lots of pairs to come forward and try the obstacle course at the same time. Be prepared for lots of noise and falling over!

Music

Dear Lord and Father of mankind

During the hymn, prepare the obstacle course to be a focus for prayer. Make a space in the middle and lay down the big cross made of lining paper, with the end shaped like an arrow pointing up towards the altar.

Prayer action

Whatever obstacles we face in life, whatever noise distracts us, God is calling us to him. Through the earthquake, wind and fire his still, small voice speaks to us.[1] In our prayers today, we will simply rest quietly in God's presence and listen. Let's begin by listening to the noise of the world around us.

1. 'Dear Lord and Father of mankind', John Greenleaf Whittier (1807–1892).

Pause as people settle into silence and tune in to the sounds of the outside world.

Through the noise and in this quietness, let's listen for the true guide who leads us through life.

Allow a short time of silence.

Lord, help us to listen to you
and show us your way.
Amen.

Conclusion

Father God,
send out your light and your truth, that they might lead us.
May we put our trust in you.[2]
Amen.

Give notices, announce the next all-age service and invite everyone to the feast.

2. From Psalm 43.

Repentance and forgiveness

Preparing the way

Theme	John the Baptist and repentance
Scripture	Matthew 3:1–6

Running order	Total: 50 minutes
Welcome	Lighting a votive candle each *(5 minutes)*
Introduction	Opening the theme
Music	Desert soundscape (see appendix) *(3 minutes)*
Activity and storytelling	Multi-media retelling of Matthew 3:1–6 *(15 minutes)*
Music	Make way, make way *(5 minutes)*
Exploring	How can we prepare the way? *(10 minutes)*
Prayer action	Washed away – interactive confession *(5 minutes)*
Music	Wait for the Lord *(5 minutes)*
Conclusion	Paving the way *(2 minutes)*

Resources

- Votive candles and matches
- Five pictures: *(see appendix)*
  - The Judean wilderness
  - A camel skin
  - Desert locusts
  - Wild honey
  - People being baptised in the river Jordan
- Desert soundscape *(see appendix)*
- A screen projector and laptop
- Plates of small rice cakes and dishes of honey
- Music and words
- Lots of small pebbles or flat stones *(pieces of slate are particularly good)*
- Felt pens *(with ordinary, water-soluble ink)*
- A large glass bowl full of water in front of the altar
- Optional music: 'Down to the river to pray' *(see appendix)*

Leaders

Minimum: 2

- Leader
- Storyteller

Optimum: 6

- Leader *(Introduction and Conclusion)*
- Activity Leader
- Storyteller
- Music Leader
- Explorer
- Prayer Leader

Suggestions for additional music

- On Jordan's bank the Baptist's cry
- Guide me, O thou great Redeemer

Service

Welcome

Light a votive candle each.

Introduction

Today we will meet the man who foretold the coming of Jesus. Come into the desert where he walked alone: the wilderness of Judea.

Turn off the lights. On the screen, using PowerPoint or a similar programme, show the first picture: the Judean wilderness. Play the music to set the scene.

Music

Desert soundscape *(see appendix)*

Activity and storytelling

This is the wilderness of Judea. It is a rocky, desolate place, with bare crags and deep crevasses. The sun scorches it all summer and in winter the snow grips these high, bare hills. It is not a place most people would choose to live. Sometimes thieves and outlaws hid there, to escape the authorities in Jerusalem. Sometimes people of faith went into the wilderness to get away from all the distractions of ordinary life and to try and get closer to God. They remembered Moses, and how God stayed close to him and his people as they made their way through the wilderness.

Today we are thinking about a man called John who was born a few months before Jesus. They called him John the Baptist, and this is his story.

Read Matthew 3:1–3.

Like Moses before him, John lived in the wilderness and depended on what God provided. Some people travelled across the desert on camels, so he made his clothes out of camel skin.

Show picture of camel skin.

There were few animals to hunt for food, so to keep his strength up, he ate big, fat desert locusts – like these.

Show picture of locusts (no doubt with accompanying cries of 'Yuck!').

There were wild bees in the desert, so he ate their honey. Do you think it made the locusts taste any better?

Show picture of wild honey.

I couldn't find any locusts today, but I have got some honey, and some rice cakes which are a bit like the sweet wafers which Moses ate in the wilderness, which he called 'bread from heaven'. Come and taste some wilderness rations . . .

Offer round the rice cakes and honey.

Now, the people who lived in the towns and villages heard about John living his extreme life in the wilderness and they became convinced that he must be close to God. This is what happened:

Read Matthew 5–6.

Show picture of people being baptised in the river Jordan.

Place glass bowl full of water in front of you, and wash your hands as you talk.

John was a Jew, and his people used washing rituals as a sign of purification. They washed before and after eating, before certain prayers and before the Sabbath. When they came to John and confessed all their sins and wrongdoings, he washed them in the river, as a sign that he was washing their sins away.

Music Make way, make way

Exploring In the desert, John called everyone to prepare a way for Jesus. What might this mean for us today? How might we prepare a way for him in our lives? Perhaps the wilderness is a good place to start. A modern writer spent some time in the desert and described it like this:

> The sky was white, too dazzling to look at, and gradually the silence of the desert took hold and

> overwhelmed me . . . there was nothing; a huge hot nothing. It was the deepest silence I have ever known. There was nothing to hear.[1]

One method of preparing the way, of letting Jesus into our lives, is simply by being silent. If we still all the noise and the chatter of our daily lives, perhaps we may be free to pay attention to God in a new way. Today, let's take a few minutes to be silent together as we contemplate the wilderness. Don't worry about what to say or even think – just be in the silence and listen . . .

Show the picture of the Judean wilderness again and let the silence last for two or three minutes.

Another means of preparing the way for Jesus is to clear away all the rubbish that blocks his path into our lives. This rubbish is made up of all the things we have said and done wrong; all the things we regret not saying and doing. This is what the Bible calls sin. None of us is perfect, but God understands what we are like. He loves us and wants to forgive our sins so that we can make a fresh start. Today we are going to call to mind everything for which we want to say, 'Sorry'. It can sometimes help to spell it out, and so we are going to do this on these stones. Take a stone, or several stones, and privately, in your own time, write on it anything for which you want to say, 'Sorry'.

Allow enough time for everyone to write on their stones.

Prayer action

In our prayers we will offer these confessions to God by putting our stones in this bowl of water. The water will wash our words away just as God's love washes our sins away. It reminds us that God forgives us and lets us start again, with a clean slate.

Allow enough time for everyone to take their stones up to the altar. People may want to do this more than once. While they are doing this, you may like to play some music: for example,

1. Sara Maitland, *A Book of Silence*, Granta Books 2008, p.195, 197.

Down to the river to pray *(see appendix). When the music and prayers have finished, say:*

Loving Father,
we are sorry.
Take all these stones
as a sign of our repentance
and wash us clean.
Amen.

Music Wait for the Lord

Conclusion *As this prayer is offered, the Prayer Leader should carefully take each of the washed stones out of the water and lay them down to form a path leading from the people to the altar.*

Lord of life,
thank you for giving us a fresh start.
Send us out as living stones
to build your church as a prophetic witness
and to pave the way for you to enter our lives.
Amen.

Give notices, announce the next all-age service and invite everyone to the feast.

Loving life

Theme	The best way to live
Scripture	Leviticus 19:1, 2, 9–18 and Matthew 5:38–48

Running order	Total: 50 minutes
Welcome	Lighting tea-lights *(5 minutes)*
Introduction	Opening the theme
Activity	Finding the Ten Commandments and fitting them together *(10 minutes)*
Storytelling	Visual response to Leviticus 19:1, 2, 9–18 *(5 minutes)*
Music	There are hundreds of sparrows *(5 minutes)*
Exploring	Why are these the best ways to live? Responding to Matthew 5:38–48 *(10 minutes)*
Music	God is love: his the care *(5 minutes)*
Prayer action	'Broken things' – confession *(5 minutes)*
Music	Let there be love *(5 minutes)*
Conclusion	Displaying the tea-lights in a heart shape

Resources

- Tea-lights and matches
- A large piece of board
- Ten Commandments puzzle pieces, hidden around the church *(see appendix)*
- Two stone tablet templates *(see appendix)*
- Blu-tack
- 10 A4 'brainstorming sheets', each with one of the Ten Commandments (as written in the service) in the middle, inside a heart shape. Leave plenty of space around the outside of the heart
- Pens and pencils
- Some tables to work on
- Music and words
- A recording of 'Broken Things', sung by Juliet Turner *(see appendix)*
- Audio equipment
- A large heart-shaped bowl or box, or a heart shape cut out of a large piece of red card *(see appendix)*
- Pieces of eggshell (make sure they are clean), placed in a bowl

Leaders

Minimum: 2

- Leader
- Prayer Leader

Optimum: 6+

- Leader *(Introduction and Conclusion)*
- Activity Leader
- Storyteller
- Music Leader(s)
- Explorer
- Prayer Leader

Suggestions for additional music

- O Lord, all the world belongs to you
- Let us build a house where love can dwell

Service

Welcome

Invite everyone to light a tea-light on the altar as they arrive. Make sure all the tea-lights are on your large piece of board: when all are lit, move them carefully to form the shape of a heart. Leave them alight on the altar.

Introduction

Today we will be thinking about the way we live and how we can get the most out of life. It has been said that every human being has a right to 'life, liberty and the pursuit of happiness'. This famous phrase was written when the USA was born, having been granted independence from Great Britain; these were among the first official words of a country which had found a new freedom.

Our story today begins with another nation with a new-found freedom. When God's people were freed from slavery in Egypt, they escaped into the wilderness, a no-man's-land where there were no rules. God loved his people and didn't want them to lose their way, so he gave them a map for living: a set of directions for 'life, liberty and the pursuit of happiness'. These directions have been called 'The Ten Best Ways'[1] for living.

Activity

Around the church, there are 10 strips of paper. Each one has an instruction on it. Can you find them all and fit them together in order?

Allow plenty of time for people to find the strips and fit them together in the right order. Use Blu-tack to stick them onto the red stone tablet shapes.

Storytelling

Invite those who have helped find the Commandments to help you read them aloud.

These are the instructions for living which God gave his people. God said:

1. For this title, the heart imagery and the story's emphasis on love, and I am deeply indebted to Jerome W. Berryman for his 'Ten Best Ways' (*The Complete Guide to Godly Play*, Volume 2, Living The Good News, 2002): his story was an epiphany for me. I have developed it for my purposes here and the Ten Commandments are in my own words.

1. I am God. Worship no other gods.
2. Worship no idols.
3. Say God's name with respect.
4. Keep the sabbath holy.
5. Honour your parents.
6. Do not kill.
7. Be faithful in marriage.
8. Do not steal.
9. Don't tell lies.
10. Don't long for things which aren't yours.

You may know these as the Ten Commandments. They are the foundation of the Bible's laws and even of our country's laws, today. They were first carved on stone tablets and are usually drawn like this. *(Hold up the two stone tablet shapes.)* God gave them to his people because he loved them, as he loves us. Because he loves us, he wants us to love him and to love each other, too. These instructions are all about love – and they should really look like this *(fix the two stone tablet shapes together to form a heart and turn them over to show the red side, making the shape clear).*

Music

There are hundreds of sparrows

Exploring

Show the ten brainstorming sheets and spread them out on tables, with pens.

So here are our Ten Commandments, our 'Ten Best Ways' to live. Why does each of these make life better? Some are obvious: clearly, life would be better for all of us if there were no murders and people didn't steal from others. Take some time now to look at each of the Commandments in turn and ask yourself: why is this a good way to live? Why does this way make life better for me and the people around me? If you like, you can write or draw some ideas around each one. Some may make you ask questions – write those down, too.

Allow plenty of time for people to circulate and think, then invite some responses. There is no need to go through each one: no. 7 in particular is a sensitive area and best left for people to ponder privately.

When Jesus talked about how we should obey God's laws, he always talked about love. He told us to love not only our friends but also our enemies; to give to anyone who asks; to go the extra mile and to turn the other cheek. He said, 'Be perfect, as your heavenly Father is perfect.' It can be hard, but that doesn't mean we should stop trying. God is love, so in all that we say and do, we should try to love God and love each other, because love is the best way to live.

Music

God is love: his the care

Prayer action

However hard we try, we are not perfect. We don't always behave lovingly towards others and we don't always live our lives in the best way we can. We say and do the wrong thing or we fail to do the right thing. Sometimes, parts of our lives and ourselves can seem messed up and broken beyond anything we are capable of fixing. That is why we need to hand over all the wrongdoing and all the broken pieces of ourselves to God. We confess what we have done wrong and say, 'Sorry' to God – and because he loves us, he forgives us and grants us a fresh start.

In a moment, we will hear a song which is a kind of prayer, offering to God the broken things in our lives and praying to be made whole again. As the music plays, take a piece of this eggshell and call to mind all those things for which you are sorry. As a sign of your prayer, place your broken piece inside the heart, trusting that God loves us all and wants to heal the brokenness we offer him.

Play 'Broken Things' and invite people to come up, take some eggshell from the bowl and place it in the heart-shaped bowl.

Loving Lord,
we are broken people.
We give all these pieces to you:
make us new and whole again.
Amen.

Music Let there be love

Conclusion *Two leaders carefully lift the board with the lit tea-lights down from the altar and lay it on the floor where people can see that the lights form the shape of a heart.*

Let us pray:
Loving Lord,
send us out into the world to love you
by loving each other
and loving life.
Let there be love.
Amen.

Give notices, announce the next all-age service and invite everyone to the feast.

Tempted

Theme	Temptation
Scripture	Genesis 2:4b–3:24 and Matthew 4:1–11

Running order	Total: 50 minutes
Welcome	Prayer cairn *(5 minutes)*
Introduction	Opening the theme
Storytelling 1	Uncovering the story of the snake in the garden *(5 minutes)*
Activity	Cut out and collage – today's temptations *(15 minutes)*
Music	Dear Lord and Father of mankind *(5 minutes)*
Storytelling 2	Uncovering the story of the temptation in the wilderness *(8 minutes)*
Exploring	What happened when Adam and Eve got it wrong? What happened when Jesus got it right? *(5 minutes)*
Prayer action	Confession – prayer with responses *(2 minutes)*
Music	What a friend we have in Jesus *(5 minutes)*
Conclusion	Closing prayer and invitation

Resources

- Lots of small, flat stones or pebbles
- A tray or wooden board on which to build the cairn
- A toy snake *(see appendix)*
- A perfect red apple
- Glossy magazines, junk mail, advertising flyers and tabloid newspapers
- Three or four large pieces of brown cardboard boxes, each cut into the shape of an apple
- Scissors and glue sticks
- Words and music
- Some soft sand *(see appendix for Ash Wednesday)*
- A large tray or piece of sheeting to spread the sand on
- A few large, round stones
- A couple of large, round bread rolls
- A figure or picture of an angel
- A crown and some gold coins *(see appendix)*

Leaders

Minimum: 1

- Leader

Optimum: 7+

- Leader *(Introduction and Conclusion)*
- Storytellers x 2
- Activity Leader(s)
- Music Leader
- Explorer
- Prayer Leader

Suggestions for additional music

- Forty days and forty nights
- Father, hear the prayer we offer

Service

Welcome

Invite people to build a prayer cairn by adding a stone to a pile or tower as a sign of their prayer.

Introduction

Today we will be thinking about saying sorry and making a fresh start. We have two stories which explain what this is all about, and the first takes us right back to the very beginning.

Storytelling 1

Gather everyone round you in a semi-circle, seated on the floor if possible. If your congregation is large, invite the children to gather round you at the front. Produce the apple and the snake and pass them round as you talk. Don't comment on the suggestions – simply accept them all, whatever they are, and let them flow. The point here is to engage your listeners in speculating about the story, not to get the 'right' answer.

Here is a lovely, juicy apple. And here is a snake. I wonder what story we might tell with these? *(Invite suggestions.)* Where does the apple grow? And where does the snake live? *(Invite suggestions.)* I wonder what is unusual about this snake in our story? *(Invite suggestions.)* This apple looks rather special, too: I wonder what might be different about it? *(Invite suggestions.)*

When the world began, God made north, south, east and west. In the east, there was a place called Eden. And in Eden, there was a garden. This garden was God's garden and it was perfect. He made it for the first two human beings he created. Their names were Adam and Eve. In the garden which God gave them, there were lots of trees, but right in the middle of the garden there was a very special tree, and on this very special tree grew this apple. *(Hold up the apple.)* God said, 'Now listen, Adam and Eve. You may eat whatever grows in the garden – except this apple. If you eat it, you will know everything about good and evil, and you will die.'

But there was someone else in the garden. The snake *(hold up the snake)* – a cunning snake who could talk. He sidled up to Eve and said, 'Mmmm – that fruit looks good. It won't kill you, you know. God just doesn't want you to be as clever as him. Why not have a bite?'

So Eve bit into the apple – and it was so delicious, she gave some to Adam, too. And suddenly they could see and understand a whole world of things, good and bad – but they knew they had disobeyed God and they were ashamed. Then God sent them away from the garden and an angel stood at the gate to keep them out.

Activity

Temptation is the theme of our service today. Adam and Eve were tempted to eat the fruit that God had forbidden, because they wanted the knowledge which the snake promised them. I wonder what temptations we face, today? What things we are tempted by? What do we want, even though we know we shouldn't? To help us think about this, we have lots of newspapers and magazines here, full of glossy pictures and big headlines. Can you cut out anything which you think represents a modern temptation, and stick your cuttings all over a cardboard apple, as a kind of collage of temptation?

Allow plenty of time for reading, cutting and sticking. When the apples are well covered, ask for volunteers to hold them up. Invite people to explain some of their choices.

Music

Dear Lord and Father of mankind

Storytelling 2

Gather people round you as before. Spread out the sand.

Here is another story. The garden with the juicy apples was a long time ago and far away. Now we are surrounded by sand. It is very dry. *(Spread out the stones.)* Here are some stones in the sand. I wonder what sort of place this is? *(Invite responses.)* What would it feel like to spend a whole day here? *(Invite responses.)* What might it be like at night? *(Invite responses.)* I wonder what it would be like to spend forty days and forty nights in this sandy, stony place? *(Invite responses.)*

Jesus spent forty days and forty nights here. But there was someone else in the wilderness. The devil – God's cunning enemy. He said to Jesus, 'Mmmm – those stones look good. They look like fresh bread rolls. You must be hungry – why don't you turn them into bread?' *(Hold up the bread rolls.)*

And Jesus said, 'People need more than bread to live – they need God's word.'

Then the devil marched Jesus up to the edge of a cliff. 'If you're so special, God will send his angels to protect you. Why don't you jump off this cliff and see if he does?' *(Hold up the angel.)*

And Jesus replied, 'Don't test God.'

Then the devil showed Jesus all the money and power in the world. 'All this could be yours if you will worship me.' *(Hold up the crown and the coins.)*

And Jesus replied, 'Worship God and no one else. Go away, you devil!'

Then the devil went away, *(take away the bread, the angel, the crown and the coins)* and angels surrounded Jesus and looked after him.

Exploring

Spread out the objects on two tables.

Take some time to look at the snake and the apple, and at the sand and stones, the bread, the angel and the treasures. Ask yourself, 'Why?'. Why were Adam and Eve tempted to eat the apple? Why was Jesus tempted by these things? And why did he resist temptation?

Allow everyone some time to explore, think and discuss.

These stories of temptation belong together. First of all, what happened when Adam and Eve got it wrong? They disobeyed God and were shut out of his perfect garden. Their story helps us to understand why there are good and bad things in life and why we can sometimes feel far away from God. But what happened when Jesus got it right? He might have been tempted to use his powers to feed himself *(hold up the bread roll),* or to see if God really was going to look after him *(hold up the angel)*. He might have been tempted to become a powerful ruler *(hold up the crown and the coins)*. But he didn't do any of these things. Jesus obeyed God – and he carried on obeying God, all through his life and in his death. His perfect obedience makes up for Adam and Eve's disobedience, and for all the things which we do wrong, too. That is why Jesus helps us to get right with God when we say sorry for those things we have done wrong. Through him, we are completely forgiven and we can make a fresh start.

Prayer action

Ask for volunteers to stand at the front and hold up the collages which people made earlier.

As we look at these pictures of some of the things which tempt us today, let's pause for a moment to bring before God all those things which we know we have done wrong, for which we want to say, 'Sorry.' *(Pause.)* After each line of this prayer, we'll repeat together the words, 'Father, forgive us.' Let us pray.

Father, forgive us.
For the times we have wanted what was not ours,
Father, forgive us.
For all we have done wrong,
Father, forgive us.
For the good things we have failed to do,
Father, forgive us.
For the times when our love let you down,
Father, forgive us.
May God forgive all our sins,
in the name of his Son, Jesus Christ.
Amen.

Music

What a friend we have in Jesus

Conclusion

Jesus, thank you for putting right
what we have done wrong
and for being with us, now and always.
Amen.

Give notices, announce the next all-age service and invite everyone to the feast.

A new birth

Theme	Belonging and being born again
Scripture	John 3:1–17

Running order	Total: 50 minutes
Welcome	Self-portraits *(5 minutes)*
Introduction	The people of God – Abraham's family tree *(2 minutes)*
Activity	Our family trees *(13 minutes)*
Music	We are marching *(5 minutes)*
Storytelling	Dramatised dialogue – Jesus and Nicodemus *(5 minutes)*
Exploring	What kind of new birth does Jesus give us? *(5 minutes)*
Music	Father, I place into your hands *(5 minutes)*
Prayer action	Melted away – interactive confession *(5 minutes)*
Music	I am a new creation *(5 minutes)*
Conclusion	Closing prayer and invitation

Resources

- Four pictures *(see appendix)*:
  - Abraham's family tree
  - Family tree template
  - New belonging
  - New beginning
- Music and words
- Either a laptop, projector and screen or an OHP and screen
- Small pieces of paper printed with a fancy frame *(see appendix for Dazzling light)*
- Lots of A4 paper
- Pencils, felt-tip pens and crayons
- A font full of hot water
- A large bag of ice-cubes, kept cold in a cooler box
- A large bowl

Leaders

Minimum: 3

- Leader
- Cast x 2

Optimum: 8+

- Leader *(Introduction and Conclusion)*
- Storyteller
- Cast x 2

  Jesus, wearing something white

  Nicodemus, wearing clothes which show power and wealth (may be traditional or modern dress)
- Activity Leader
- Music Leader(s)
- Explorer
- Prayer Leader

Suggestions for additional music

- As the deer pants for water
- Jesus is greater than the greatest heroes

Service

Welcome

Invite everyone to take a fancy frame and draw a quick self-portrait to leave on the altar as a way of saying, 'Here I am, Lord.'

Introduction

Today we are going to be thinking about birth and belonging, and we'll start by looking at families. In the earliest stories in the Bible, God chose one family to be his special people. This family belonged to a man called Abraham, and his family tree looked like this.

Show Abraham's family tree picture.

Here is Abraham – and here is his son, Isaac, and his grandson, Jacob, and his great grandson, Joseph, who had the multi-coloured coat. Joseph and his brothers were the fathers of the twelve tribes of Israel. God told Abraham that his enormous family would be specially blessed, so that anyone who belonged to the family would be blessed, too.

Activity

What about our own families? Can we make a family tree for them?

Show family tree template.

Here is the pattern of what a family tree might look like: here's me in the middle, and here are all the people who are part of my family. Can you draw a family tree like this to show who belongs to your family?

Leave the template up and allow plenty of time for people to draw their own family trees. You may like to invite some people to share what they have drawn.

Music

We are marching

Storytelling

The first family we belong to is the one we are born into, and we can join new families by being adopted or getting married, but Jesus had something different to say about birth and belonging. In our story today an important man asks Jesus lots of questions and gets some surprising answers. *(Introduce your actors.)* This is Jesus, and this is Nicodemus. He is a rich and influential religious leader, called a Pharisee. It is the middle of the night, which is probably the only time when Jesus isn't surrounded by crowds. It is a perfect time for Nicodemus to have a proper conversation with Jesus.

Nicodemus Teacher, we know that God is on your side, because no one can do the miracles you've been doing without God's power.

Jesus Absolutely – and no one can see God's kingdom without being born from above.

Nicodemus What? But how can anyone be born again once they are grown up? Who can go back into the womb and come out a second time?

Jesus The truth is, no one can enter God's kingdom without being born twice – physically and spiritually. So don't be surprised that I said to you, 'You must be born from above.' It is like the wind – you can see what it does, but you don't know where it comes from or where it's going to. When God's Holy Spirit gives someone a new birth, you can see that their life has changed and they are like a new person, even though you may not understand where the change has come from.

Nicodemus But how does that work?

Jesus Nicodemus, don't you get it? You're a respected teacher, and I'm telling you what I know to be true – why don't you understand? If I have told you about things which happen on earth and you don't believe them, how can you believe what I'm telling you about heavenly things? Here's the thing: no one has gone up into heaven except the one who came from there – God's Son. So God's Son must be lifted up, so that everyone who believes in him can live forever with God.

God loved the world so much that he gave his only Son, so that everyone who believes in him will not die, but live forever in heaven. God did not send his Son into the world to criticise and condemn people, but to love them and save them. That is what I am here to do.

Exploring

So Jesus said we must be 'born again', 'born from above' – and Nicodemus reacts exactly as we would: 'What do you mean?' he asks. 'How can anyone be born twice? How would that work?'

Show the 'New belonging' picture.

When we were physically born, we took our place in our family tree. *(Indicate the picture frame with the outline of a person.)* But if we are like this person here – if we believe in Jesus with our whole heart – then we have a whole new kind of spiritual family tree to belong to. It might look a bit like this: rather like our pictures of who belongs in our families. Here is God – the Father, the Son and the Holy Spirit – and here are all the people in his family. This family keeps on growing. More people are joining all the time, and there is always room for more because God wants us all to belong to him for ever.

Show the 'New beginning' picture.

This is the other kind of new birth which Jesus offers us. He gives us the chance to start afresh, with a clean slate – like this. Whatever we have done wrong and whatever we regret, we can say sorry to God and be completely forgiven. We can make a new beginning. In our prayers today, we will have an opportunity to say sorry to God and to leave everything in his hands.

Music

Father, I place into your hands

Prayer action

Today, we will use these ice cubes in our prayers. (*Tip the bag of ice cubes into the bowl.)* Think of them as the bad things which you feel sorry for, the wrongdoing which gives you a cold, sad feeling inside. Let's take a moment to think what we each need to say sorry for. *(Pause.)*

The water in this font which we use in baptism represents the fresh start which Jesus offers us. It washes us clean and takes our sins away, so that we can start again. When you are ready, take your ice cube as a sign of your prayer and drop it into this water. Say sorry to God in your heart and watch your ice cube melt away and disappear, just as Jesus takes all our sins away so that we can start afresh.

Place the bowl of ice cubes next to the font and allow enough time for everyone to take an ice cube and drop it into the water, then watch it melt.

Forgiving Lord,
take from us all those things
for which we are sorry
and melt them away in your love.
Touch what is good in us
and make us clean
so that we can start again.
Amen.

Music

I am a new creation

Conclusion

Lord Jesus,
We thank you for offering us a new birth.
As we belong to you, may you keep watch
over our going out and our coming in,
from this time forth for evermore.[1]
Amen.

Give notices, announce the next all-age service and invite everyone to the feast.

1. Adapted from Psalm 121:8.

Being the Church

What do we do now?

Theme	Mission: Impossible?
Scripture	Acts 1:6–14

Running order	Total: 50 minutes
Welcome	Incense prayers *(5 minutes)*
Introduction	Opening the theme
Storytelling	*Either:* The Ascension, retold with pictures *Or:* If today is your church's celebration of Ascension, you could use Storytelling 1 and 2 from the Ascension Day service instead *(10 minutes)*
Music	I cannot tell *(5 minutes)*
Activity	Finding out about Jesus' mission *(10 minutes)*
Music	At the name of Jesus *(5 minutes)*
Exploring	'Is this Mission: Impossible?' – finding out how we can do his work *(10 minutes)*
Prayer action	'Be still' – contemplative prayer *(5 minutes)*
Conclusion	Closing prayer and invitation

Resources

- A packet of incense *(see appendix for The Ascension)*
- A small charcoal brazier for use outside, or a thurible or other incense-burner for use inside. If you have lots of people, the outside option is preferable, as too much incense at once will choke a small burner
- Charcoal and matches
- A sign which reads, *O Lord, let my prayer be counted as incense before you*
- Music and words
- A choir to sing 'Be still, for the presence of the Lord' *or* a recording and equipment to play it on
- Spread around the church, things which show Jesus' ministry: these may be pictures; children's Bible story-books; a film clip; objects such as water, wine, bread and a rough wooden cross
- A whiteboard, a flip chart or two large boards, with marker pens
- Three gold envelopes *or* important-looking files/boxes, each containing a piece of Scripture on a card *(see the Exploring section of the service)*

Either:

- Pictures of the Ascension and James Bond with his gadgets *(see appendix)*
- Laptop, projector and screen for the 'Picture reveal' storytelling *(see appendix)*

Or if you have not used the Ascension Day service and would prefer a less hi-tech option:

- The resources for Ascension Day Storytelling 1 and 2.

Leaders

(See Ascension Day if using second Storytelling option)

Minimum: 2

- Leader
- Storyteller/Technician

Optimum: 6

- Leader *(Introduction and Conclusion)*
- Storyteller/Technician
- Activity Leader
- Explorer
- Music Leader
- Prayer Leader

Suggestions for additional music

- Christ's is the world
- Come and celebrate

Service

Welcome

Place your small charcoal burner or brazier and dish of incense granules next to the sign which reads, *O Lord, let my prayer be counted as incense before you*. As people arrive, your Prayer Leader should be on hand to light the charcoal and help people add a few grains of incense as a sign of their prayer.

Introduction

Today we will be remembering the moment when the resurrected Jesus was lifted up into heaven. Our incense prayers remind us that our prayers, too, rise up to heaven. We are going to tell the story of the Ascension with the help of a painting which we will discover bit by bit.

Storytelling

Begin with the medieval picture of the Ascension completely covered up. Then uncover the two grey-bearded disciples by the trees on the left.

After Jesus rose from the dead, he stayed on earth for forty days. This gave his disciples a chance to ask him all the unanswered questions he had left them with when he died. When he was alive, they knew that he was on a mission to save the world and that it was their job to follow him and help him. When he died, they were left wondering, 'What now?' But when he rose again, he showed that he could even defeat death. The disciples must have felt a great surge of hope: surely anything was possible, now that Jesus, the all-powerful Saviour, was back again? One of them asked him a question: 'When will you make everything right in Israel, Lord? Is now the time?'

Uncover the face of Jesus.

Jesus replied: 'Only God knows when that will happen. It is not for you to know. But I have a job for you: God will give you great power – the power of his Holy Spirit – and then I need you to do my work on earth. I need you to be my representatives not just here, in Jerusalem, but all over the world.'

Uncover the whole sky.

Before any of the disciples had a chance to say anything, Jesus was lifted up, up into heaven and out of sight.

Uncover the rest of the picture. Pause for a moment to give people a chance to look at it all.

Two angels appeared and said to the disciples, 'What are you all looking at? Jesus has gone back up into heaven, and one day he'll come back the same way.'

Cover the whole picture, apart from the group of five dark-haired figures on the right-hand side.

So that left the disciples with a question: 'What do we do now?' They had been following Jesus as he carried out his world-saving mission, but now he had left that mission to them! Jesus had promised them that they would be given the power of God's Holy Spirit, but they had no idea when or how that would happen. They must have been amazed at what had just happened – but also confused, excited and perhaps frightened. So they stuck together and went back to Jerusalem to wait, and pray, and see what would happen next.

Music I cannot tell

Activity So the disciples had a mission: to do Jesus' work in the world. But what exactly was Jesus' work? What sort of things did he do while he was alive? All around the church today there is evidence of things that Jesus did. There may be pictures, objects, stories to read: take some time now to find as much of this evidence as you can and investigate it.

Allow plenty of time for people to explore the items you have hidden around the church, then gather everyone together. Invite contributions and try to value them all; then on the whiteboard/flip chart, write the question, 'What was Jesus' mission?' Ask for some answers and write them down: these might include things like, 'He came to heal, love, share, save us, give us eternal life.'

Music At the name of Jesus

Exploring

Look again at the answers gathered by the previous activity.

So if this was Jesus' work, Jesus' mission, then this is what he told his disciples to do for him. This is what he told his church – and us – to do for him. I wonder what it might mean for us to do his work in the world?

Write the question, 'How can we do Jesus' work in the world?' on the whiteboard/flip chart and invite people to think about it and/or discuss it amongst themselves for a few minutes. Then ask for contributions and write them on the board. Try to broaden the definition of 'doing Jesus' work' beyond obvious professions, such as being a minister or a doctor. Encourage people to think of ways in which those who are not employed can also do God's work (this would include children, the retired, the unemployed and mums who are at home full-time with their children).

Doing Jesus' work in the world is the mission of the church – it is our mission, should we choose to accept it. But is it 'Mission: Impossible'? Perhaps some of those disciples worried that it might be.

Let's think for a moment about a different kind of mission: the kind given to spies and undercover agents like James Bond.

Show the James Bond picture.

However complicated and dangerous the mission, James Bond is never sent off without being given the tools he needs for the job – his amazing gadgets like a watch with a laser beam, a pen that can fire a bullet or a bowler hat which conceals a throwing weapon. Bond is never sent into the field without the essential equipment for his mission.

Show the picture of Jesus' Ascension again.

When Jesus gave his church its mission, he knew that we, too, would need some really special help.

Invite three volunteers to discover the contents of the three gold envelopes/special containers and to read aloud what they find there.

First of all, there is the power of God the Father who made us:

> Ascribe power to God,
> whose majesty is over Israel;
> and whose power is in the skies.
> Awesome is God in his sanctuary,
> the God of Israel;
> he gives power and strength to his people.
>
> *Psalm 68:34, 35*

Then, there is the power of God the Son, who was one of us:

> The God of all grace, who has called you to his eternal glory in Christ, will himself restore, support, strengthen, and establish you.
>
> *1 Peter 5:10*

Finally, there is the power of God the Holy Spirit, who is active in the world and in our hearts:

> You will receive power when the Holy Spirit has come upon you; and you will be my witnesses in Jerusalem, in all Judea and Samaria, and to the ends of the earth.
>
> *Acts 1:8*

This is what makes Mission: Impossible into Mission: Possible – God promises us his power and presence as we try to do his work. We are never alone. And for Jesus' disciples on the day of his Ascension, there was the promise of the Holy Spirit, God's power which would inspire and encourage them more than they would ever have thought possible.

Prayer action

So whatever work we have to do, whatever we have to face, we are not alone: God is with us. When we feel as if we can't cope by ourselves, we need to open our hands in prayer and ask God for the strength we need. For our prayers today, we will reflect on the words of the hymn which begins, 'Be still, for the presence of the Lord, the Holy One, is here.' Whoever is feeling tired or frightened or weak or overwhelmed, rest in God's presence and ask him for the strength you need.

Listen to the music and let people settle into stillness. Pause for a moment when the music finishes.

Almighty God,
no work is too hard for you;
in faith may we receive from you[1]
all that we need to do your work.
Amen.

Conclusion

Living Lord,
as we go out into the world
may we live and work in your name,
knowing that you are with us
today and always.
Amen.

Give notices, announce the next all-age service and invite everyone to the feast.

1. Adapted from David J. Evans, 'Be still, for the presence of the Lord' © 1986 Thankyou Music.

One for All

Together in unity

Theme	Being a united and welcoming church
Scripture	Genesis 45:1–15 and Matthew 15:21–28

Running order	Total: 50 minutes
Welcome	Flame flags *(5 minutes)*
Introduction	Opening the theme
Music	O Lord, all the world belongs to you *(5 minutes)*
Storytelling 1	Joseph reunited with his brothers – film clip/music *(5 minutes)*
Storytelling 2	The Canaanite woman – dramatised dialogue *(5 minutes)*
Music	Bind us together, Lord *(5 minutes)*
Exploring	Who is 'inside' and 'outside'? Active reflection on our own church *(10 minutes)*
Activity	Learning and practising 'Praise God, from whom all blessings flow' (to Tallis' canon) *(10 minutes)*
Prayer action	United in harmony – Singing the above as a round *(5 minutes)*
Conclusion	Closing prayer and invitation

Resources

- Short lengths of bamboo pole or similar for the flame flags *(see appendix)*
- Red, yellow and orange paper, cut into rough strips
- Pens
- Sellotape
- DVD or music clip of *Joseph and the Amazing Technicolor Dreamcoat*, plus equipment to play it on *(see appendix)*
- A small circle of inward-facing chairs, at the front to one side
- On a large, clear area of floor, a simple outline of your church building marked out in masking tape
- Music and words

Leaders

Minimum: 3

- Leader
- Cast x 2

Optimum: 7

- Leader *(Introduction and Conclusion)*
- Storyteller
- Cast x 2
  Jesus, wearing white
  Woman, wearing bright colours
- Explorer
- Activity / Music Leader
- Prayer Leader

Suggestions for additional music

- In Christ there is no east or west
- Let everything that has breath

Service

Welcome

As people arrive, invite them to write their prayer on a paper flame and attach it to a flag.

Introduction

The theme of our service today is being together in unity, particularly in this – our church family. There is an old joke about four shipwreck survivors who made a life for themselves on a desert island. When they were finally rescued, they proudly showed their rescuers around. 'Look!' they said. 'Here are the houses we made for ourselves – and here are the two churches we built.'

'Two churches?' said their rescuers. 'Why two?'

'This one here is *our* church,' they replied, 'and that one over there is the one we don't go to.'

As we think about our own togetherness today, we will be looking at how easily a sense of belonging can become a matter of 'us' and 'them'.

Music

O Lord, all the world belongs to you

Storytelling 1

Our first story is a tale of jealousy and betrayal among brothers. Lots of you will know this story: it starts with a favourite son and a multi-coloured coat.

Ask people who they think it is: you could invite those who know Joseph's story to recount it, with some prompting, instead of telling it yourself with the following script.

Joseph's brothers were jealous of him, so they sold him as a slave and told their father he was dead. But Joseph was taken to Egypt where he impressed Pharaoh with his ability to interpret dreams and predict a famine. So while people all around are starving, Joseph is in charge of food storage and distribution in Egypt, and thanks to him, the Egyptian people are doing fine. Joseph's starving brothers come to Egypt in search of food. They kneel before him, not realising that he is the brother they sold as a slave. Joseph tests their love and decides to forgive them. This is what happens next:

Play the film clip/music, showing Joseph being reunited with his brothers and father.

Storytelling 2

Stand in the middle at the front. On your left is the circle of inward-facing chairs with Jesus standing in the middle. On your right is Canaan: the woman should enter from there.

Our second story today is about 'us' and 'them'. Jesus was a Jew. The Jews called themselves 'the house of Israel' and Jesus' followers said to themselves, 'He's one of us'. *(Indicate the chairs.)* Here is the house of Israel with Jesus in the middle. He calls them his lost sheep, and he is their shepherd. The people who came from the land of Canaan – over there – *(indicate your other side)* were definitely not 'one of us', and many Jews were suspicious of their worldly, pleasure-seeking ways.

The woman enters.

Over here is a woman from Canaan. She is desperate because her daughter is very sick and she has come to ask for Jesus' help.[1]

Woman: Have mercy on me, Lord, Son of David; my daughter is tormented by a demon!

Storyteller: But he did not answer her at all. And his disciples came and urged him, saying, 'Send her away, for she keeps shouting after us.' He answered:

Jesus: I was sent only to the lost sheep of the house of Israel.

The woman crosses to the edge of the circle and kneels.

Woman: Lord, help me.

Jesus: It is not fair to take the children's food and throw it to the dogs.

Woman: Yes, Lord, yet even the dogs eat the crumbs that fall from their masters' table.

Jesus: Woman, great is your faith!

He opens the circle of chairs and lets her in. She kneels in front of him and he puts his hand on her head.

Let it be done for you as you wish.

Storyteller: And her daughter was healed instantly.

Music

Bind us together, Lord

1. The lines are taken directly from Matthew's Gospel (NRSV): you may prefer to use a different translation.

Exploring

What both our stories have in common is a sense of 'them' and 'us' – of people being shut out and then, happily, welcomed in. Joseph's brothers resented him so much that they physically got rid of him, and when they begged from him in Egypt he could have held a grudge and sent them away empty-handed. Instead, he welcomed the whole family back with open arms and invited them to share the good life in Egypt.

The woman in our story was initially shunned by Jesus, who said she was nothing to do with him – but her humility and faith won through and she was welcomed into the circle of those who received his help.

These stories remind us that past ill-treatment and grudges can cause us to shut people out; so can a feeling that they are 'not one of us', or not 'our sort' of people. In our own lives and in the life of our church, we may have felt excluded, or we may have been one of those on the inside, perhaps unwittingly shutting people out. Today we will take some time to think about this by exploring the shape which is marked out on the floor. This is the outline of our church. It divides the space inside from the area outside. Let's take some time now to walk around, both inside and out, and ask ourselves and each other, 'Who is on the inside of our church? Who is left on the outside, and why?' Ask yourself, 'Where am *I*?'

Allow some time for people to walk, think and talk around the space. You may like to join in with discussions as they happen, or ask for some reflections afterwards, depending on the sensitivity of the issues raised.

Activity

It is no accident that there is a lot of music in today's service. Music is a wonderful symbol of unity, as different voices or instruments join together to create harmony. Today we are going to learn a simple hymn by heart so that we can sing it as a round – perhaps in two, three or even four parts.

Teach the words line by line, to the tune of Tallis' canon:

Praise God, from whom all blessings flow,
praise him, all creatures here below,
praise him above, ye heavenly host,
praise Father, Son and Holy Ghost.[2]

Practise singing this all together, then as a round, in just two parts at first.

Prayer action

For our prayers today, we are going to join together in singing God's praise as a round. We all have different voices and new people will join in the singing at different points, but together we unite in harmony to praise God.

Sing a few repetitions of the round in four parts before indicating that each part should fall silent in turn.

God who is Three and One,
unite us in your forgiving, welcoming love.
Amen.

Conclusion

Today's Psalm says, 'How good and pleasant it is to dwell together in unity'. As we go out into the world, let's pray for unity: not the cosy sense of togetherness which means keeping ourselves separate from everyone who is different, but the deep unity which holds us all together as children of God. Let us pray:

Lord of all,
may we live together in love, welcoming the outsider with open arms.
May we live together in peace, forgiving others as we ourselves are forgiven.
May we live together in joy, showing your good news to the world.
In Jesus' name.
Amen.

Give notices, announce the next all-age service and invite everyone to the feast.

2. Thomas Ken (1637-1710).

Doing God's work

Theme	Discerning God's will
Scripture	Exodus 1:8–2:10; Matthew 16:13–20; Romans 12:1–8

Running order	Total: 50 minutes
Welcome	Clay imprints *(5 minutes)*
Introduction	Opening the theme
Storytelling 1	Moses in the basket – film clip *(5 minutes)*
Music	God moves in a mysterious way *(5 minutes)*
Storytelling 2	Jesus names Peter the Rock – dramatised dialogue *(3 minutes)*
Exploring	How do we discern God's will for us? Visual exploration of the Church's gifts of grace which form the body of Christ *(10 minutes)*
Activity	What are our gifts? Writing down our gifts and making paper-chains *(12 minutes)*
Prayer action	Linked together – active offertory prayer using one long paper-chain *(5 minutes)*
Music	Amazing grace *(5 minutes)*
Conclusion	Closing prayer and invitation

Resources

- A piece of clay, rolled out to fill a large tray or board, just thick enough for people to make fingerprints in it. Cut the top edges to form the simple shape of a church and cover it tightly with clingfilm until ready for use
- A DVD of *The Prince of Egypt* and equipment to play it on *(see appendix)*
- 'The body of Christ': large, labelled body parts and A4 copies of the complete body *(see appendix)*
- A board and Blu-tack
- Music and words
- Strips of coloured paper, about 20cm long
- Pens and pencils
- Sellotape

Leaders

Minimum: 3

- Leader
- Readers x 2

Optimum: 8

- Leader *(Introduction and Conclusion)*
- Storyteller
- Readers: Jesus and Simon Peter
- Explorer
- Activity Leader
- Music Leader
- Prayer Leader

Suggestions for additional music

- Take me, Lord, use my life
- Help us to help each other, Lord

Service

Welcome As people arrive, invite them to leave their fingerprint in the clay as a way of saying, 'Here I am, Lord'.

Introduction Today we will be thinking about how we can tell what God wants us to do with our lives. Our stories today are about two people for whom God had big plans – Moses and Jesus' disciple, Simon Peter. Let's begin with Moses, whose adventures began when he was just a baby.

Storytelling 1 *Show the clip from* The Prince of Egypt, *from the beginning of the film to the end of Moses' rescue by Pharaoh's daughter.*

Music God moves in a mysterious way

Storytelling 2 The baby Moses, who only just escaped drowning, grew up to become the man chosen by God to free his people from slavery in Egypt. We will be hearing more of his story on another occasion. In our Gospel story, Jesus chooses his disciple, Simon, for a special job. This is what happened.[1]

Jesus: Who do people say that the Son of Man is?

Simon Peter: Some say John the Baptist, but others Elijah, and still others Jeremiah or one of the prophets.

Jesus: But who do you say that I am?

Simon Peter: You are the Messiah, the Son of the living God.

Jesus: Blessed are you, Simon son of Jonah! For flesh and blood has not revealed this to you, but my Father in heaven. And I tell you, you are Peter, and on this rock I will build my church, and the gates of Hades will not prevail against it. I will give you the keys of the kingdom of heaven, and whatever you bind on earth will be bound in heaven, and whatever you loose on earth will be loosed in heaven.

Exploring So God had a mission for Moses, and Jesus had a purpose and a new name for Simon, who became Peter, the rock on whom the church is built. These men clearly

1. The lines are taken directly from Matthew's Gospel (NRSV): you may prefer to use a different translation.

knew what God expected of them in their lives, because he told them directly. But how can we tell what God wants us to do? This is the subject of today's New Testament reading, which comes from Paul's letter to the Church in Rome.

Paul describes the Church as the body of Christ, and he uses this image to help each of us understand our own purpose. He says that Jesus is the head of the Church.

Place the head labelled 'Christ' at the top of the board.

Christ's body is the Church: individually, we all make up that body which continues to do Christ's work on earth. Paul explains that a body needs different parts, like hands and a heart and feet, because each part has its own particular job to do in keeping the whole body healthy and working properly. This is how the Church should work, too. Paul says that there are those whose gifts lie in caring and helping: they make up one part of the body of Christ which is the Church.

Place the body labelled 'Carers and helpers'.

Then there are those who are good listeners and friends *(place the arm with these labels)* and those who are good at giving and sharing *(place the other arm).* There are gifted teachers and leaders *(place the hands with these labels).* All these help make up the body of Christ which is the Church.

Then Paul says that there are the dreamers: the people who have visions of how things could be. They are like Martin Luther King Jr, who said, 'I have a dream,' and described his vision of a world without racism. The dreamers spur us on and make us wonder, 'What if . . . ?' They too help make up the body of Christ which is the Church.

Place the foot labelled 'Dreamers'.

Finally Paul says there are the challengers. *(Place the other foot.)* These are the people who tell us we could do better and urge us to try harder. The challengers are like the foot which gives us an occasional kick to stop us getting too comfortable with the way things are.

What Paul's image shows us is that we are all different, and we are all good at different things: we each contribute our own particular talents to keep the Church alive and kicking and doing Christ's work in the world. This image also shows that we are called into relationship with one another, not a solitary existence. Moses was called to lead a nation, and Peter was called to found the Church: both men were called into relationship with others and renewed closeness to God. So when we are thinking about what God wants us to do, we need to remember that we are not looking at ourselves in isolation. I wonder which part of the body of Christ each of us might be? Take some time now to look at this image and ask yourself, 'Where am I in this picture?'

Spread copies of the 'Body of Christ' picture around the church. Allow plenty of time for people to look, think and discuss. You may like to invite some contributions.

Activity

When we are trying to discover what God wants us to do with our lives, the biggest clues we have are our gifts and talents. Everyone is good at something, even if you haven't yet discovered what it is. This picture of the Church, the body of Christ, reminds us that gifts and talents can come in all shapes and sizes. Some people have the ability to be leaders; others have a special gift for friendship. Some talents may lead to public roles and recognition, while others are more quietly appreciated by the individuals who have been listened to with kindness and patience. You may be good at something which hardly anyone else knows about.

We are going to take some time today to think about our own particular gifts. Take some strips of paper and on each one, write or draw something which you are good at. No one else need see it – simply add your gift or talent to the pile of paper strips in the middle of the table.

Allow plenty of time for people to write down their gifts.

The image of the Church as the body of Christ reminds us that our individual gifts and talents are joined together: they work together for the good of the whole. Now we are going to join all these gifts together to make the longest paper-chain we possibly can.

Demonstrate how to form the strips into inter-linking loops, sticking the ends with Sellotape.

Prayer action

This paper-chain is made up of all our gifts and talents joined together. Each link is important because it helps to join the chain together and make it strong. Each one of us is important: we are connected to each other and to God like the links in this chain. In preparation for our prayers today, let's carry this chain so that it reaches as far as possible round our church.

Invite everyone to help carry the chain so that it encircles your worship space as far as possible.

In a moment of quiet, let us pray for all the individuals whose gifts and talents are joined together here. Let us pray for God's guidance in showing us all how we may use these abilities to do his will.

Pause for a short time.

Heavenly Father, we do not stand alone:
our lives are linked together and held fast in your love.
We offer you these gifts and talents which we freely received;
help us to work together in Jesus' name.
Amen.

Music

Amazing grace

Conclusion

Lord Jesus,
we are your body, your hands and feet on earth.
Send us out into the world to do your work.
Amen.

Give notices, announce the next all-age service and invite everyone to the feast.

Old Testament stories

The Creation

Theme	The Creation
Scripture	Genesis 1:1–2:3

Running order	Total: 50 minutes
Welcome	Wildlife TV clip or sound recording *(5 minutes)*
Introduction	Opening the theme
Storytelling/Activity	Illustrated interactive retelling of Genesis 1:1–2:3 *(23 minutes)*
Exploring	What does the Creation story tell us? *(7 minutes)*
Music	Who put the colours in the rainbow? *(5 minutes)*
Prayer action	Natural treasures – thanksgiving *(5 minutes)*
Music	If I were a butterfly *(5 minutes)*
Conclusion	Wildlife TV clip or sound recording

Resources

- *Optional:* screen, laptop and projector
- *Optional:* two clips from nature programmes such as *The Blue Planet* or *Springwatch*. The first one should last for several minutes and be visually spectacular (such as the scenes of whales and dolphins hunting in *The Blue Planet*). The second one may be shorter and should feature sleeping lions or other animals resting
- If you don't want to show a TV clip, a recording of birdsong is a lovely alternative. There are lots of free downloadable sound effects on the internet (e.g. www.partnersinrhyme.com)
- Sound equipment
- Music and words
- A very long sheet of lining paper (at least 14 ft), marked into seven equal sections, titled 'DAY ONE', 'DAY TWO' and so on. Stretch the paper out in front of the altar, roll it out along the aisle or stick it to a long stretch of accessible wall
- A variety of art materials: crayons and pencils; felt-tip pens; scraps of coloured paper and fabric; glue sticks, PVA glue, glue-pots and glue-spreaders; Sellotape; shiny and glittery scraps; animal stencils; scissors; long-arm stapler
- Your chosen version of the Creation story *(see appendix)*
- A basket or two full of natural treasures: shells, feathers, smooth pebbles, acorns, catkins, leaves, buds, flowers. You could either collect these yourself beforehand or – if you are not using the TV clips – begin your service by inviting everyone into the church grounds to hunt for their own treasures

Leaders

Minimum: 3

- Leader/Storyteller
- Activity Leader
- Prayer Leader

Optimum: 7+

- Leader *(Introduction and Conclusion)*
- Technician
- Storyteller
- Activity Leader(s)
- Music Leader
- Explorer
- Prayer Leader(s)

Suggestions for additional music

- All things bright and beautiful
- For the beauty of the earth
- Dance and sing
- Mountain maker, ocean tamer

Service

Welcome

Invite people into a darkened church where a clip from a nature programme is playing on your screen at the front with no soundtrack (or have the recording of bird-song playing as people arrive). The idea is to encourage people to sit in quiet contemplation of nature's wonders before the service begins. When everyone has been seated for a few minutes, turn on the lights and switch off the clip / sound recording.

Introduction

Today we will be telling the story of what happened in the beginning, when God created everything we know out of nothingness. It was the beginning of 'life, the universe and everything'.

Storytelling/Activity

Indicate the long strip of lining paper.

We are going to illustrate our story as we tell it. Here is the outline of our storytelling frieze and here is a wealth of art materials. You can draw or trace, cut out shapes to make a collage or simply add some pieces of colourful background. Whatever you choose to do, be creative and make a big and bold picture for each part of our story – the story of the Creation.

Read Genesis 1:1–5 in your chosen version and encourage illustration of DAY ONE: darkness, nothingness and the coming of light. Remind people that there are no stars, moon or sun yet! Collages and cut-outs are best secured with staples or Sellotape as well as glue. Attach them to the lining paper.

DAY TWO: read Genesis 1:6–8 and encourage illustration of sky and water (NB no fish yet!).

DAY THREE: read Genesis 1:9–13 and encourage illustration of land and sea, plants, trees and fruit.

DAY FOUR: read Genesis 1:14–19 and encourage illustration of the sun, moon, stars and planets.

DAY FIVE: read Genesis 1:20–23 and encourage illustration of birds, sea creatures and freshwater creatures – from whales to tadpoles, crabs to crocodiles.

DAY SIX: read Genesis 1:24–31 and encourage illustration of animals, insects and human beings (be prepared for children's unflinching depiction of a naked Adam and Eve!).

DAY SEVEN: read Genesis 2:1–3 and encourage imaginative illustration of God resting!

Allow some time for people to finish their illustrations and attach them to the lining paper, then encourage everyone to stand back and look at what they have created.

Exploring

Let's look at all the things God did on each day of the Creation. Can we describe what God did by making new names for him? For example, on day 4, we could call God the 'Moon-maker' or 'Star-shaper'. On day 3 we could call him the 'Fruit-grower' or the 'Sea-stirrer'. Names like these are called kennings: for the first six days, can you come up with as many kennings for God as possible? Write them all around our pictures of the Creation.

Allow plenty of time for people to fill each section with kennings, then read some of them out.

Look at all these different names for one Creator! They reflect all the wonderful abundance and variety in the Creation. God didn't just make the bare essentials: he made nearly a million different species of insect and he made birds with rainbow-coloured feathers and different patterns of snowflakes and leopards with spots and tigers with stripes and us with our freckles and our different colours of skin.

But that's not all. Look at the seventh day. What did God do then? *(Invite answers.)* After all that creative effort, God said, 'Job done – time to rest.' Even God's abundant, generous work of creation involved some 'time out', and this pattern is repeated in the natural world today. Fields are left fallow for a season, animals hibernate, plants die back and overwinter in the ground and every living creature needs time to sleep. Whenever we plan our own days and weeks and years, we need to remember the seventh day which God blessed. It is the day of rest which rounds off the week, like the vital full stop at the end of the sentence.

So the story of the Creation tells us two vital things: First of all, we should be thankful, because God made 'life, the universe and everything' and it was *good*. We can be thankful by doing all we can to look after the environment and to protect this beautiful planet which he gave us. Secondly, we should rest as well as work, because that is the pattern which God's Creation established and which all of nature follows. Thanksgiving, work and rest – these are some of life's essentials, as God showed us in the very beginning.

Music

Who put the colours in the rainbow?

Prayer action

Pass round the baskets and invite everyone to choose a natural treasure for their prayer.

The earth is full of God's glory. All these natural treasures we have are part of that glory, because they are part of the world which God created for us. Today we are going to offer these treasures to God in prayer as a way of recognising that he gave us all this wealth. You may like to lay your treasure on the altar just as it is, or you may like to make a pattern or a shape with other treasures. Whatever you choose, take your time to bring your offering to the altar and make it your prayer which says, simply, 'Thank you'.

Allow plenty of time for everyone to bring their offerings forward, then gather them together in prayer:

Light-maker, *(add some of the kennings which people invented earlier)*
we offer you these treasures from the abundance
you have given us.
We thank you that everything we have
is a precious gift,
for all life and beauty, growth and glory
come from you.
Show us how to cherish and protect
the world you created.
Amen.

Music

If I were a butterfly

Conclusion

Show your second TV clip with no soundtrack or play the birdsong recording. As it plays, say:

Generous Creator,
send us out to do your work in the world
and to rest when that work is done.
Amen.

Give notices, announce the next all-age service and invite everyone to the feast.

Noah's Ark

Theme	Faith in action
Scripture	Genesis 6:9–22, 7:24, 8:14–19; Matthew 7:21-29

Running order	Total: 50 minutes
Welcome	Salt dough prayers *(5 minutes)*
Introduction	Opening the theme
Storytelling	Interactive retelling of the Flood with soft toys *(10 minutes)*
Music	Think of a world without any flowers *(5 minutes)*
Exploring	What does it mean to put our faith into action? *(10 minutes)*
Activity	Making paper doves *(10 minutes)*
Prayer action	The wings of a dove – intercessions *(5 minutes)*
Music	The wise man built his house *(5 minutes)*
Conclusion	Closing prayer and invitation

Resources

NB Prior publicity needed! On your posters, invite everyone to bring along a toy animal

- Some additional soft toy animals, placed among the people
- Salt dough *(see appendix for Crib Service)*. Colour one half blue and the other green and form them into a rough sphere to suggest the earth
- Basic Noah costume (tunic and headcloth)
- A long piece of blue fabric
- A large cardboard box, cut along its seams so that it lies flat
- Parcel tape for reconstructing the box
- Music and words
- DVD of *Evan Almighty (see appendix)*
- Laptop, projector and screen
- Templates for dove and wings *(see appendix)*
- Hole punch
- Pens, scissors and string
- Something near the altar from which to suspend the doves: the altar rail or rood screen, or a pole balanced between two chairs

Leaders

Minimum: 1

- Leader

Optimum: 6+

- Leader *(Introduction and Conclusion)*
- Storyteller (+ helper)
- Explorer
- Music Leader
- Activity Leader
- Prayer Leader

Suggestions for additional music

- Christ is made the sure foundation
- Heaven shall not wait

Service

Welcome

As people arrive, invite them to create something out of salt dough as a sign of their prayer.

Introduction

Today we will be telling the story of Noah and the Ark. It is such a big story that we will need everyone's help to tell it. Who would like to be Noah? *(Pick a volunteer and send him/her to a helper to get into costume.)* Who has got an animal with them today? You are in charge of the creatures in our story. Who would like to be in charge of the Flood? *(Pick two volunteers and give them the long strip of blue fabric between them.)* Everyone else: we will be providing sound effects.

Storytelling

Begin with an empty space in front of you and call your characters and props forward as you name them.

A long, long time ago, when the world was young, there lived a good man called Noah who believed in God.

Bring Noah forward.

But God was sad because his beautiful world was being spoiled. Wherever he looked, there was violence and wickedness, so he decided to wash the earth clean and start again. God wanted to save Noah, so he told him: 'You must build an enormous ark, with enough room in it for all your family and for two of every kind of creature which lives on the earth. Make sure you take every kind of food with you, too – enough for a long journey. Because I am going to make a great flood which will wash over the earth, and nothing and no one will survive it unless they are on your ark.'

Bring out the flat cardboard box and invite Noah to stand in the middle.

So Noah did what God told him: he built a huge ark.

Bring up the sides of the box around Noah and tape them together to make the walls of the ark.

Then he invited all the creatures on earth to come into the ark!

Everyone brings forward their soft toys and adds them to the ark.

When they were all safely on board, it began to rain.

Tap your fingers lightly on the floor or a chair and encourage everyone else to do so.

The rain got heavier *(drum your fingers loudly)* and heavier *(drum loudly with your hands, again encouraging general participation)* until the earth was covered with water.

Encourage the drumming to continue as your Flood helpers spread out the blue fabric around the ark, rippling it slightly to create waves.

Finally, the rain stopped. *(The drumming stops.)* Noah stepped out on deck and looked to the north, south, east and west – he could see nothing but water. The ark sailed on for days, and then months, but no one ever shouted, 'Land ahoy!' Noah sent out ravens and then doves to look for land, but they always came flying straight back to him. Then one day, he sent out a dove, and she came back with a fresh olive leaf in her beak. At last, Noah had proof that there was dry land somewhere, and before long the water disappeared *(the Flood helpers take the blue cloth away)* and everyone could leave the ark – Noah and his family and all the animals. *(Invite the toys' owners to retrieve them.)* God told them all to spread out across the world and have families, so that once again his beautiful earth would be full of life.

Applaud Noah and your helpers and invite everyone to return to their seats.

Music Think of a world without any flowers

Exploring So there was Noah, busy being a good man who believed in God, when God gave him an extraordinary job to do. Imagine being told to build an enormous boat when you don't live anywhere near the sea!

A film called *Evan Almighty* imagines what life would be like for a modern-day Noah. The hero, Evan, is a popular man who goes into politics because he wants to change the world. He gets a great job in Washington and finds himself with a big house, a big car and lots of power. Then strange things start happening to him. Animals begin to follow him wherever he goes; huge deliveries of wood arrive at his house; someone buys a big piece of land on his behalf. Then God arrives and tells him that he must build an ark. This God has a sense of humour and even makes Evan look like Noah, with a long beard which he can't shave off and robes which he can't avoid wearing! Eventually, Evan gives in and starts building his ark. His family is baffled, his neighbours laugh at him and his colleagues think he has gone mad. This is what happens on the day when God has told Evan that the flood will come: crowds and reporters have gathered to see what will happen.

Play the film clip from the scene where they are aboard the ark and waiting for the flood, ending with the ark's arrival on Capitol Hill.

By bringing Noah's story up to date, this film may make us wonder, 'What might God be asking *us* to do? We may not have to build an ark, but what job might God have for us?' Today's Gospel reading stresses the importance of putting our faith into action:

> Everyone then who hears these words of mine and acts on them will be like a wise man who built his house on rock. The rain fell, the floods came, and the winds blew and beat on that house, but it did not fall, because it had been founded on rock. And everyone who hears these words of mine and does not act on them will be like a foolish man who built his house on sand. The rain fell, and the floods came, and the winds blew and beat against that house, and it fell—and great was its fall!

If we hear Jesus' words and believe in them, then that belief has to lead to action. We have to 'walk it like we talk it'. In Jesus' story, acting on our beliefs is like building a storm-proof house: our faith has a firm foundation which will keep us strong. Noah's faithful actions – and Evan's – saved many lives. What life-changing and even world-changing things might happen if we put *our* faith into action?

Activity

In preparation for our prayers today, we will make paper doves like the one which brought Noah the sign he hoped for – proof of dry land appearing from the flood.

Show the dove template and demonstrate how to make the wings and insert them. Allow plenty of time for people to make their doves and attach the string.

Prayer action

Even when the flood waters are all around us, we always have hope; even if we can do nothing else about a situation which is overwhelming us, we can pray. These doves are a reminder that our prayers are always carried to God. Take a moment now to think of anyone who needs your prayers today. *(Pause.)* Take your dove's wings and write or draw your prayers along the folds. Then put the wings back, come up to the altar and let your dove fly.

Allow plenty of time for people to complete their prayers and suspend their doves in front of the altar. Then gather everyone together.

God, our refuge and strength,
hear our prayers for those in need.
May you keep them strong in hope
and steadfast in faith.
Amen.

Music

The wise man built his house

Conclusion

God of power and might,
give us the strength to put our faith into action
and to do your work in the world.
Amen.

Give notices, announce the next all-age service and invite everyone to the feast.

The burning bush and the Ten Plagues

Theme	Letting go of life in order to find life
Scripture	Exodus 3:1–15; Matthew 16:24–26

Running order	Total: 50 minutes
Welcome	'Living water' prayers *(5 minutes)*
Introduction	Opening the theme
Storytelling 1	Reading Matthew 16:24–26 *(5 minutes)*
Exploring	Why do we need to lose our life to find it? *Finding Nemo* film clip and exploration *(10 minutes)*
Music	Follow me *(5 minutes)*
Storytelling 2/Activity	The burning bush – Moses' call to freedom. Finding pictures and objects to tell the story *(15 minutes)*
Prayer action	Letting go – party popper prayers *(5 minutes)*
Music	Thuma mina *(5 minutes)*
Conclusion	Closing prayer and invitation

Resources

- A wide, deep tray of fine soil or potting compost, sown with grass seed
- A watering can
- A sign next to the water: 'Jesus said, "Those who drink of the water that I will give them will never be thirsty."'
- A DVD of *Finding Nemo* and equipment to play it on *(see appendix)*
- Music and words
- Pictures for Storytelling 2 *(see appendix)* Show them on screen *or* print them off and hide them around the church:
  - Burning bush
  - Red Sea shore
  - Bugs
  - Lightning
  - Locust
- Hidden around the church, objects for Storytelling 2:
  - A bottle or bowl of red water
  - A toy frog
  - Toy horses/cows
  - Plasters and bandages
- Party poppers, enough for one each (usually available from the party supplies section of big supermarkets)

Leaders

Minimum: 2

- Leader
- Reader

Optimum: 7 or 8

- Leader *(Introduction and Conclusion)*
- Storyteller(s)
- Reader: Jesus
- Explorer
- Activity Leader
- Music Leader
- Prayer Leader

Suggestions for additional music

- Take my life, and let it be
- Father, hear the prayer we offer

Service

Welcome

As people arrive, invite them to water the seeds as a sign of their prayer.

Introduction

There is a phrase we hear a lot these days, in streets and playgrounds, which can be hurtful if it is said to us: 'Get a life!' It's a put-down which says that whatever we are doing with our time isn't really worth that much. Bullies say it to make people feel small – but 'getting a life' which feels real and worthwhile for the person living it should be a wonderful, positive thing. Our service today is about what 'getting a life' might really mean.

Storytelling 1

Jesus sometimes told his disciples off when they got things wrong. One day he explained to them what was going to happen to him. He described his horrible death on the cross and told them that he would rise from the dead three days later. Peter said, 'No way! This can't happen to you, Lord!' and Jesus told him off for thinking only about one man's experiences, rather than God's bigger plan. Then he said this to all his disciples, and us:

Jesus reads Matthew 16:24–26.

What on earth does he mean, 'Those who want to save their life will lose it, and those who lose their life for my sake will find it'? *(Invite suggestions, valuing whatever is offered.)* This is the question we will be thinking about today.

Exploring

To help us think about why we need to lose our life in order to find it, we will watch part of a very different story. Who has seen the film, *Finding Nemo*? *(Invite a show of hands.)* This is the story of an orange and white clownfish called Marlin. He is an anxious, over-protective father who is searching the Pacific Ocean for his lost son, Nemo. He is helped by a cheerful, forgetful fish called Dory. They know that Nemo is in Sydney and they have reached Sydney harbour – but there's a hitch. They are trapped inside the body of a whale.

Show the film clip.

This little scene contains the lesson of the whole film, and it is one which can help us with our thinking today. Trapped inside the whale, with the water pouring down the whale's throat, Marlin's every instinct is to cling on to the whale's tongue for dear life. But Dory can speak whale and understands the bigger plan. She encourages Marlin to trust enough to let go – and it is only by doing so that they escape to freedom in the whale's waterspout.

Look at their conversation about 'letting go'. Marlin is frightened and anxious: 'How do you know something bad isn't going to happen?'

Dory is full of cheerful trust: 'I don't!' she yells – before letting go anyway.

Marlin is just as fearful of letting his son have some freedom; it is a feeling which many of us may recognise when we are faced with a big change in our lives. If we let go of things we are sure about – the place where we live, the school we go to, the job we do, the friends we know – then how do we know something bad isn't going to happen? Dory shows us the kind of faith we need to have. We don't know for sure, but we just have to trust in God – and let go. If we do, we may find that we too have been catapulted into new life.

Music

Follow me

Storytelling 2/Activity

The Activity Leader should be in charge of helping people find the objects, then making sure that they are passed to the Storyteller at the right moment. If you plan to show the pictures on the screen, the Activity Leader should take charge of the technology.

Our second story today is also about being called to lose everything in order to find life. This is the beginning of the story *(show the picture of the burning bush)* and this is the far-off happy ending *(show the picture of the far shore of the Red Sea)* but in between there are lots of horrible happenings. Some pictures and objects around the church can help us tell the story. Can you find them for me?

People hunt for the objects and bring them to the front, ready to add them to the story.

God had great plans for a man called Moses. One day, in the desert, God appeared to Moses in a burning bush.

Show the picture of the burning bush.

He said, 'My people, the Israelites, are miserable slaves in Egypt. I will rescue them and give them freedom in a land of their own. Moses, I have chosen you to speak to Pharaoh and lead my people out of Egypt.'

Moses said, 'Who, me?'

God said, 'Yes, you.'

So Moses said to Pharaoh, 'Let my people go!'

And Pharaoh said, 'No!'

So God gave Moses the power to turn all the water in the river Nile into blood. Everyone was thirsty and all the fish died.

Someone finds the red water.

But Pharaoh wouldn't listen. Then God made a plague of frogs overrun Egypt. There were frogs everywhere!

Someone finds the toy frog.

Pharaoh said, 'Get rid of the frogs! Then I'll let your people go.'

But he broke his promise when the frogs disappeared. So then God sent lots of crawling bugs; then he sent a plague of flies which buzzed everywhere.

Show the picture of bugs; encourage everyone to buzz like flies.

Pharaoh said, 'Get rid of the flies! Then I'll let your people go.'

But he broke his promise when the flies disappeared.

So then God sent a plague which killed all the Egyptian animals; then he sent a horrible skin disease which gave everyone blisters; then he sent lightning and burning hail.

People find the toy cows and horses, the plasters and bandages; show the picture of lightning.

Pharaoh said, 'Get rid of the lightning and hail! Then I'll let your people go.' But he broke his promise when the lightning and hail disappeared. Then God sent a plague of locusts, which ate every living thing in Egypt.

Show the picture of the locust.

Then God covered the land in darkness for three days.

Turn off the lights.

Still Pharaoh refused to let Moses and his people go. Finally God sent the most terrible plague of all. He sent his angel of death to kill every firstborn child and animal in Egypt, and finally Pharaoh relented. 'Go!' he said to Moses. 'Take your people and leave my country!' The Israelites escaped into the wilderness and across the sea. At last, they were free.

Turn on the lights and show the picture of the Red Sea shore.

When God appeared to Moses in the burning bush, he called him to lead his people to freedom – but this meant Moses had to let go of everything he had and get involved with the difficult, messy business of persuading Pharaoh to let the Israelites go. God gave his people a new life – but to find it they first had to leave their homes and head out into the wilderness. Even though they were slaves, they still had a roof over their heads and food and water to live on: going into the wilderness with Moses meant leaving all this security behind.

In our stories today, we have heard about people letting go in order to find new life. They remind us that sometimes we have to stop holding on to the things and situations that make us feel safe: sometimes we have to let go and trust in God. Jesus said, 'I came that they may have life, and have it abundantly.' This is both the eternal life he promises us in heaven and the fuller, richer life we can find here and now if we dare to let God take over and transform our lives. Remember what Marlin the clownfish said about his son:

'I promised I'd never let anything happen to him.'

Dory replied, 'That's a funny thing to promise . . . You can't never let anything happen to him, then nothing would ever happen to him.'[1]

If we trust in God and let things happen to us, we might just find the abundant life which Jesus promises us.

Prayer action

As we think today about holding on and letting go, we will use these party poppers as a sign of our prayers. Inside each one is a rainbow of coloured streamers – but they can't spring out unless we pull the string and brace ourselves for a bang and some smoke. God may be waiting to make a change in our lives, and it might involve some difficulty and upheaval – but only by letting him make that change happen will we release our life's hidden potential and discover its true colours.

Let us call to mind those people known to us who are looking for the courage to face change in their lives. *(Pause for a moment.)* When we say, 'Amen', release your party popper as a sign of your prayer.

Father, as we hold on to what we know,
give us the courage to trust in you and let go.

Release the party poppers.

Amen!

1. Andrew Stanton, screenplay for *Finding Nemo,* Walt Disney Pictures 2003.

Music Thuma mina

Conclusion Living Lord,
as we go out into the world,
may we seek to follow you.
Lead us into life.
Amen.

Give notices, announce the next all-age service and invite everyone to the feast.

Note: place the tray of grass seeds in a sunny spot and keep well watered.

Gospel stories, miracles and parables

It's a miracle!

Theme	Water into wine
Scripture	John 2:1–11

Running order	Total: 50 minutes
Welcome	Making footprints *(5 minutes)*
Introduction	Opening the theme
Storytelling	Visual retelling of John 2:1–11 *(10 minutes)*
Music	Life for the poor was hard and tough *(5 minutes)*
Activity	Finding 20 gallons *(5 minutes)*
Exploring	*How* much wine?! *(10 minutes)*
Music	Jesus calls us here to meet him *(5 minutes)*
Prayer action	Palmful – receptive prayer *(5 minutes)*
Music	Give me joy in my heart *(5 minutes)*
Conclusion	Closing prayer and invitation

Resources

N.B. Some advance planning needed!

Organise your congregation to collect:

- 45 clean, empty 2-litre plastic milk containers (or 30 3-litre ones). Place them in boxes around the church before the service begins

You will also need:

- A sheet of lining paper and felt-tip pens, in front of the altar
- Music and words
- A small table
- A box containing the following:
  - A white tablecloth
  - Some flowers
  - A glass jug with water in it
  - An opaque china jug with a large measure of *Ribena* in the bottom
  - A wine glass
- Lots of reels of Sellotape
- Several pairs of scissors
- Six large cut-out shapes of stone jars *(see appendix)*
- Empty font or large glass bowl
- Another large jug full of water (two if there are lots of people)
- Some towels

Leaders

Minimum: 1

- Leader

Optimum: 6+

- Leader *(Introduction and Conclusion)*
- Storyteller
- Activity Leader
- Music Leader(s)
- Explorer
- Prayer Leader(s)

Suggestions for additional music

- Joy to the world
- Christ's is the world

Service

Welcome

Invite people to come up to the altar and draw round their feet on the sheet of lining paper as a way of saying, 'Here I am, Lord'.

Introduction

Today's story is about a famous miracle: the Bible describes it as a 'sign' that Jesus is God's son. This miracle reveals his identity and shows us something of God. This is the story . . .

Storytelling

Stand behind the bare table.

In Galilee, where Jesus grew up, a wedding wasn't a private function. When people got married, they invited the whole village; they invited people from the next town; they invited friends of friends and second cousins twice removed.

Lay the table with the white cloth and the flowers.

When there was a wedding in Cana, Jesus' parents were there and so was Jesus with all his friends. Everyone was celebrating, eating and drinking. Now as you may imagine, lots of happy people get through a lot of party food and an awful lot of wine. The bridegroom had served his finest wine first, but as the merrymaking continued and people began not to notice what they were drinking, he made do with the cheaper wine. But soon that began to run out, too, until there was not a drop left. The bride and groom were horrified: they had offered hospitality to hundreds of well-wishers who had come to celebrate with them, and they had let their guests down! Jesus' mother, Mary, looked for him in the crowd. 'They've run out of wine!' she said.

Jesus replied, 'What has that got to do with you or me? My time has not yet come.'

But Mary found the servants and said to them, 'That's my son. He will help – do whatever he tells you.'

Place the china and glass jugs on the table.

Jesus pointed to six enormous stone jars and told the servants, 'Fill those jars with water.' *(Pour the water from the glass jug into the china jug.)* It took them a while to fetch so much water, but when each jar was full to the brim, he said to them, 'Now pour some out and take it to the chief steward to taste.'

Pour the water, which has now turned dark red, into the wine glass.

The chief steward took one sip and gasped. *(Sip from the glass.)* It was delicious wine! He found the bridegroom and said, 'I thought you had served the best wine first, but you have saved the best 'til last! I've never tasted wine like it!'

So the wedding celebrations continued joyfully, and everyone who saw Jesus turn water into wine believed in him, because the miracle was a sign which revealed the glory of God.

Music Life for the poor was hard and tough

Activity In our telling of today's story, we didn't really turn water into wine: we used a trick. Who would like to taste what it did turn into? *(Invite a volunteer to come up and identify the Ribena).* And who can guess how the trick worked? *(Invite suggestions, then explain how you did it.)*

But when Jesus turned water into wine, it wasn't a trick. It really happened. And instead of showing how it was done, Jesus' miracle showed people about God. Today we will explore what it showed them and us. First of all, let's get something to help us imagine exactly what happened in the story. The water which turned into wine was in a stone jar which – the Bible tells us – held 20 or 30 gallons of water. Now 20 gallons is about 90 litres – that is 45 of these 2-litre milk containers. *(Show one container.)* What would all that water look like together? Who can find some of these bottles around the church?

Volunteers bring all 45 milk containers to the front in a pile.

Now, can we build all these 2-litre containers into a tower, perhaps in the shape of one of those enormous stone jars in our story?

All volunteers help stick the containers together in rows and then build them up into a tower.

Imagine each of these containers is full of water. This huge tower is what 20 gallons of water look like in one place – but that is not all . . .

Exploring

This tower represents one stone jar which Jesus miraculously filled with wine.

Unroll the cut-out shape of a jar and ask two helpers to hold it in front of the tower.

But the Bible tells us there were *six* jars like this!

Unroll the cut-out shapes of five jars and ask your helpers to hold them up in a line next to the tower.

And not only that – it was the finest quality wine, the best wine anyone had ever tasted!

The miracle of all this wine really does reveal the glory of God. Why? Just think about what Jesus could have done instead. He could have made just enough for everyone to have another cupful; he could have made some basic, ordinary-tasting wine, reasoning that most of the guests were too drunk to notice. Most important of all, he could have decided to do nothing because – as he said to his mother – a shortage of wine at someone else's wedding really wasn't his problem. After all, no one was dying – this was a social crisis, not a life-threatening emergency.

And yet – by the power of God, Jesus made not simply *enough* wine, but more than any of us have ever seen at a wedding. He made not just basic stuff, but the finest quality wine. And he did not judge whether this was a situation which 'deserved' divine assistance: he turned water into wine and so helped a community to continue celebrating a wedding.

This miracle shows us the God who is more generous than we can ever believe or deserve; the God who loves to give abundantly and without judgement. This is the God who is revealed to us by his Son, Jesus.

Music

Jesus calls us here to meet him

Prayer action

We are used to asking for things in prayer, but it is also important that we open ourselves up to receiving whatever God gives us. Above all, God is generous: he gave us this beautiful world and he gave us his son, Jesus. Jesus loved to give, too: we have learnt today how he gave more wine than people could drink, with plenty to spare. Our prayer today reminds us to open our hands and receive from God, because he pours his grace upon us like a never-ending stream. You are all invited to come up and hold out your hands like a bowl to receive the water as a sign of God's abundant generosity.

You may need two leaders to do this simultaneously. Each person comes up and holds out their cupped hands over the bowl or font. As you pour water into their hands, say:

The palmful of the God of Life.
The palmful of the Christ of Love.
The palmful of the Spirit of Peace.
Trinity
of grace.[1]
Amen.

Music

Give me joy in my heart

Conclusion

Turn the sheet of lining paper with footprints on it so that the footprints are facing towards the door of the church, or heading down the aisle.

Generous Lord,
as we have received good things from you,
so send us out with open hands,
ready to give freely
as a sign of your grace overflowing in the world.
Amen.

Give notices, announce the next all-age service and invite everyone to the feast.

1. Adapted from source unknown (Early Scottish), *The SPCK Book of Christian Prayer.* SPCK, 1995, p.454.

Alive!

Theme	The promise of life
Scripture	Ezekiel 37:1–14 and John 11:1–45

Running order	Total: 50 minutes
Welcome	Creating a cross made of seeds *(5 minutes)*
Introduction	Opening the theme
Storytelling 1/Activity	The dry bones come alive – interactive story with puppets *(15 minutes)*
Music	Dem Bones *(see appendix) (5 minutes)*
Storytelling 2	Retelling the raising of Lazarus – an eyewitness account *(5 minutes)*
Music	Breathe on me, Breath of God *(5 minutes)*
Exploring	What is Jesus' promise? Unfolding the promise-crosses *(5 minutes)*
Prayer action	Bulbs – receptive prayer *(5 minutes)*
Music	Jesus the Lord said: 'I am the Bread' *(5 minutes)*
Conclusion	Instructions for planting bulbs – and prayer

Resources

- Lots of seeds – various sorts, the bigger the better (e.g. sunflower, pumpkin or runner bean seeds)
- A shallow bowl for the seeds
- A tray with the outline of a cross chalked on it
- 4 to 6 sets of 'body bits' *(see appendix)*
- Brass split pins
- One or two tables with chairs behind them at the front of church
- Some wooden bricks (children's building bricks or ones from the construction game, 'Jenga')
- Words and music
- 'Dem bones' words *(see appendix)*
- Promise-crosses *(see appendix)* placed all around the church
- Lots of cheap bulbs, enough for one each. Choose ones which are appropriate for planting at this time of year
- A basket or bowl for the bulbs

Leaders

Minimum: 2

- Leader/Storyteller 1
- Storyteller 2

Optimum: 7+

- Leader *(Introduction and Conclusion)*
- Activity Leader(s)
- Storytellers x 2
- Explorer
- Music Leader
- Prayer Leader

Suggestions for additional music

- Spirit of the Living God
- Breathtaking

Service

Welcome

As people arrive, invite them to come up to the altar and play with the seeds, then add a handful to the seed-cross as a sign of their prayer.

Introduction

Today we will hear two dramatic stories from the Bible which are about life and death. For the first story, I will need some helpers. I need people who are good with their hands to make some puppets for our story. We also need sound effects – who is good at making a noise?

Choose 4 to 6 puppeteers and sit them down at the tables in front of you with a set of body bits each and some split pins. Hand out the wooden blocks to everyone else. While you are rehearsing the sound effects, your Activity Leader(s) should be briefing the puppeteers about what they will need to do to fit their figures together and when.

First of all, we need a quick sound effects rehearsal. First, we need a gentle clicking sound, like this *(demonstrate with your own bricks)*. So when I say, 'clicking', you do this: *(demonstrate and encourage them all to join in, fairly quietly)*. Now, we need a bigger sound when I say 'rattling' *(demonstrate and encourage them all to join in)*. Now we need the biggest noise of all when I say 'mighty clattering': *(encourage the noise)*. Finally, when I say 'silence', we need this: *(put your finger to your lips, pause breathlessly and silence should fall!)*.

You may want to run through the cues and the sound effects once more.

Storytelling 1/Activity

Is everybody ready to help tell the story? Once there was a man called Ezekiel who was a prophet chosen by the Lord. One day, the Lord came close to Ezekiel – as close as your breath is to you now – and said 'Come with me.' The Lord took Ezekiel to the dusty desert and showed him a dry valley full of dry, dry bones. The bones were scattered all around – bone upon bone upon bone – and there was no sign of life anywhere.

There was silence. *(Put your bricks down and your finger to your lips.)*

Ask each puppeteer to show a handful of bones.

Then the Lord said to Ezekiel, 'Tell these bones this prophecy: 'Listen, dry bones, hear the word of the Lord. You ribs, I will fill you with breath. You legs and arms, I'll join you together with muscles and sinews. I will cover your whole body with flesh and blood and skin and put breath in you and you will live! Then you will know that I am the Lord.' So Ezekiel spoke this prophecy aloud in the desert air.

During this part, the puppeteers should be encouraged by the Activity Leader(s) to start making their skeleton puppets.

At first, there was silence. Then, in the silence, there was a clicking *(encourage the sound effects)* – the bones began to move! Then the clicking grew to a rattling *(encourage the sound effects)* and the rattling grew to a mighty clattering *(encourage the sound effects)* as each bone found the bone it belonged to and the bones joined together again.

Allow time for the skeleton puppets to be fixed together, then ask your puppeteers to hold them up for all to see.

Then, with a slither and a squelch, flesh and blood and skin covered all the bones. Where there had been dry bones, there were now bodies – but there was no breath in them.

The puppeteers attach the still body puppets over the skeletons and hold them up. During the next part, they attach the alive body puppets.

Then the Lord said to Ezekiel, 'Tell this prophecy to the breath: Come from the north wind and south wind, from the east wind and west wind, O breath; breathe into these bodies and make them live.' So Ezekiel spoke this prophecy aloud to the desert winds, and the people came to life and stood up. Ezekiel looked around the dry valley and saw a huge crowd of living, breathing people, and they were the people of God.

The puppeteers hold up all the puppets and make them move.

Music Dem Bones *(see appendix)*

Storytelling 2

Leader Our next story is told by an eyewitness. This is his/her story.

Storyteller I've known the family for years, of course. Lazarus and his sisters, Mary and Martha – they've been good neighbours. They were good to Jesus, too: their door was always open, and Jesus and his friends used to drop in whenever they felt like it for a meal or a bed for the night. For Jesus, their house in Bethany was like a home from home. So we couldn't understand why he didn't come running when he first heard that Lazarus was so ill. The fever was terrible, but we knew that if anyone could cure him, it was Jesus. They waited and waited but he didn't come, and despite everything Martha and Mary did, Lazarus died.

They buried him in the family cave and us neighbours helped to roll the big stone in front of the entrance. Every day, one of the girls was there by the cave, crying. Then four days later – four days, mind you! – Jesus turns up. I was there in the house with some of the others who had come in to help Mary and Martha. Well, I don't know what the girls said to him, but by the time I saw him he was looking pretty upset. He asked where Lazarus was buried, and when they led him there we all followed. I had never seen Jesus cry before, but there were tears running down his face. I thought, 'Well, those tears won't do Lazarus much good now. Why didn't you come when you could have saved him?'

When we get down to the cave, Jesus asks us to move the stone away. We thought he was mad – the smell from inside was already terrible. But he insists, so some of us cover our faces and shoulder the big rock out of the way. I still can't believe what happened next, but I saw it with my own eyes. Jesus goes right up to the mouth of the cave and bellows, 'Lazarus, come out!' We listen as the echo of that almighty yell bounces around the stones. Nobody moves. Then suddenly – out walks Lazarus! Still wrapped in his grave-clothes, but large as life!

Much later, after all the feasting and celebrations, Martha told me what Jesus had said to her before he brought her brother back from the dead. He said, 'I am the resurrection and the life. Those who believe in me, even though they die, will live, and everyone who lives and believes in me will never die.'

Music

Breathe on me, Breath of God

Exploring

Today's stories are about death and coming back to life – what we call 'resurrection'. Our second story finished with Jesus' amazing promise and now we are going to look at what that promise is. All around the church today, you will see colourful little paper crosses. How many can you find?

Encourage everyone to collect the promise-crosses and distribute them.

There are enough for everyone to take one home to keep in a safe place. They are small enough to tuck in a wallet or under your pillow.

These crosses are promise-crosses: if we unfold them bit by bit, you will find the promise which Jesus makes to us all. *(Unfold your cross as you talk.)* Let's start with the top. Jesus said 'I AM' – (*then unfold the arms of the cross)* – 'THE RESURRECTION AND THE LIFE'. Then, all down the rest of the cross is his promise to us: 'THOSE WHO BELIEVE IN ME, EVEN THOUGH THEY DIE, WILL LIVE.' So Jesus promises us that, because of him, even though we will die, we will live forever with God. His promise is the promise of life.

Prayer action

Our stories about new life remind us of creation's most familiar miracle. In nature, many plants grow and die before they grow again the next year. Life is followed by death which is followed by life again, and Jesus gives us the promise of life after death, too. In our prayers today, we will use these bulbs as a sign of the promise of life which Jesus gives us all. Each bulb looks dried-up and dead, but if it waits in the cold, dark earth for long enough it will spring into new life. Take a bulb as a sign of the gift of life which is given to us and hold it in your hands as we pray.

Pass round the basket of bulbs and pause once everyone has one.

Father, all creation is in your hands.
After the winter, green life will come again.
After death, new life will be ours
through your Son, Jesus Christ.
We thank you for the promise of life.
Amen.

Music

Jesus the Lord said: 'I am the Bread'

Conclusion

Please take your bulbs home and plant them as a living reminder of God's promise of life. *Give brief planting instructions for the bulbs.*

Let us pray:

Creator God, Giver of life,
thank you for making us.
Loving Son, death-defier,
thank you for saving us.
Breathing Spirit, life-force,
thank you for sustaining us
now and for ever.
Amen.

Give notices, announce the next all-age service and invite everyone to the feast.

One for All

The big picnic*

Theme	Feeding the five thousand
Scripture	Matthew 14:13–21

Running order	Total: 50 minutes
Welcome	Clay imprints *(5 minutes)*
Introduction	Opening the theme
Activity	Sharing the picnic *(10 minutes)*
Storytelling	Retelling Matthew 14:13–21 *(10 minutes)*
Music	5000+ hungry folk *(5 minutes)*
Exploring	What does this story tell us about God and about us? *(10 minutes)*
Prayer action	Kneaded dough – offertory prayers *(5 minutes)*
Music	Longing for light *(5 minutes)*
Conclusion	Closing prayer and invitation

*Note: This is ideal for an open-air service.

Resources

- *If holding this service outside*, lots of picnic rugs and some deck-chairs
- A piece of clay, rolled out to fill a large tray or board, just thick enough for people to make fingerprints in it. Cut the top edges to form the simple shape of a church and cover it tightly with clingfilm until ready for use
- Lots of bread rolls in baskets
- Tinned sardines, drained and arranged on plates
- Paper napkins
- Jugs of water and lots of cups
- Baskets and dishes for leftover food
- A bag for rubbish
- Music and words
- Salt dough *(see appendix for Crib Service)*

Leaders

Minimum: 1

- Leader

Optimum: 6

- Leader *(Introduction and Conclusion)*
- Activity Leader
- Storyteller
- Explorer
- Music Leader
- Prayer Leader

Suggestions for additional music

- Gather around, for the table is spread
- Let us talents and tongues employ

Service

Welcome

As people arrive, invite them to leave their fingerprint in the clay as a way of saying, 'Here I am, Lord'.

Introduction

Today we will be hearing the story of the biggest picnic in the Bible. It was a miraculous picnic which Jesus shared with a huge crowd. Before we hear the story, let's share the picnic food they ate: bread and fish, enough for everyone!

Activity

Invite everyone to tuck in: keep passing round the food until everyone has had enough; walk round with the baskets for leftovers.

Storytelling

Jesus was a celebrity in Galilee. Everyone wanted to hear him speak; everyone wanted to get close to him; everyone knew someone who had been cured by him, and more and more sick people trailed him wherever he went. He walked through the fishing villages around Lake Galilee surrounded by crowds. They followed him down onto the beach one day and pressed round him as he got into a boat and rowed out into the middle of the lake to find some peace.

For a while he drifted quietly, then he rowed towards the other side of the lake where the hills were high and lonely. But the crowds didn't give up that easily. Some men climbed trees and strained their eyes until they spotted Jesus' little boat and could work out where he was heading. They shouted directions to the eager crowds, who ran and stumbled along the rocky shoreline.

Everyone they passed got caught up in the excitement. 'Where are you going?' the people in the next village asked them.

'Round to the east side of the lake – that's where Jesus is going!'

Fishermen dropped their nets, vineyard workers left their baskets, mothers strapped their babies to their chests and set off. They all joined the bustling crowd that hurried through the villages, around the northern edge of the lake and onto the quieter eastern shore.

As Jesus rowed closer, a noise drifted across the water. It sounded like a flock of gulls – then he saw that the beach was filled with expectant crowds. Among them, his harassed disciples were struggling to keep order as people pushed into the water to reach the boat first. But Jesus felt great compassion for those who had trekked so far to see him; he waded ashore and began to heal everyone who came to him.

This went on all day, until everyone was tired and hungry. The disciples said to Jesus, 'Tell people to get going now, because it's late and there's nowhere to eat around here. We all ought to head back to the villages and find some food.'

Jesus replied, 'There's no need for anyone to go anywhere. You feed them.'

The disciples looked at each other. 'How, Lord? Nobody has brought any food – well, apart from that lad over there who has got a few bread rolls and some fish: a packed lunch, basically.'

Jesus said, 'That'll do. Bring it here.' He took the five bread rolls and the two little fish and he looked up to heaven. Then he blessed the food and broke the bread and gave the little picnic to the disciples to share out. Then, very quietly, something amazing began to happen. The disciples kept on handing out bread and fish and the more they gave it away, the more they had to give. That little picnic miraculously grew as people shared it, until every person in that enormous crowd was full up – and that was about five thousand men, as well as women and children. When the disciples gathered up the leftover fish bones and bits of crust, they filled twelve baskets full, and no one was left hungry.

Music 5000+ hungry folk

Exploring

Today's story focuses on a crowd of hungry people. The disciples must have walked through the crowd asking if anyone had brought anything to eat, until one boy piped up, 'I have! I've got some bread and fish!' I'd like to ask everyone here that question: 'Who has got something to eat?' Don't worry, we're not going to take it and share it out! But if we *were* hungry here, today, what would we have between us to eat?

Invite a show of hands and ask for contributions. Ask people, 'What food have you got with you today? Why have you brought it?' Accept all answers, from rusks to cough sweets. If there are no other contributions, ask those in charge of the post-service feast to say what food is in store.

Now, how many people are here today? Who would like to count them for me?

Let your volunteers count up as you continue.

The Bible tells us that at Jesus' big picnic there were 'five thousand men, besides women and children.' So although we often call this miracle 'The feeding of the five thousand', that was only the number of men. There could have been just as many mums and twice as many kids – and we all know how much they can eat! But in all those thousands of people, only one person had brought a picnic. Whereas there are *(insert your total here)* people here today and among us, we have this much food *(mention some of the food that people have brought with them)*. I wonder why those people who walked all that way to see Jesus didn't pack a picnic first?

Invite contributions.

This story shows us how Jesus' first followers followed him: they just dropped everything and went. They didn't worry about preparing for every eventuality and, as things turned out, Jesus provided what they needed when they needed it. Their example may make us think about how we follow Jesus: do we need to be less concerned with what we might need, and more ready simply to trust in God and get on with whatever it is he is calling us to do?

This story also shows us something about God. When Jesus fed all those people, he didn't provide the bare minimum: he didn't say, 'No more than half a roll and one piece of fish each.' He miraculously shared so much food that there were twelve baskets of leftovers. We left this much *(show the basket of leftovers):* imagine twelve baskets like this and people who were so full that they could afford to leave their crusts. Jesus' miracle shows us how generous God is: he doesn't ration his grace but lavishes it on us, his people.

Finally, this story shows us what part each one of us might play in God's miracles. Jesus made this miracle happen, but what else made it possible? *(Invite contributions.)* Jesus didn't make food appear from thin air: he used a humble picnic, generously shared by a young boy. Our own humble gifts can be used by God to make amazing things happen, too. So next time you hear people talking about doing God's work and think to yourself, 'Yes, but what can *I* do?' – think of that little boy's picnic and remember what miracles God can do with the smallest and most ordinary of ingredients.

Prayer action

There is a poem written about this story from the point of view of the boy's mother. She made the bread that morning from her ordinary, everyday dough. She struggles to believe his story about the miraculous picnic, and the poem ends with her asking this question:

It can't be true . . . but if it is . . .
What kind of dough did these hands knead
this morning?[1]

In our prayers today, we will each have a piece of dough to knead. As you work it in your hands, ask yourself, 'What kind of dough might these hands knead? What part might I have to play in God's plan?' Rest quietly in God's presence and ask what you are being called to do; let the dough take the shape of your prayer.

Allow plenty of time for everyone to make their prayers.

1. Cordelia Baker-Pearce, 'Just a housewife' in *Celebrating Women,* ed. Hannah Ward, Jennifer Wild, Janet Morley, SPCK 1995.

Giving Lord,
we are your hands on earth:
show us what you need us to do
and give us the strength to do it,
in Jesus' name.
Amen.

Music Longing for light

Conclusion Lord of plenty,
we thank you for your abundant grace.
Help us to share your goodness with the world.
Amen.

Give notices, announce the next all-age service and invite everyone to the feast.

One for All

Walking on the waves

Theme	Trusting in God and not being afraid
Scripture	Matthew 14:22–33

Running order	Total: 50 minutes
Welcome	'Living water' prayers *(5 minutes)*
Introduction	Opening the theme
Storytelling	Dramatised, interactive retelling of Jesus walking on the water *(10 minutes)*. Note: This does not need prior rehearsal for anyone except Jesus
Exploring	What kind of waves overwhelm us? Written brainstorm *(10 minutes)*
Music	Dear Lord and Father of mankind *(5 minutes)*
Activity	Making floating crosses *(10 minutes)*
Prayer action	Floating crosses – written, active intercessions *(5 minutes)*
Music	Do not be afraid *(5 minutes)*
Conclusion	Closing prayer and invitation

Resources

- A wide, deep tray of fine soil or potting compost, sown with grass seed
- A watering can
- A sign next to the water: 'Jesus said, "Those who drink of the water that I will give them will never be thirsty."'
- Two long bamboo canes (at least 2m)
- A tall cross-shaped mast made out of two bamboo canes tied together
- Two long pieces of blue material
- A long sheet of lining paper with the simple outline of waves on it
- Lots of pens and pencils in sea colours
- *Optional*: blue and green paint, water and brushes
- Music and words
- Templates for the floating crosses *(see appendix)*
- Biros and pencils (not felt-tip pens)
- Scissors
- A large tray of water, with room to float lots of paper crosses on the top. A large font may be suitable

Leaders

Minimum: 2

- Leader
- ***Jesus***

Optimum: 7

- Leader *(Introduction and Conclusion)*
- Storyteller
- ***Jesus***, wearing white
- Explorer
- Activity Leader
- Music Leader
- Prayer Leader

Suggestions for additional music

- Lead us, heavenly Father, lead us
- Nada te turbe

Service

Welcome

As people arrive, invite them to water the seeds as a sign of their prayer.

Introduction

Our story today is very dramatic, so with everyone's help we are going to act it out.

Storytelling

This story happened on Lake Galilee. Who would like to play the part of the water in the lake?

Pick two or four volunteers and give them the ends of the blue material to hold flat on the floor.

Now when we think of Lake Galilee, we might imagine a little boating lake, or a big, calm place like somewhere in the Lake District. Wrong. It is big – thirteen miles long and eight miles wide – and while it is often calm, a wicked wind can race down the Jordan Valley and whip up a storm before you can say, 'Man overboard!'

Encourage your volunteers to ripple the material to make big waves.

When this happens, waves ten feet high can crash into the lakeside towns and villages. You wouldn't want to be caught out in the middle of the lake in a storm like that.

Lay the material flat again.

On this occasion, Jesus wanted some time to himself to pray, so he headed up into the mountains and sent the disciples off across the lake in a little fishing boat. It was late afternoon, and the waters were calm, so the disciples climbed cheerfully into the boat. Who would like to volunteer to be a disciple in our story?

Invite your volunteers forward and stand them behind the blue fabric. Position one volunteer at the front and one at the back, (with anyone else in between) and give them the ends of a pair of long bamboo canes to hold. They should hold their ends together so that the canes form points fore and aft before curving round to suggest the sides of the boat. The disciples in the middle can help hold the shape. Give one person the simple cross-shaped mast to hold up in the middle.

Peter and the other fishermen took charge of the rowing *(pick a volunteer Peter: he/she and some others mime rowing)* and all went well until they were right in the middle of the lake, about four miles from the shore. Night had fallen and the wind was starting to get up.

Encourage everybody to make quiet sound effects for the wind.

Soon the gusts turned into a gale *(encourage louder effects)* which stirred up the waves *(encourage the wave-makers to ripple the fabric)* until the little boat was being battered to and fro by a huge storm! *(Encourage sound effects, wild wave-making and boat-swaying. The person holding the mast tips it from side to side.)*

The disciples yelled out in panic. *(Encourage yelling.)* Then they couldn't believe their eyes. *(Jesus enters, treading on the blue material.)* They saw a pale figure walking towards them across the waves. 'It's a ghost!' someone yelled and they all screamed. *(Encourage screaming.)* But the figure shouted:

Jesus — It's me – Jesus! Do not be afraid!

Storyteller — Peter said, 'Lord, if it's really you, call me to walk over to you on the water.' And Jesus said:

Jesus — Come.

Storyteller — Well, Peter tried. He stepped out of the boat *(Peter does so)* as the waves surged even higher *(encourage wilder wave-making)* and started to walk on the water, but as the wind whistled around him *(encourage sound effects)* he got really scared and started to sink. *(The wave-makers start to raise their material up towards Peter's head.)* Peter cried out for help. *(Encourage Peter to shout out.)* And Jesus grabbed his hand and said:

Jesus Where's your faith? Didn't you trust me?

Storyteller Then they clambered back into the boat and suddenly, amazingly, the storm stopped. *(The blue material lies still again.)* And everyone in the boat worshipped Jesus, because they knew for sure that he was the Son of God.

Exploring

Jesus asked Peter, 'Where's your faith? Didn't you trust me?' and his question makes us think about what this story might mean to us. Peter wants to follow Jesus' call and walk on the waves, and he starts to do so, full of faith and trust – but when the wind gets up and the waves roll, he gets frightened and starts to sink. In our own lives, I wonder what kind of waves overwhelm us? What things happen to shake our faith and make it hard for us to trust in God?

Show the wave picture.

We will explore these questions together with the help of these enormous waves. Gather round this paper and paint, draw or write on it anything in life which can make us feel overwhelmed – anything which makes us feel as if we're in the middle of a stormy sea.

Allow plenty of time for people to think and add to the wave picture. You may like to read out some of the contributions.

Music

Dear Lord and Father of mankind

Activity

'Do not be afraid,' said Jesus. Whatever storms we face in life, we can still take his words to heart. Today we are going to make little crosses to use in our prayers which have at their centre these encouraging words. Cut out a cross and fold in the arms to hide the words, *(demonstrate this)* then on the back of the circle write the names of anyone you would like to remember in prayer. Think of people you know who are feeling overwhelmed at the moment or who are finding life stormy and difficult. You may like to cut out and fold several crosses for your prayers.

Prayer action

In a moment, we will float these folded crosses on the water as a sign of our prayers. Make sure you keep the folded side upwards. When Jesus walked on the water, he told Peter, 'Do not be afraid,' and then he calmed the storm. We pray now for all those known to us who feel as if they are struggling like Peter to keep afloat. We pray that they might be strengthened and encouraged: we lay these, our floating prayers, on the water in Jesus' name.

Everyone lays their folded-up crosses on the water. Gather round and watch as the arms of the crosses slowly unfold to reveal the words, 'Do not be afraid.'

Storm-stilling Lord,
be with us in life's rough seas
and tell us, 'Do not be afraid'.
Help us to trust in you.
Amen.

Music

Do not be afraid

Conclusion

Wave-walking Lord,
call us to you and give us the courage
to brave the storms of life with you by our side.
Amen.

Give notices, announce the next all-age service and invite everyone to the feast.

Note: place the tray of grass seeds in a sunny spot and keep well watered.

The road to Emmaus

Theme	The cost of discipleship
Scripture	Luke 24:13–35

Running order	Total: 50 minutes
Welcome	Adding leaves to the living prayer tree *(5 minutes)*
Introduction	Finding the meal table
Activity	Wondering about the uneaten meal *(10 minutes)*
Storytelling	Retelling Luke 24:13–35 *(10 minutes)*
Music	We'll walk the land *(5 minutes)*
Exploring	'What is the cost of spreading the good news?' – brainstorming the pros and cons of returning to Jerusalem *(10 minutes)*
Prayer action	Bread-breaking – sensory contemplative prayer *(5 minutes)*
Music	Gather around, for the table is spread *(5 minutes)*
Conclusion	Closing prayer and invitation

Resources

- A living 'prayer tree': some budding branches in a large pot or vase, filled with water and pebbles to weigh it down *(see appendix for Seeing and believing)*
- Prayer leaves *(see appendix for Seeing and believing)*
- A wooden table laid with the barely-eaten meal to which Jesus and his friends sat down in Emmaus. You might include the following: a lamp or candle; plain wooden or pottery dishes; simple, middle Eastern food such as olives, dates, grapes, nuts and sardines. There should be a round loaf of bread (warm if possible) which has been broken in two and a jug of wine, poured out into three full glasses. There might be crumbs on the floor and some spilt wine to indicate a hurried exit
- Music and words
- Two big boards or pieces of lining paper, with a title each: *Stay in Emmaus?* and *Go back to Jerusalem?*
- Marker pens

Leaders

Minimum: 1

- Leader

Optimum: 6

- Leader *(Introduction and Conclusion)*
- Activity Leader
- Storyteller
- Explorer
- Music Leader
- Prayer Leader

Suggestions for additional music

- I am the bread of life
- In the garden Mary lingers
- Rejoice, the Lord is King!

Service

Welcome

Invite people to add prayer leaves to the living prayer tree as they arrive.

Introduction

We will begin today's story not at the beginning, but at the end. Here is the scene which is left at the end of our story: gather round and let's see if we can imagine what might have happened here.

Gather everyone around the table with the uneaten meal. If your congregation is large, ask the children to come forward.

Activity

Allow some time for people to look at the table. Then ask questions which invite them to explore the scene with their senses, for example:

What things can you see here?
What does the bread taste like?
What does the drink smell like?
Is this food hot or cold?
Is the lamp / candle still warm?

Then invite some deductions and inferences. Try to value all contributions – you are not looking for the 'right' answer. Here are some questions you might ask:

I wonder what part of the world this meal comes from?
I wonder what might have happened here?
I wonder where the people have gone?
I wonder why they left without finishing their meal?
I wonder why there is food on the floor?

Storytelling

This is what happened. When Jesus died on the cross, the religious leaders in Jerusalem hoped that that was the end of all this rabble-rousing talk of kings and saviours. What the Roman governor hated most was trouble, and excited crowds on the brink of a riot counted as trouble with a capital T. So when the rumour started to spread that Jesus had come back from the dead, all the powerful people wanted to hush it up. Anyone who had been a friend of Jesus was in danger of being arrested, and worse. Anyone who talked about Jesus, who told people he was still alive, could find themselves in big, big trouble in Jerusalem, both with the religious leaders and the Romans.

So two of Jesus' friends decided to get out of town, and fast. They walked the long, stony road westwards out of Jerusalem, heading for a village called Emmaus, where they would be safe for a while. It was a good four hours' walk and the afternoon sun blazed in their faces, so they covered their heads to shade their eyes and to keep out the dust which they kicked up as they hurried along.

It was hard going, but at least they could finally talk freely about everything that had happened. Was Jesus really alive? How could he be? What would happen to them all now? What about all those promises Jesus had made about being the Saviour?

Suddenly, as if from nowhere, they heard footsteps behind them. Panic! Had someone followed them? Were they going to be arrested? But it was only another traveller like them, with his head all wrapped in cool cloths to keep off the sun. He joined them. 'What's the news?' he asked.

'If you've come from Jerusalem like us, then you'll know!' said one of the disciples, grimly.

'Tell me,' said the stranger.

So they told him everything: all about Jesus and how they had hoped he was the Messiah; all about his horrible death and the strange rumours of angels and an empty tomb.

The stranger listened to it all. He said gently, 'You don't get it, do you? All these things had to happen to the Messiah, just like the prophets said.' And very patiently, starting at the beginning of Jewish history, he explained everything about the Messiah, their Saviour.

Before they knew it, they had reached Emmaus and night was falling fast. You don't want to get caught out alone on these roads at night, so the friends persuaded the stranger to come and share a meal with them. They were all welcomed at the house where they had been expected; their hands and feet were washed and they sat at the table. Then the stranger reached for the bread and broke it, saying: 'This is my body, which is given for you. Do this in remembrance of me.'

Only one person had ever blessed bread like that with them before – Jesus. The friends looked and suddenly saw – it was him! Jesus, large as life, sitting with them at the table! Before they could speak, he vanished as suddenly as he had appeared on the road.

'I knew it!' said one of the friends. 'Did you hear how he talked about the scriptures while we were walking? I felt as if my heart was on fire, just listening to him! We've got to tell the others!'

'What? Back to Jerusalem – now?' said his companion.

He was right to be scared. Did they really want to leave this delicious meal and this safe, warm house and head back into the night, walk for another four hours in the dark and then go back through the dangerous streets of Jerusalem, where they might be arrested just for saying Jesus' name?

But what else could they do? They had to tell their friends that they had met Jesus and that he was alive!

Music We'll walk the land

Exploring Those two disciples had a big decision to make once they realised they had met Jesus, risen from the dead. I wonder what was going through their minds? Let's imagine they had time to list the pros and cons of their situation: what would be good about staying where they are in Emmaus, sixteen miles away from Jerusalem? What might make them want to go back to their friends, in hiding in the city? We have two big decision-boards here. Think about the good and bad things about staying put in Emmaus, and the good and bad things about going back to Jerusalem. If you were Jesus' friends that day, what might you write?

Allow plenty of thinking and writing time, then read out some of the contributions.

The friends had to ask themselves, 'What is the cost of spreading the good news?' And they chose to risk everything by going back to Jerusalem and telling the truth about what they had experienced. I wonder whether anything in this situation reminds us of ourselves? Do we ever risk anything to tell people about our experience of God? We may not be arrested, but we might be afraid that people will laugh at us, or think we've gone mad. Think of this story about the friends on the road to Emmaus and ask yourself, 'What does it cost me to tell people about Jesus?'

Prayer action

Take the broken bread from the meal table.

For our prayers today, we will use the bread which Jesus broke to share with his friends. Take some and eat it, and as you do so, rest quietly in God's presence and let the taste of fresh bread give shape to your prayer. You may be thankful for having good food to eat, or you might reflect on how Jesus made himself known to his friends through the simple, homely act of breaking bread. You might pray about how we share our food with others. Whatever your prayer might be, take and eat this bread and let us pray.

Pass the bread round on two plates. Allow enough time for everyone to take a piece and eat it.

Bread-breaking Lord,
as we share this bread together
we thank you for sharing yourself with us.
Amen.

Music

Gather around, for the table is spread

Conclusion

As we go out into the world today, let's remember the stranger on the road to Emmaus who was suddenly recognised as Jesus. Let us pray:

Lord Jesus,
may we be ready to recognise you in friends and strangers,
to meet you where we least expect you
and to love you wherever we find you.
Amen.

Give notices, announce the next all-age service and invite everyone to the feast.

The forgiven debtor

Theme	Celebrating new life
Scripture	Exodus 14:19–31; Matthew 18:21–35

Running order	Total: 50 minutes
Welcome	Clay imprints *(5 minutes)*
Introduction	Opening the theme
Storytelling 1	Crossing the Red Sea – film clip *(10 minutes)*
Music/Activity	Shout for joy and sing your praises – leading into singing and dancing *(10 minutes)*
Storytelling 2	Dramatised retelling of the story of the forgiven debtor *(5 minutes)*
Exploring	How much are we forgiven? Calculating the sums in the parable *(10 minutes)*
Prayer action	Washed clean – active confession *(5 minutes)*
Music	Bless the Lord, my soul *(5 minutes)*
Conclusion	Closing prayer and invitation

Resources

- A piece of clay, rolled out to fill a large tray or board, just thick enough for people to make fingerprints in it. Cut the top edges to form the simple shape of a church and cover it tightly with clingfilm until ready for use
- A DVD of *The Prince of Egypt* and equipment to play it on *(see appendix for Doing God's work)*
- Music and words
- Percussion instruments
- Streamers and worship flags *(see appendix)*
- King's throne
- A simple scroll
- A long bill covered in red numbers
- Whiteboard *or* OHP and screen
- Pens for whiteboard/OHP slides
- A large tray or dish of water, with a pile of small pebbles on one side and a cloth with a cross in the middle on the other
- Felt-tip pens (with ordinary water-soluble ink)

Leaders

Minimum: 5

- Leader
- Cast x 4

Optimum: 9+

- Leader *(Introduction and Conclusion)*
- Music/Activity Leader(s)
- Storyteller
- Cast x 4
  Guard, with some armour or a weapon
  King, wearing a crown and a cloak
  First Slave, wearing a simple tunic
  Second Slave, wearing a simple tunic
- Explorer
- Prayer Leader

Suggestions for additional music

- Forgive our sins as we forgive
- Take this moment

Service

Welcome

As people arrive, invite them to leave their fingerprint in the clay as a way of saying, 'Here I am, Lord'.

Introduction

Our first story today is one of the most dramatic in the Bible. The story so far is that God's people, the Israelites, have escaped from Egypt where they were slaves. Moses leads them into the wilderness – but they are being pursued by Egyptian soldiers. This is what happened.

Storytelling 1

Show the film clip from The Prince of Egypt *– the Israelites crossing the Red Sea and the Egyptian army drowning.*

Music/Activity

When God's people reached the seashore and knew they were finally free, they danced and sang for joy. We are going to sing now – and as the music continues, you are all invited to sing or dance or play an instrument to celebrate God's goodness.

Hand out percussion instruments, streamers and worship flags before you sing the hymn, 'Shout for joy and sing your praises' Sing it twice and then as the musicians continue to play the tune, encourage as many people as possible to join in by playing instruments or dancing. You could even lead a conga around the church!

Storytelling 2

Our second story is about finding freedom of a different kind – the freedom which comes from having our sins forgiven. Peter asked Jesus how often he should forgive someone who had sinned against him. Was there a limit to forgiveness? In reply, Jesus told this story.

The king is on a throne at the front of the church.

Guard: *(Reading from a scroll)* By royal command: his majesty wishes to settle all accounts with his slaves today. Call the first slave!

First slave: Here I am, your majesty.

King: *(Producing a long bill covered in red numbers)* Now let me see – you owe me . . . 10,000 talents.

First slave — Your majesty, I don't have that sort of money!

King — Very well: I will sell you and your family and everything that you own, in payment of your debt.

First slave — Please, no! Please be patient – I'll pay it all back eventually, I promise! I just need more time!

King — You could never live long enough to pay back all this. But I will take pity on you: I will write off all your debts. You no longer owe me anything at all.

(He screws up the bills.)

First slave — Your majesty! I don't know what to say except – thank you!

He turns and walks down the aisle, where he meets the second slave and grabs him round the neck.

You! Where's that 100 denarii[1] you owe me? I want it now!

Second slave — Please, no! Please be patient – I'll pay it all back eventually, I promise! I just need more time!

First slave — No way – I'm locking you up until your debt is paid.

Guard — Your majesty! You'll never guess what that slave has just done! *(He whispers in the king's ear.)*

King — WHAT?! Bring him back here.

The guard drags the first slave back.

King — You wicked slave! I forgave you a huge debt – could you not have shown the same mercy to your fellow-slave?

First slave — I – I –

King — Guard! Throw him into the dungeon and torture him until his whole debt is paid.

The guard drags the slave off.

Exploring

Set up the whiteboard or OHP and screen.

There is a lot to think about in this parable of sin and forgiveness. Let's start by looking more closely at the sums of money involved: 10,000 talents and 100 denarii.

1. Pronounced 'di-*naar*-e-ee'.

Write down '10,000 talents' and '100 denarii'.

What's that in today's money? First of all, let's work it all out in denarii. 1 talent = 6000 denarii.

Write down '1 talent = 6000 denarii'.

So how many denarii in 10,000 talents?

Allow people some time to work it out.

60 million denarii! That's how much the first slave owed; the second owed 100 denarii.

Write down '60,000,000 denarii' and '100 denarii'.

But what would a denarius be worth today? In Jesus' time, it was the normal day's wage for a labourer. Today, a day's work done for minimum wage would earn you about £40.[2] So let's say 1 denarius = £40 in today's money.

Write down '1 denarius = £40'.

Now, you do the maths. How much did both slaves owe in today's money?

Allow some time for people to come up with an answer. Ask for contributions.

The answer is: in today's money, the second slave owed £4000 and the first slave owed £2,400 million![3]

Write down '£2,400,000,000' and '£4000'.

Put into a currency we can understand, these numbers describe what forgiveness is like. The amount owed by the first slave is mind-bogglingly huge. Even the sale of everything he has could not begin to cover this debt. Our minds struggle to grasp such a vast sum of money: in the same way, we struggle to comprehend terrible

2. Based on a 7 hour day @ £5.80 per hour. Adjust these figures as necessary, in line with the current minimum wage.
3. Figure based on the fact that a UK billion is a million million. In the USA a billion is a thousand million.

evil in the world. We look at the Holocaust, the terrorist attacks of September 11th, the Rwandan genocide and other horrors and we struggle to grasp the full extent of their wickedness, let alone the possibility of ever forgiving such things. The slave's huge debt reminds us of the unimaginable extent of human sinfulness.

What about the king to whom the debt is owed? We have to ask ourselves, if this king's slave owes him this much money, and this slave is only one of many with whom the king is settling accounts, then just how rich is the king? If he can afford to lend and be owed £2,400 million, how great is his wealth? This time our minds struggle to grasp an amount *even bigger* than the vast debt. And then he releases the slave from his debt! This is a king who can afford to go without the £2,400 million he was owed! Jesus says, this king is like God: his story shows us just how mind-bogglingly huge God's goodness is. Like the king's unimaginable riches, his mercy defies our ability to reckon it up, which is why when we talk about God's goodness we often use the word 'infinite' – it might as well be endless because there's so much of it, we have to give up counting.

Now, next to all these millions of pounds, there is the debt of £4000 which the second slave owes. Tiny in comparison to the other debt, but still not so small that you wouldn't miss it. The behaviour of the first slave tells us a lot about ourselves and forgiveness. Remember how he grabbed his debtor by the throat and demanded payment? We can receive God's forgiveness on a grand scale, and rejoice that Jesus died for all our sins, but still hold bitterly onto a grudge we bear. How many of us still remember the hurt someone caused us, by an unkind word or action, ten, twenty or thirty years ago? Like £4000 compared to £2,400 million, the wrongdoing may be relatively small, but we won't let it go because the injustice still rankles.

This story forces us to look at the link between the amazing forgiveness we receive from God, and the hard forgiveness we need to practise in our own lives. Both slaves ended up in prison and for us, the alternative to forgiving each other is that we become trapped in an endless, vicious cycle of paying each other back. Forgiveness sets us free: it is this freedom which God longs to give us, and wants us to give each other.

Prayer action

Bring forward the tray of water and lay the pile of stones with the felt-tip pens on one side, and the cloth with the cross on the other.

The people of God walked through the waters of the Red Sea to freedom: when they got to the other side, they danced and sang for joy. When we confess our sins and God forgives them, we too can enjoy new-found freedom and a fresh start. To remind us of this connection between forgiveness and the celebration on the seashore, we are going to use water in our prayers today.

As we rest in God's presence, let's call to mind something for which we each need to say sorry. Take a pen and write or draw whatever it is on one of these stones. *(Pause while people do this.)* Then, on the other side, write something which is hard to forgive – a wrongdoing you suffered, or a wrong which was done to others. *(Pause while people do this.)*

These stones are double prayers for forgiveness: the forgiveness which each of us needs, and the forgiveness which we find it so hard to grant others. We will offer these prayers to God by washing them in this water so that the stones emerge clean and as good as new on the other side.

Allow plenty of time for people to come forward and wash their stones and place them by the cross on the other side of the water.

Lord of limitless forgiveness,
may your love wash away our sins
and the sins of those who have wronged us.
May your mercy set us free
in Jesus' name.
Amen.

Music Bless the Lord, my soul

Conclusion Merciful Lord,
as we go out into the world,
may our hearts be open to receive
the uncountable riches of your grace.
Amen.

Give notices, announce the next all-age service and invite everyone to the feast.

The workers in the vineyard

Theme	God's generosity
Scripture	Exodus 16:2–15; Matthew 20:1–16

Running order	Total: 50 minutes
Welcome	'Living Water' prayers *(5 minutes)*
Introduction	Opening the theme
Storytelling 1	Visual retelling of Exodus 16:2–15 *(5 minutes)*
Activity	Feast of manna *(5 minutes)*
Music	Guide me, O thou great Redeemer *(5 minutes)*
Storytelling 2	Dramatised retelling of Matthew 20:1–16 *(10 minutes)*
Music	Father welcomes all his children *(5 minutes)*
Exploring	What is God's generosity like? Hot-seating the workers *(5 minutes)*
Prayer action	Empty bowl – receptive prayer and contemplation with Taizé chant: In the Lord I'll be ever thankful *(10 minutes)*
Conclusion	Closing prayer and invitation

Resources

- A wide, deep tray of fine soil or potting compost, sown with grass seed
- A watering can
- A sign next to the water: 'Jesus said, "Those who drink of the water that I will give them will never be thirsty"'
- A tray of dry sand
- Some stones and dry twigs
- A plate of cooked chicken *(see appendix)*
- A plate of puff pastry with honey *(see appendix)*
- A jug of water and a glass plus lots of plastic cups
- Music and words
- A large clock
- Five large baskets or cardboard boxes
- A bundle of *Monopoly* money or similar

Leaders

Minimum: 7

- Leader
- Cast x 6

Optimum: 12

- Leader *(Introduction and Conclusion)*
- Storytellers x 2
- Cast x 6
  Five workers, wearing scruffy clothes
  The Landowner, smartly dressed
- Activity Leader
- Explorer
- Music Leader

Suggestions for additional music

- God of life, God of love
- Great is thy faithfulness

Service

Welcome

As people arrive, invite them to water the seeds as a sign of their prayer.

Introduction

Our service today is about God's generosity. God loves to give – and in our first story, he gives food to hungry people. This is what happened.

Storytelling 1

Gather people around you; spread out the sand and the stones.

This is the desert. It is a hot, barren place. Water doesn't last long.

Sprinkle some water from the watering can and watch as the sand absorbs it.

Nothing much grows here.

Scatter a few dry twigs.

There is not much to eat. Moses led God's people through this wilderness. They had escaped from slavery in Egypt, and at first they were overjoyed to be free. But after six weeks in the desert, they began to complain.

'At least when we were slaves, we had enough to eat!'

'We could have died in Egypt with full bellies – instead, Moses has brought us out here to starve!'

God heard his people's complaints. He said to Moses, 'Tell your people, "In the evening I will give you meat, and in the morning I will rain bread from heaven – as much as you can eat. Then you will know that I am the Lord your God."'

That evening, a flock of quails settled around the people's tents. The little birds were easy to catch and that night, everyone ate delicious roast quail for supper.

Produce the plate of chicken pieces.

The next morning, God's people woke up to find their camp was white with dew. When the dew lifted, the desert was covered in something pale and flaky: what on earth was it?

Produce the plate of puff pastry pieces with honey.

It tasted like wafers made with honey and the people called it 'manna'. This was the 'bread from heaven' which God sent every night.

Once God had fed his people, he gave Moses the power to make streams of fresh water spring from the rocks.

Produce the jug of water and pour some into a glass.

The people of God had everything they needed and for the next forty years, they lived in the wilderness.

Activity

Let's eat some of this wilderness food: the roast quail and the bread from heaven, washed down with fresh water.

Allow plenty of time for everyone to share the food and water. While you eat, you may like to explain that nobody really knows what manna was, except that it was white 'like coriander seed', it tasted like wafers made with honey and it went bad quickly. Quail is a game bird that tastes a bit like pheasant – a stronger flavour than chicken.

How would we like to live on this for forty years? *(Invite responses.)*

Music

Guide me, O thou great Redeemer

Storytelling 2

Our second story today is one which Jesus told to describe God's generosity and his way of doing things.[1] The story begins in the early morning, with a landowner in the marketplace. He is looking to hire workers for his vineyard.

1. Keith White in *Through the eyes of a child*, ed. Anne Richards and Peter Privett, Church House Publishing 2009, p.48.

The Storyteller stands at the front holding the large clock. It reads 7 o'clock.

Landowner: Grape-pickers wanted! Anyone want a day's work picking grapes?

First worker: I do! How much do you pay?

Landowner: The usual – forty pounds for the day.

First worker: Deal. *(They shake hands.)* Where do I start?

Landowner: Here's a basket, there's the vineyard – now get picking.

'The vineyard' runs the length of the aisle. The workers should mime picking grapes, and move further up the aisle as each new worker joins. Encourage plenty of acting – sweating, sore backs, heavy baskets and so on!

The Storyteller shows the clock: it reads 9 o'clock.

First worker: I've been working for over two hours – I'm ready for breakfast!

Landowner: Grape-pickers wanted! Anyone else want a day's work picking grapes?

Second worker: I do! How much do you pay?

Landowner: I'll pay you a good wage. Here's a basket, there's the vineyard – now get picking.

The Storyteller shows the clock: it reads 12 o'clock.

First worker: We've been working for hours.

Second worker: It must be nearly lunchtime.

Landowner: Grape-pickers wanted! Anyone else want work picking grapes?

The third worker raises his/her hand.

Landowner: Here: basket, vineyard – you know what to do.

First worker: It's so hot!

Second worker: There's no shade!

Third worker: These baskets are really heavy!

The Storyteller shows the clock: it reads 3 o'clock.

Landowner: Grape-pickers wanted! Anyone else want work picking grapes?

The fourth worker raises his/her hand. The landowner points in the direction of the other workers and the fourth worker joins in the picking.

The Storyteller shows the clock: it reads 5 o'clock.

Landowner — *(To the fifth worker, who is lounging about.)* Have you been here all day doing nothing?

Fifth worker — *(Shrugs)* Nobody hired me.

Landowner — Well I'm hiring you now. Go and help in my vineyard.

The Storyteller shows the clock: it reads 7 o'clock.

Landowner — Job done! Now it's pay-time. Those who arrived last, line up first. *(Handing money to each in turn)* £40 for you.

Fifth worker — Great! Thanks!

Landowner — £40 for you.

Fourth worker — Thanks!

Landowner — £40 for you.

Third worker — Er – thank you.

Landowner — £40 for you.

Second worker — What?

Landowner — And £40 for you.

First worker — That's not fair! We slogged away all day in the heat, and we did most of the work!

Second worker — Yeah – we should get more than them!

Landowner — Did you agree to work for £40, or not?

First worker — Well yes, but –

Landowner — Then I have treated you fairly. I have chosen to give the last worker the same as I gave you. Am I not allowed to do what I want with my own money? Or are you envious because I am generous?

Music

Father welcomes all his children

Exploring

Let's line up all our characters. I wonder how we would feel if we were them?

Line up your actors and invite responses.

Let's begin with the one who started work at dawn and slaved away all day in the heat. How do you think this worker felt when they were paid?

How about the worker who lazed around in the market-place all day and turned up to start work at teatime? How do you think they felt about their pay?

Invite responses.

Let's think about the landowner. I wonder why he decided to pay all these workers the same? Do you think it was fair? Do you think it was a good thing to do?

Invite responses.

Jesus said that the landowner in the story is like God. His story challenges us because it shakes up our idea of what is fair and right – we absolutely sympathise with the grumpy pair who worked all day and felt they deserved more than those who turned up at the last minute. But in fact this story shows us something wonderful about God: he is not restricted by human rules about who deserves what, and how much; he is purely and simply generous. He gives to all of us in abundance, and his goodness is more than any of us could possibly deserve. Our first story today reminded us that God even fed an entire nation in the desert for forty years! In spite of their grumbling and lack of faith, God's people received as much food as they could eat.

So if God's goodness cannot be earned or deserved, what are we to do? Think of these workers, lining up to receive their wages *(cup your hands like a bowl).* Remember the people in the wilderness without food or water, who were completely dependent on the bread which God provided. We simply need to open our hands and receive whatever God wants to give us.

Prayer action

Cup your hands like a bowl.

We are going to use this gesture in our prayers today. Simply hold out your hands like an empty bowl and rest quietly in God's presence, waiting for whatever he may give.

All sit or kneel with cupped hands. Pause for a moment's silence.

Whatever we need, whatever we pray for in the lives of others, may we look to the Lord.

Begin the Taizé chant: In the Lord I'll be ever thankful. Repeat several times, growing louder and then softer, before settling into silence.

Generous Lord,
may we always hold open a space in our lives
so that you might fill it with your abundant grace.
Amen.

Conclusion

God of all goodness,
whatever our needs, let us look to you.
May your grace run in the dry places like a river[2]
and your goodness flow through our lives.
Amen.

Give notices, announce the next all-age service and invite everyone to the feast.

Note: place the tray of grass seeds in a sunny spot and keep well watered.

2. From Psalm 105:41.

The wise and foolish bridesmaids

Theme	Keeping our 'lamps' burning
Scripture	Matthew 25:1–13

Running order	Total: 50 minutes
Welcome	Balloon prayers *(5 minutes)*
Introduction	Opening the theme
Storytelling	Retelling the parable of the wise and foolish bridesmaids – with visual aids *(5 minutes)*
Music	This little light of mine *(5 minutes)*
Exploring	How can we keep our light shining? Stations and discussion *(10 minutes)*
Music	Jesus bids us shine *(5 minutes)*
Activity	Making little lamps *(15 minutes)*
Prayer action	Little lights – active prayer *(5 minutes)*
Conclusion	Closing prayer and invitation

Resources

- Balloons and a balloon pump
- Lengths of ribbon or string
- Scissors
- Permanent-marker pens
- A fixture near the altar onto which balloons may be tied (have one or two already on there)
- Three traditional terracotta oil lamps with wicks *or* three large candles, plus a picture of an oil lamp *(see appendix)*
- Matches and tapers
- For the Storytelling: a table with one lit lamp or large candle and a taper, and *either* a pair of scissors, a bottle of olive oil and the other two lamps *or* the remaining two large candles, unlit
- Music and words
- Two stations:
  - Several lit lamps and lanterns of different kinds (traditional and modern), candles and torches; a sign saying, 'What is our lamp?'
  - Several lamps and lanterns which have gone out, blown-out candles and torches with failing batteries; a sign saying, 'What happens when the lamp burns out?'
- Lots of tea-lights
- A quantity of Model Magic, clay or salt dough *(see appendix for The Maker's mark)*

Leaders

Minimum: 1

- Leader

Optimum: 6

- Leader *(Introduction and Conclusion)*
- Storyteller
- Music Leader
- Explorer
- Activity Leader
- Prayer Leader

Suggestions for additional music

- O for a closer walk with God
- We are marching

Service

Welcome

As people arrive, invite them to blow up a balloon and write or draw their prayer on it, then tie it with ribbon and add it to the bunch by the altar.

Introduction

Today's service is about light. In Jesus' time, people made the most of daylight. Housewives, farmers, builders and carpenters worked hard to finish their day's work before sunset. Travellers left the roads as night fell and found somewhere to stay for the night. When the sun went down, darkness took over.

Turn out the lights.

No streetlamps, no electric light. If you needed light in your home, you used one of these *(show the oil lamp/ picture)*: a simple pottery lamp, with a wick like a candle and a hole so that you could fill it up with olive oil.

Fill up a lamp and light it, or light a large candle.

To keep this lamp burning, you needed to top it up regularly with more oil, otherwise it would burn out. Our story today involves a night-time wedding party and lots of lamps like this. In Jesus' time, weddings began with an evening procession from the bride's home. Bridesmaids accompanied the bride and groom and held lamps to light their way through the night.

Storytelling

Tell this story in as dark a church as possible. Have a table beside you with the lit lamp or candle and a taper, and either a pair of scissors, a bottle of olive oil and two more lamps, or two more large candles, unlit.

It was sunset. The beautiful bride and her ten bridesmaids gathered together to wait for the bridegroom to come and lead them all to the wedding. Five of the bridesmaids lit their lamps and sat down to wait. *(Light the first lamp/candle.)*

'What if we run out of oil?' asked one.

'Oh, we won't – he's bound to be here soon,' said another.

But the bridegroom didn't come. The other five bridesmaids lit their lamps, too. *(Light the second lamp/candle.)*

'I brought some spare oil, just in case,' said one.

'We are the bridesmaids, after all,' said another. 'It's our job to be ready and waiting. I've brought some spare oil with me, too.'

Still the bridegroom didn't come. Eventually, the bride and her bridesmaids fell asleep with the lamps still burning. At midnight, there was a shout.

'HE'S HERE! THE BRIDEGROOM'S HERE!' Suddenly all the bridesmaids were up, straightening their dresses and bustling about, getting ready to go out into the night. They reached for their lamps and saw that they had almost gone out.

Blow out both lamps/candles.

The first five bridesmaids panicked. 'Oh no! Our lamps are going out! Can you let us have some of your spare oil?' But the five bridesmaids who had come prepared didn't have enough to share, so the others rushed off to the village to find some more oil.

The five who were left trimmed their wicks *(trim the wick of one lamp/candle),* refilled their lamps with oil *(refill one lamp and relight it/light the candle)* and joined the wedding party. They set off through the night, lighting the path for the bride and groom.

Walk forwards, holding the lamp/candle high.

They all went into the wedding feast and shut the door. Later, the other five bridesmaids rushed up and found the door closed. And no matter how loudly they shouted, no one came to let them in.

Pause and then turn on the lights.

Music This little light of mine

Exploring There is a lot to think about in today's story about the wise and foolish bridesmaids. Jesus told it as a way of describing God's kingdom, so he expected his listeners to think about how the story might apply to them and their own lives. Let's begin by looking at the lamps in the story: the lamps that burned out, which belonged to the foolish bridesmaids, and the lamps that carried on burning brightly, which belonged to the wise bridesmaids. Take some time now to visit these two stations and think about the questions which you find there.

Introduce the two tables: the first has lots of lit lamps, candles and torches, and a sign saying, 'What is our lamp?' The second has lamps which have gone out, blown-out candles and torches with failing batteries, and a sign saying, 'What happens when the lamp burns out?' Allow plenty of time for people to visit the stations, think and discuss, then invite responses. Try to find value in every answer.

The bridesmaids had to wait for the bridegroom and be ready to accompany him to the wedding feast. That was their job. They were not just guests who had come along for a party: their whole purpose in being there was to follow the bridegroom through the dark and join him at the feast.

Jesus' parable suggests that he is the bridegroom and we are the bridesmaids. Our job is to follow him in a confusing, uncertain world, like bridesmaids in the dark. We need to be prepared for this journey: we need to keep our lamps burning brightly. But how? What might the lamps in the story represent for us? And how do we keep them alight?

Show the first lamp/candle.

Our lamp could be our faith: sometimes it burns brightly and sometimes it grows dim. The wise bridesmaids kept their lamps topped up with oil, and we can keep our faith burning brightly if we attend to it and make sure it doesn't run out of fuel. We can pray, get to know the Bible better and try to show others what God's love is like. All these things can help our faith burn brighter.

Show the second lamp/candle.

Our lamp could be our spirit. The Bible says, 'The human spirit is the lamp of the Lord'[1] – and when God's Holy Spirit inspires us, he makes our lamp burn extra brightly, making us feel fired up and full of energy. We should always be ready for the Holy Spirit to refresh us, just as the wise bridesmaids were ready to fill up their lamps with extra oil.

Show the third lamp/candle.

Keeping our lamp burning is also about being wise. The foolish bridesmaids didn't pay attention to what was really important, which was their job of being ready to accompany the bridegroom. Their lamps went out, they ran out of oil, they were left in the dark and shut out of the feast. If we don't pay attention to what is important in our lives, then we will find that we miss out on the best that life has to offer. Being wise means making the right choices and paying attention to what is most important. It means entering into a relationship with God and becoming the best people we can be – in other words, the people God wants us to be. No one else can do this for us; remember that the wise bridesmaids didn't share the oil they had brought for their lamps. We have to choose for ourselves, and if we concentrate on following Jesus, he will lead us towards that close relationship with God which can be ours in life and even after death – and that happiness is greater than a hundred wedding feasts.

Music Jesus bids us shine

Activity As a reminder of our theme today, we will make our own lamps like the ones used in our story. Instead of oil and a wick, we will use a tea-light to make the light which our lamp carries.

Using either a traditional lamp or a picture of one as a model, demonstrate how to shape the clay around the tea-light to form a holder and a spout. Then invite everyone to have a go and allow plenty of time for people to make their lamps.

1. Proverbs 20:27.

Take these lamps home and leave them to dry for about a day. Once they are dry, they are easy to decorate with felt-tip pens or paint.

Prayer action

Turn out the lights.

Let's use our lamps in our prayers today. As we light them, we will rest in God's presence and reflect on what this light means to each of us. Let's ask God how each of us might let our light shine.

Move through the church, lighting lamps as you go. Pause once all the lamps are lit.

Lord of light,
may we be beacons of shining faith
and radiant wisdom.
May our lives blaze brightly with your Spirit's fire.
Amen.

Conclusion

Lord Jesus,
as we go out into the world,
may we always be prepared to follow you.
Amen.

Give notices, announce the next all-age service and invite everyone to the feast.

Special occasions

Crib Service

Theme	Celebrating Christmas
Scripture	Luke 1:78, 79

Running order	Total: 50 minutes
Welcome	Lighting all four Advent Candles and then a votive candle each *(5 minutes)*
Introduction	Opening the theme
Activity	Hand-made Nativity scene – dressing up *(5 minutes)*
Music	Once in royal David's city *(5 minutes)*
Storytelling	Dramatised reading of *Jesus' Christmas Party* by Nicholas Allan *(10 minutes)*
Music	*(Around the crib)* The Virgin Mary had a baby boy *(5 minutes)*
Exploring	Why is Christmas special? *(5 minutes)*
Music	Hark, the herald-angels sing *(5 minutes)*
Prayer action	Hand-made prayers – interactive thanksgiving *(5 minutes)*
Music	O come, all ye faithful *(5 minutes)*
Conclusion	Closing prayer and invitation

Resources

- Advent wreath, votive candles and matches
- A copy of *Jesus' Christmas Party* by Nicholas Allan *(see appendix)*
- Basic standby Nativity costumes:
  - Brown fabric (e.g. scarf/shawl) for Joseph/shepherds
  - Some sheepskin/fur for shepherds
  - Blue/white fabric for Mary
  - A manger/wooden crate
  - Shiny or velvety cloaks for kings
  - Three cardboard crowns
  - Pieces of white sheet
  - Some tinsel haloes
- Props:
  - A toy lamb
  - Some hay
  - Two blankets and a smaller blanket
  - A baby Jesus doll
  - A large shiny star on a long stick
- A screen in front of the Nativity scene *(perhaps a large blanket held by two adults)*
- Music and words
- A cloth or a tray for the finished prayers to lie on (the oil and salt in the dough could damage altar linen)
- Lots of salt dough *(see recipe in appendix)*
- Wet wipes for hands

Leaders

Minimum: 2

- Leader
- Dresser/helper

Optimum: 7+

- Leader
- Activity Leader
- Dresser(s)/helper(s)
- Storyteller
- Music Leader
- Explorer
- Prayer Leader

Suggestions for additional music

- Away in a manger
- Ding dong, merrily on high

Service

Welcome

Light all four Advent Candles and then a votive candle each.

Introduction

Welcome to our crib service today. Who is excited about Christmas? Who has got lots of presents under their Christmas tree? Today we'll be exploring why Christmas is so special – and why our presents remind us of 'the reason for the season'.

Activity

No crib service can happen without a bit of dressing up, and that is what we are going to begin with today – but we need everyone's help. We couldn't afford any special costumes, so we thought that with all these creative, artistic people here we could manage to make some costumes ourselves. First we need a Mary and a Joseph. *(Invite volunteers.)*

Now we need something plain and brown for Joseph to wear *(invite people to lend a scarf, a shawl etc.)* and something blue for Mary – and perhaps something white as well. *(Take the donated items and dress Mary and Joseph. Repeat this procedure for each of the following, using items lent by the congregation or previously planted by you around the church, for children to run and find.)*

Now we need a manger and some hay – can anyone find anything that might do?

Now we need our shepherds – and something woolly and warm for them to wear. And is there a little lamb anywhere?

Now we need three kings – does anyone have anything shiny or velvety which might be fit for a king to wear? I wonder if there are any crowns hidden anywhere?

And of course we need some angels – and something white and sparkly for them to wear . . .

Last of all, we need the big star which shone over the place where Jesus was born. Can anyone see a really big, shiny star we could use?

I think that is everything we need for our handmade Nativity scene: in a moment, we'd like you all to help us tell our story today.[1]

During the hymn, gather all your Nativity actors at the back of the church and draw up the screen at the front. Place the manger behind the screen with the baby Jesus in it. Have an adult helper behind the screen ready to help set up the Nativity scene as the actors arrive, and to hold up the star at the appropriate moment.

Music Once in royal David's city

Storytelling Dramatised reading of *Jesus' Christmas Party* by Nicholas Allan.

Note: All speeches may be spoken by the Narrator, or by confident (and audible!) actors.

You will need helpers here to usher your volunteer actors in the right direction. The Narrator reads the story aloud and the actors arrive in turn by coming down the aisle and 'knocking' on the door by the first pew. They then disappear 'round the back' by going behind the screen, where they take up their positions around the crib. At the point where the bright light wakes the innkeeper up, the helper behind the screen should raise the star above it. The chorus of singing may be provided by the angels themselves, or by a quick burst of a recording of the 'Hallelujah Chorus' from Handel's Messiah. *When the Innkeeper storms 'round the back', remove the screen to reveal the Nativity scene. When he wakes up all the guests at the inn, he should encourage everyone to get out of their seats and gather around the crib at the front.*

Music *(Sung around the crib)* The Virgin Mary had a baby boy

Exploring So we told today's story ourselves. We told it with our handmade costumes and with our bodies, and we all became part of the story at the end when we joined in the celebrations in the stable.

Who here has made something themselves for Christmas? Who has made a cake or mince pies? Who has

1. I am indebted to the team at St John's, Ivybridge for this idea of improvised borrowing and dressing-up in the crib service.

made their own Christmas cards? Who has given some home-made presents? When we give someone a hand-made present, it shows them how much we love them. Those presents remind us of the most special thing about Christmas. That baby in the stable was God's present to all of us, the most special present he could give – the gift of himself. On that first Christmas Day, God was born as a human being called Jesus – a human being who was going to live and die for us. On that first Christmas Day, he showed us how much he really loves us.

And what difference does God's love make to us? Well – remember the grumpy innkeeper in our story? In the book called *Jesus' Christmas Party*, the innkeeper is drawn with a big black cloud over his head. The angrier he gets, the bigger the shadow of his black cloud. Today's Bible reading looks towards Jesus' birth and talks about what it means to all of us who – for whatever reason – feel as if we are living with a dark cloud over us.

> By the tender mercy of our God,
> the dawn from on high will break upon us,
> to give light to those who sit in darkness and in the shadow of death,
> to guide our feet into the way of peace.

When the innkeeper saw the baby Jesus, the black cloud disappeared. Jesus had shown him the light of God's love, which is a light for all of us, too. *That* is why we celebrate Christmas!

Music

Hark, the herald-angels sing

Prayer action

When God became one of us on that first Christmas day, he didn't make sure he had a specially-built palace. He was born as an ordinary baby and made do with what there was: he slept in an animals' feeding trough instead of a cradle. When we say our prayers, they don't have to be especially fine and grand, either. We can make our prayers out of everyday things. Today, we're not even going to use words for our prayers. We're going to make them out of dough. These will be our handmade prayers.

Invite everyone to take a dumpling-sized piece of dough.

Hold your dough and let your hands play with it. As you do so, think of all the special presents you have been given – not just for birthdays and Christmas, but those gifts which are so great and precious that we can never say a big enough 'thank you'. Think of the life you have, the people you love, the friendships you share and the beautiful world we live in. Think of God who made it all and the love he showed us by giving us his son, Jesus. Think of something or someone you'd like to thank God for and make your dough into a shape for your prayer. If you want to thank God for someone you love, you might make a heart shape. You might make a shape that only you and God will understand. Whatever it is, take some time now to make your handmade prayers.

As people finish their prayers, invite them to bring the dough shapes up to the altar. If lots of people are milling around and looking at the finished shapes, you may like to invite them to gather round the prayers on the altar as they are offered to God.

Loving Father,
we offer you these handmade prayers
and thank you for all the good things we have,
in the name of Jesus
who gave himself to us
for our sake.
Amen.

Music O come, all ye faithful

Conclusion May God bless us all this Christmas.
May our hearts and homes be places of peace and joy,
love and hospitality,
generosity and thankfulness.
In Jesus' name,
Amen.

Don't forget to return all borrowed items of clothing to their owners! Then give notices, announce the next all-age service and invite everyone to the Christmas feast.

Mothering Sunday

Theme	A mother's love
Scripture	Colossians 3:12–17

Running order	Total: 50 minutes
Welcome and introduction	Opening the theme
Activity and prayer	Patchwork of prayer *(10 minutes)*
Storytelling	*No Matter What* by Debi Gliori *(7 minutes)*
Music	For the beauty of the earth *(5 minutes)*
Exploring	What is a mother's love like? *(8 minutes)*
Music	Lord of all hopefulness *(5 minutes)*
Gift-giving and prayer	Handing out posies and lighting candles *(10 minutes)*
Music	He's got the whole world in his hand *(5 minutes)*
Conclusion	Closing prayer and invitation

Resources

- A copy of *No Matter What* by Debi Gliori *(see appendix)*
- Music and words
- Lots of small squares of paper in different colours. The blocks of paper sold as telephone memo pads are good for this
- Felt-tip pens in a variety of colours
- Some reels of Sellotape and several pairs of scissors
- A sari or very long piece of material *(see appendix)*
- A nest of cushions on the floor
- Posies of spring flowers
- Lots of votive candles, each placed in a circle of yellow card which is shaped like daffodil petals *(see appendix)*
- Matches and tapers

Leaders

Minimum: 1

- Leader (and solo Storyteller)

Optimum: 8+

- Leader *(Introduction and Conclusion)*
- Storytellers x 3
- Music Leader(s)
- Explorer
- Activity / Prayer Leader
- Gift-giving / Prayer Leader

Suggestions for additional music

- Do not be afraid
- Jesus, good above all other

Service

Welcome and introduction

You may like to invite those who arrive early to make a start on the patchwork of prayer, before introducing it as the opening part of the service.

Today is Mothering Sunday. We all come here with our own particular feelings about our mothers – and those feelings are as varied as we are. We will begin today with an activity to bring all those feelings to God: we are going to make a Mothering Sunday patchwork of prayer.

Activity and prayer

First of all, take one of these little squares of paper. Then pick a coloured pen and write or draw your own prayers for today – prayers for yourself, or for others who need your prayer. Fill your square with as much writing or drawing as you would like. When you have covered your prayer square, bring it up to the altar and lay it face down with all the others to make a patchwork of prayer.

Allow enough time for everyone to fill their square and bring it to the front. Keeping the squares face down, the leader and/or the helpers should assemble them into a rectangle. Tape the squares to each other as they arrive, with no spaces in between. When the last prayers have been attached, invite everyone to return to their seats and lift the sheet of prayers to show it the right way round. It should look like a small patchwork quilt, each square densely covered with coloured words or pictures. Then say:

Let us pray.
Mothering God,
we offer you this, our patchwork of prayer,
as varied and unique as the people who made it.
We pray for the mothers we have,
the mothers we have lost,
the mothers we are and
the mothers we would like to be,
in Jesus' name.
Amen.

Storytelling

No Matter What by Debi Gliori.

Gather all the children present at the front so that they are close to the storyteller(s) and can see the pictures. The story could be read by one person, but ideally there should be three readers. The Storyteller reads the narrative parts and shows the colourful pictures. Before the service, the people reading the parts of Small and Large should write out their own (short) parts so that they can read from their own scripts.

Music

For the beauty of the earth

Exploring

'I'll always love you, no matter what.' What a wonderful sort of love that is. The mother in our story loved her grumpy child like this, and promised to carry on loving him, whatever he turned into. It is how Mary loved her son, Jesus, however much the path God chose for him made her worried and unhappy. And most important of all, it is how God loves us: even when we get things wrong again and again, even when we turn away from him and forget him, his love never lets go.

Today I'd like to show you a picture of what this sort of love is like. For this, I'll need two helpers to be my models: children, would one of you like to volunteer yourself and your mum?

Bring your volunteers to the front.

Once there was a mother in India who always wore a sari, like this. It was a very, very long piece of material which she wore as a kind of dress by folding and winding it around herself, like this.

Dress your volunteer mum in the sari (see appendix).

This mum had a *son/daughter [depending on the volunteer]* who loved a cuddle.

Encourage the child to cuddle his/her mum.

And, like a lot of children, *he/she* liked to keep hold of a bit of mum's clothes.

Give the child the trailing end of the sari to hold.

Sometimes, the cuddle was so long and snuggly that the child fell asleep.

Ask the child to close his/her eyes.

When that happened, *his/her* mum didn't make *him/her* let go. Very gently, she laid her child down and began to tuck *him/her* up with her sari.

She lays the child down on the cushions and you help her to unwind the sari gradually as she tucks up the sleeping child.

She twisted and turned until the whole length of the sari was completely unwound, so that she could tuck her child up with it while *he/she* slept. And when the child woke up, *he/she* felt as if *his/her* mum had never left *him/her*, because her sari had stayed with *him/her* all the time.

Ask your helpers to hold one end of the sari as you walk down the aisle holding the other end, unwinding it as you talk.

This is what God's love is like. It wraps itself around us all and unwinds endlessly, giving everything, so that wherever we are and whatever we do, we know that we are still enfolded in his love, like the sleeping child snuggled in his/her mum's sari. Remember that this is how we should try to love each other, too. This is what the Bible says:

> Clothe yourselves with compassion, kindness, humility, meekness, and patience. Bear with one another and, if anyone has a complaint against another, forgive each other; just as the Lord has forgiven you, so you also must forgive. Above all, clothe yourselves with love, which binds everything together in perfect harmony.

We should all 'clothe ourselves with love', rather like this long, unwinding sari which wraps around those we love and binds them to us.

Music Lord of all hopefulness

Gift-giving and prayer

Mothering Sunday is often a time for presents and flowers, so here we have these beautiful posies for all the mums who are with us today. Please come forward and take one to give to your mum, or to a mum you know.

Hand out the posies.

The rest of us will not go home empty-handed. We all have a Mothering Sunday candle to take home, to remind us that God loves us like a mother as well as a father.

Light your own candle and then move through the church, lighting candles as you go. As you do so, say:

As we light our candles, let's have a moment of silence in which to bring our own prayers before God. *(Pause.)*
God, our Mother and Father in heaven,
guard us, guide us, keep us, feed us[1]
now and always,
no matter what.
Amen.

Blow out the candles.

Music He's got the whole world in his hand

Conclusion

As we go our own ways,
may God our Mother always watch over us, her children.
Amen.

Give notices, announce the next all-age service and invite everyone to the feast.

1. J. Edmeston (1791-1867) 'Lead us, heavenly Father, lead us'.

Harvest Festival

Abundant gifts*

Theme	Receiving and sharing God's goodness
Scripture	Luke 12:22–30

Running order	Total: 50 minutes
Welcome	Offering Harvest gifts *(5 minutes)*
Music	We plough the fields and scatter *(5 minutes)*
Introduction	Opening the theme
Exploring 1	What can't we do without? Active brainstorm *(5 minutes)*
Storytelling	Reading Jesus' words in Luke 12:22–30 *(5 minutes)*
Activity	Sensory exploration of the things we need *(10 minutes)*
Music	Thank you, Lord *(5 minutes)*
Exploring 2	What do we do with what we have been given? *(5 minutes)*
Prayer action	Fruits of the earth – edible thanksgiving *(5 minutes)*
Music	Who put the colours in the rainbow? *(5 minutes)*
Conclusion	Closing prayer and invitation

* Note: This service could be followed by a Parish Harvest Feast.

Resources

- Catalogues and advertising magazines (such as those produced by supermarkets)
- Two sheets of lining paper, labelled 'Like' and 'Need'
- Scissors
- Sellotape
- Music and words
- Around the church: five different tables, one for each of the senses *(see appendix)*
- Three signs: 'STOP WORRYING', 'SHARE' and 'GIVE THANKS'
- Five bowls containing the following: sunflower seeds; carrot sticks; herbs and salad leaves; raisins and chopped apple; Rice Krispies and puffed wheat

Leaders

Minimum: 1

- Leader

Optimum: 6

- Leader *(Introduction and Conclusion)*
- Music Leader
- Explorer
- Storyteller
- Activity Leader
- Prayer Leader

Suggestions for additional music

- God, whose farm is all creation
- This world you have made

Service

Welcome

As people arrive, invite them to bring forward their gifts of harvest produce and arrange them around the altar.

Music

We plough the fields and scatter

Introduction

Today is our Harvest Festival. In the days before supermarkets, when people grew all their own food, a good harvest meant that they were not going to starve during the winter. They had all the food they needed to feed their families until more crops grew in the spring. A plentiful harvest, safely gathered in, was definitely a good excuse for a party. These days, we still celebrate harvest to give thanks for all the good things we have, and to remember those who do not have enough.

Exploring 1

Stand in front of the tables with catalogues and advertising magazines and the two sheets of lining paper, labelled 'Like' and 'Need'.

Our ancestors needed a good harvest in order to live, and we are going to begin today by thinking about what we need. Shops are very good at telling us what we must have, what is 'essential'. Let's have a look at some of these catalogues and adverts now and ask ourselves, 'What would I like to have?' and 'What do I really need?' Cut out as many pictures as you can and stick them onto these two big sheets of paper – one for the things we need, the other for the things we'd like.

Allow plenty of time for people to choose their pictures and stick them on, then hold up the two sheets and invite people to explain their choices.

Jesus had something to say about the things we need, and the things we spend our time wanting and worrying about.

Storytelling

Read Jesus' words in Luke 12:22–30.

Activity

'Don't worry,' said Jesus. 'Your Father knows what you need.' He reminds us that God has already given us an abundance of good things to use and enjoy. Today we are going to explore some of those gifts. Around the church are five different tables, one for each of the senses. Take some time to visit each one and touch, taste, smell, hear or look at whatever you find there. Ask yourself, 'Why has God given us this? Why do we need it?'

Allow plenty of time for people to visit each station.

Music Thank you, Lord

Exploring 2 Let's think about some of the things God has given us which we have been exploring today. Why do we need them?

Invite answers, valuing all contributions.

All these good things are wonderful to have and appreciate, but that's not all. These gifts require a response from us. The first thing to do, says Jesus, is STOP WORRYING *(hold up the sign or invite a child to hold it for you)* – in other words, trust in God, because he knows what we need. This is really difficult, especially when times are hard, but Jesus is right: worrying does not gain us anything – not an extra penny, nor a single extra hour of life. All worrying does is rob us of the enjoyment of what we have. If we try to appreciate all the wonderful things God has given us in creation, we might start to trust that God is unbelievably generous and will provide for us. We may not get all the things we *want*, but God knows what we really *need*.

The second thing to do is SHARE *(hold up the sign)*. All these good gifts are not ours to keep and hoard, but to share with those who have less than us. That is why we have brought harvest offerings today: the food we have given will be shared with those in our community who need it most. This is one of the ways in which God provides for people's needs – not by making things appear out of thin air, but by using us as his hands on earth, to take the natural resources we have been given and share them out.

The third thing God's gifts tell us to do is GIVE THANKS *(hold up the sign)*. Before we eat, when we share and whenever we can, we need to remember that all good things come from God. Our prayers today are edible prayers of thanksgiving.

Prayer action

Harvest has traditionally been celebrated with a feast. In our prayers today, we will have a feast to remind ourselves of the good things we have received from this fertile earth that God gave us. Please take and eat a little of whatever you like and thank God in your heart for it.

If there are lots of people, stay seated and pass round three or four bowls of each foodstuff. Otherwise, gather in a circle and pass round a bowl of each foodstuff as you say:

Creator God,
thank you for the fruits of the earth:
for the seeds, *(pass round the sunflower seeds)*
for the roots, *(pass round the carrot sticks)*
for the green leaves, *(pass round the herbs and salad leaves)*
for the fruit *(pass round the raisins and chopped apple)*
and for the grain *(pass round the Rice Krispies and puffed wheat).*
Thank you for the abundance of your gifts;
thank you for the human hands which help them grow;
thank you for the skills that make them into good things to eat.
Amen.

Music

Who put the colours in the rainbow?

Conclusion

Lord of growth and harvest,
you crown the year with your goodness,
and your paths overflow with plenty.[1]
May we remember the hungry,
may we share this goodness with all
and may we be truly thankful.
Amen.

Give notices, announce the next all-age service and invite everyone to the harvest feast.

1. Psalm 65:11.

One for All

All Saints' Day

Blessed

Theme	The Saints and the Beatitudes
Scripture	Matthew 5:1–12

Running order	Total: 50 minutes
Welcome	Halo of light – lighting a circle of candles *(5 minutes)*
Introduction	Opening the theme
Activity	Discovering the saints – interactive 'information stations' *(15 minutes)*
Music	O when the saints go marching in *(5 minutes)*
Storytelling	Reading the Beatitudes with visual aids *(5 minutes)*
Exploring	Who is blessed? Hot-seating the listeners to the Sermon on the Mount *(10 minutes)*
Music	Bind us together, Lord *(5 minutes)*
Prayer action	Prayer bunting – creative intercessions *(5 minutes)*
Conclusion	Closing prayer and invitation

Resources

- A double row of tea-lights arranged in a circle around the Paschal candle or other large candle
- Matches and tapers
- A piece of board for the tea-lights to stand on
- 'Information stations' about the saints *(see appendix)*
- Music and words
- 8 signs: 'POOR IN SPIRIT', 'MOURNER', 'MEEK', 'HUNGRY AND THIRSTY FOR RIGHTEOUSNESS', 'MERCIFUL', 'PURE IN HEART', 'PEACEMAKER', 'PERSECUTED FOR FOLLOWING JESUS'
- 8 white robes or tunics
- A baby doll wrapped in blankets
- A long piece of ribbon or bias binding
- Lots of coloured triangles of paper or card
- A stapler or two, plus spare staples
- Pens and pencils

Leaders

Minimum: 10

- Leader
- ***Jesus***
- ***Eight people***

Optimum: 15

- Leader *(Introduction and Conclusion)*
- Activity Leader
- Storyteller
- ***Jesus***, wearing white
- Explorer
- Cast
  Eight people, dressed in ordinary clothes
- Music Leader
- Prayer Leader

Suggestions for additional music

- For all the saints
- Let saints on earth in concert sing

Service

Welcome

As people arrive, invite them to light one of the tea-lights around the Paschal candle as a sign of their prayer.

Introduction

Today we celebrate the festival of All Saints. This is sometimes called All Hallows – which is why the night before is called All Hallows' Eve – or Hallowe'en. But who are the saints we celebrate today? We will begin our service by finding out a little more about some of them.

Activity

Around the church are three interactive 'information stations' where there are things to read, look at, explore and do to help us learn more about the saints. Take your time to visit each station and see what you discover there.

Allow plenty of time for people to visit the stations. You may like to invite responses afterwards.

Music

O when the saints go marching in

Storytelling

We honour the saints because they are men and women of faith who showed Christ-like qualities during their lives and are now close to him in heaven. With Jesus, they continue to pray for us. They are blessed children of God who are part of the Church family which unites all Christians, on earth and in heaven. In our story today, Jesus told his listeners in Galilee – and us – about some other people who would become blessed children of God. What kind of people do you think he said would be close to God in heaven, like the saints?

Invite the children to respond.

Let's hear what Jesus said.

The volunteers who hold up the signs may be anyone – not necessarily those who will speak their parts later on.

Jesus — Blessed are the poor in spirit, for theirs is the kingdom of heaven.

Invite someone to hold up the sign: 'POOR IN SPIRIT'.

Blessed are those who mourn, for they will be comforted.

Invite someone to hold up the sign: 'MOURNER'.

Blessed are the meek, for they will inherit the earth.

Invite someone to hold up the sign: 'MEEK'.

Blessed are those who hunger and thirst for righteousness, for they will be filled.

Invite someone to hold up the sign: 'HUNGRY AND THIRSTY FOR RIGHTEOUSNESS'.

Blessed are the merciful, for they will receive mercy.

Invite someone to hold up the sign: 'MERCIFUL'.

Blessed are the pure in heart, for they will see God.

Invite someone to hold up the sign: 'PURE IN HEART'.

Blessed are the peacemakers, for they will be called children of God.

Invite someone to hold up the sign: 'PEACEMAKER' .

Blessed are those who are persecuted for righteousness' sake, for theirs is the kingdom of heaven. Rejoice and be glad, for your reward is great in heaven, for in the same way they persecuted the prophets who were before you.

Invite someone to hold up the sign: 'PERSECUTED FOR FOLLOWING JESUS'.

Exploring

These are the people Jesus said were blessed. Many of them were a surprise to his listeners at the time. Let's hear what some of the people in that first congregation in Galilee might have thought.

The first person comes forward from his/her place in the congregation and stands at the front.

First person — I'm not important. I'm just a shepherd here in Galilee. I'm used to people being cleverer than me and whenever I hear preachers at the synagogue, they're always holier than me. I'm not worth much – but Jesus said that I'm blessed, and the kingdom of heaven is mine!

The first person puts on the white robe/tunic and holds up the sign, 'POOR IN SPIRIT'.

The second person comes forward from his/her place in the congregation and stands at the front.

Second person — I've been mourning my father's death. I have been following the pattern for mourning laid down by our forefathers. Since he died, I haven't cut my hair or listened to music; I haven't been to a single party. I miss him so much and at the moment, everything I do is coloured by the fact I am mourning him. But Jesus said I am blessed – and he promised me comfort.

The second person puts on the white robe and holds up the sign, 'MOURNER'.

The third person comes forward from his/her place in the congregation and stands at the front.

Third person — I'm not what you'd call a confident person. I've never wanted to put myself first. I'll let others win races or get prizes. I've always just taken what I was given and tried to make the best of it. But Jesus said I'm blessed! No one ever told me I was special before. Jesus said that the earth will belong to people like me.

The third person puts on the white robe and holds up the sign, 'MEEK'.

The fourth person comes forward from his/her place in the congregation and stands at the front.

Fourth person — I get so angry when I see how unfair the world is. I see rich people hogging all the wealth, and powerful people abusing their power. And I see masses and masses of poor people, struggling to survive with no safe homes, no clean water and not enough food. When will they have justice? When will life be fair for everyone? These questions gnaw at me like an empty belly – but Jesus said that I am blessed and that one day, I will be satisfied.

The fourth person puts on the white robe and holds up the sign, 'HUNGRY AND THIRSTY FOR RIGHTEOUSNESS'.

The fifth person comes forward from his/her place in the congregation and stands at the front.

Fifth person I caught the thief who was stealing from my vineyard last night. My grape harvest is just ready, and he was stripping it, vine by vine. He was afraid I was going to beat him to within an inch of his life – and I did think about it. But when I saw his face, and how scared he was, I felt sorry for him. I let him go, and gave him a job as a grape-picker this week. My brother thinks I should have killed him – but Jesus said that I'm blessed, and that God will have mercy on me.

The fifth person puts on the white robe and holds up the sign, 'MERCIFUL'.

The sixth person comes forward from his/her place in the congregation and stands at the front, holding a doll wrapped in a blanket.

Sixth person My daughter is tiny – she hasn't had a chance to get things wrong like the rest of us. She's so little that people often overlook her: her big brothers say, 'She's only a baby.' She's an innocent, trusting child – I wish more people could be like her. Jesus knows she's special, because he said that she is blessed and will see God.

The sixth person wraps the white robe around the child and holds up the sign, 'PURE IN HEART'.

The seventh person comes forward from his/her place in the congregation and stands at the front.

Seventh person I'm always caught in the middle when there's an argument in our family. Everyone else is trying to shout the loudest but I try and calm things down and stop the fight. I stay in the middle, acting as a go-between. The others always moan at me because they want me to take sides, but Jesus says I'm blessed and that I'm one of God's children.

The seventh person puts on the white robe and holds up the sign, 'PEACEMAKER'.

The eighth person comes forward from his/her place in the congregation and stands at the front.

Eighth person My family won't speak to me. They think I've gone mad because I said I want to follow Jesus wherever he goes in Galilee – I'll even follow him to Jerusalem! But my father doesn't believe that Jesus is anyone special, and he says he'll disown me if I leave my job as a fisherman. Some of my friends are ignoring me, too – but Jesus says I'm blessed, and told me that the kingdom of heaven belongs to people like me.

The eighth person puts on the white robe and holds up the sign, 'PERSECUTED FOR FOLLOWING JESUS'. All eight people should now be standing at the front in white robes, holding their signs.

Explorer — Look at all these people whom Jesus blessed. None of them felt like obvious candidates for a special place in heaven – but that is what Jesus promised them. He told them that they would share what Paul called 'the riches of his glorious inheritance among the saints.'[1] Let's pause for a moment to consider whether we too could share those riches. I wonder whether we are like any of these people? I wonder whether we could try to be more like them, for example by being peacemakers or showing mercy?

Pause for a short time.

Music

Bind us together, Lord

Prayer action

Today we celebrate all the saints. Christians everywhere are members of one body, one family, and the saints are part of that family, too. So when we pray, we do not pray alone: Jesus prays with us, the Church prays with us, and so do all the saints in heaven. For our prayers today, each of us will write or draw our prayer on one of these flags and attach it to this string to make bunting. As well as being a sign of celebration, this bunting is also a symbol of our praying church: it is a connected, continuing community of prayer.

Let us call to mind whatever it is we wish to bring to God in prayer today.

Pause for a moment, then start to write on your own flag and encourage others to do the same. Allow enough time for everyone to staple their flags to the ribbon, then stretch the bunting in front of the altar.

1. Ephesians 1:18.

Father God,
in communion with all the saints,
and with our brothers and sisters in Christ across the world,
we offer you these prayers today
in Jesus' name.
Amen.

Conclusion

Bring forward the board with the Paschal candle and its halo of tea-lights.

Like the saints, let us seek the Lord.
Look upon him and be radiant.
Living Lord,
may we trust in you and be blessed.[2]
Amen.

Give notices, announce the next all-age service and invite everyone to the feast.

2. From Psalm 34:1–10.

Remembrance Sunday

We will remember

Theme	Remembering the fallen; Christ's sacrifice
Scripture	Luke 22:7–20

Running order	Total: 60 minutes
Act of Remembrance	The laying of wreaths and the two minutes' silence *(15 minutes)*
Welcome	The National Anthem *(5 minutes)*
Introduction	Opening the theme
Storytelling	Retelling the story of the Last Supper with visual aids *(5 minutes)*
Music	And did those feet in ancient time *(5 minutes)*
Exploring	Why do we need to remember? Naming those we wish to remember on paper poppies *(5 minutes)*
Music	Eternal Father, strong to save *(5 minutes)*
Activity	Meditation montage – 'Brothers in arms' by Dire Straits *(10 minutes)*
Prayer action	Bitter-sweet rosemary – sensory prayers *(5 minutes)*
Music	Make me a channel of your peace *(5 minutes)*
Conclusion	Closing prayer and invitation

Resources

- Music and words
- Laptop, projector and screen
- Pictures of Passover food and a poppy field *(see appendix)*
- Unleavened bread: matzo or other flat bread
- Five earthenware goblets or glasses
- An earthenware or glass jug full of red grape juice
- A volunteer who is confident in using computers. This is an ideal job for a teenager or two. Their brief is to create the following:
  - A 'meditation montage' of images to accompany 'Brothers in Arms' by Dire Straits *(see appendix)*
- In every pew / row of seats, enough for one each of the following:
  - Paper poppies *(see appendix)*
  - Pens
  - Sprigs of rosemary

Leaders

Minimum: 2

- Leader
- Activity Leader / Technician

Optimum: 6

Note: For this service, you might invite the uniformed organisations to take some of the following roles.

- Leader *(Introduction and Conclusion)*
- Music Leader
- Storyteller
- Explorer
- Activity Leader / Technician
- Prayer Leader

Suggestions for additional music

- At this table we remember
- Broken for me
- I vow to thee, my country

Service

Act of Remembrance

The laying of wreaths and the two minutes' silence.

Welcome

The National Anthem

Introduction

Today is Remembrance Sunday and we gather together to honour the memory of all those who died so that we might be free. We remember too those who are still fighting in our name around the world. We begin today with a story which is all about remembering.

Storytelling

This is the story of the last meal Jesus ate with his friends. It was a special meal for Passover: this is a festival which Jewish people still celebrate today. Gathered round the Passover meal table, they remember how God rescued his people from slavery in Egypt, and they eat the food which their ancestors ate before walking to freedom.

Show the picture of Passover food.

They eat flat bread which has been made without yeast, to remember that their people escaped from Egypt in a hurry and didn't have time to let the dough rise. Here's some of that bread. *(Show the flat bread.)* It's called unleavened bread: who would like to try some?

Pass round the bread, keeping one piece back.

At the Passover meal, Jews also eat bitter herbs, to remember how their people suffered when they were slaves. They drink four cups of wine to remind them of the promises God made to redeem his people.

Pour out the four cups of wine.

This is the last meal Jesus shared with his friends before he died. He took some unleavened bread and thanked God for it, then broke the bread and said to them, 'This is my body which is given for you. Do this in remembrance of me.'

Break the remaining piece of bread.

Later he took a cup of wine and said, 'This is my blood. It is a new promise which I give to you; it is poured out for the forgiveness of everyone's sins.'

Pour out the wine into the fifth cup.

Later that night, Jesus was arrested and handed over to the Romans to be crucified.

Music And did those feet in ancient time

Exploring Our story today is full of remembering. Every element of the Passover meal is a reminder of the history of God's people, who went from slavery in Egypt to freedom and the promise of a land of their own. In the Passover meal there are memories of pain and loss; there are joyful memories of liberation and God's promise of redemption. For Christians, this meal evokes pain and joy, too: it reminds us of the pain of Christ's sacrifice on the cross, the joy of sins forgiven and the promise of everlasting life.

On this Remembrance Sunday, there is sadness and joy in our remembering. Those who have fought for our country remember the pain of war and the grief of losing comrades. Loved ones left at home know what it is like to wait in fearful hope. Those who are lucky enough to have no direct experience of war can only remember, with joy and gratitude, those to whom we owe our freedom and safety today.

Around a table where there is bread and wine, the Jewish people remember their nation's suffering, and we remember how Christ died for us. Both stories end with liberation and joy. It is right to remember the sacrifices of war which made our freedom possible, and to hold the pain together with the joy. One symbol of remembrance which we use today is the poppy. This wild flower flourishes in the fields of northern France where the trenches of the First World War were dug. Poppy seeds need light in order to germinate, so seeds which had been ploughed deep into the ground sprang into new life when the earth was churned up by trench-digging and explosions. Fields full of poppies grew as a result and became our symbol of remembrance today.

Show the picture of a poppy field.

Poppy seeds should not stay buried: they need to be brought into the light so that they can grow and blossom into new life. The story of Christ's sacrifice needs to be told so that we remember the new life he gave us by freeing us from sin and death. And especially today, our own memories of war and sacrifice need to be brought into the light, so that we may rejoice in our hard-won freedom.

Ask people to share out the paper poppies and pens.

Let's take a moment now to call to mind those we remember today. Write their names on these poppies as a sign of remembrance, then keep the poppies to offer later in prayer.

Allow some time for people to think and write on their poppies.

Music

Eternal Father, strong to save

Activity

Today we will use some music and images to help us remember.

Play the meditation montage accompanying 'Brothers in arms' by Dire Straits.

Prayer action

Ask people to share out the rosemary sprigs.

As we remember with sadness and joy, we will use this herb, rosemary, in our prayers. Rosemary is evergreen, just as our memories stay with us, year after year. It also has a strong, bitter-sweet taste and smell, just as our memories of those we have loved and lost can be vivid and bitter-sweet. We remember them with tears and with pride. Today, we will use this rosemary as a token of our remembrance and a sign of our prayers.

Take a sprig and rub it between your fingers. As the bitter-sweet smell fills your senses, rest in God's presence and call to mind all those whom you want to remember today. In a moment of silence, let us remember those we have lost.

Long pause.

We remember those still caught up in conflicts around the world. We remember too all those who lose their lives in wars which are not of their making.

Let us bring forward our remembrance poppies and rosemary as we offer our prayers to God.

Invite people to bring their poppies and rosemary to the altar – or collect them in offertory plates if your congregation is very large.

Lord of all time and space,
we remember today those we lost long ago;
those we lost in far-away places;
those who died by our side
and those who left us only recently.
May their memory stay green
in our lives and in our prayers.
Amen.

Music Make me a channel of your peace

Conclusion Living Lord,
as we go out into the world, may you give us your peace in our hearts.
Amen.

Give notices, announce the next all-age service and invite everyone to the feast.

Appendix

Resources for activities

Advent

Baby

Print out, copy onto A4 paper and cut along the straight solid lines for the activity; enlarge and trace or copy by hand for the whiteboard/OHP.

Christmas Day

Angel picture

Posters of classical paintings are a useful source (try shops in big art galleries), as are children's books, for example: *This is the star* by Joyce Dunbar, illustrated by Gary Blythe (Doubleday, 1996). Shops attached to religious houses often have postcards and prints by monastic artists: I have seen some startling interpretations of the familiar 'angel and shepherds' scene. For this activity, you will probably need to produce a large, colour copy of the picture you choose. This may involve some expense, but if you cut the picture into large pieces which can then be laminated, you will have a durable resource.

God is with us

'Hallelujah'

This much-loved song has been recorded by a range of artists. Choose the one you prefer: the spare, haunting version recorded by Jeff Buckley is the one I would recommend in this context. It can be found on his album, *Grace* (Sony, 1994).

Meditation montage

This is a slide show of images which accompany the music. The aim is to encourage reflection and to deepen our understanding of the many different and perhaps unlikely situations in which we can praise God. You may like to include some of the lyrics in the montage, such as:

Love is not a victory march,
it's a cold and it's a broken Hallelujah.
Hallelujah . . .[1]

Images which might be shown as these lines are heard include marching soldiers and flags, a couple embracing tearfully, two hands holding each other or Mary at the foot of the Cross. Look on the internet for copyright-free images, for example at www.shutterstock.com. The best computer programs for creating slide shows are PowerPoint for PCs and Keynote for Macs. If a volunteer is preparing this montage for you, you may need to exercise some editorial control over the choice of images. The main thing to remember is that the aim is not to preach, but to encourage reflection.

Blue paper and cut-out shapes
In addition to the pieces detailed on the printable sheet, you will need the following (one of each per table, plus a set of cut-out shapes):

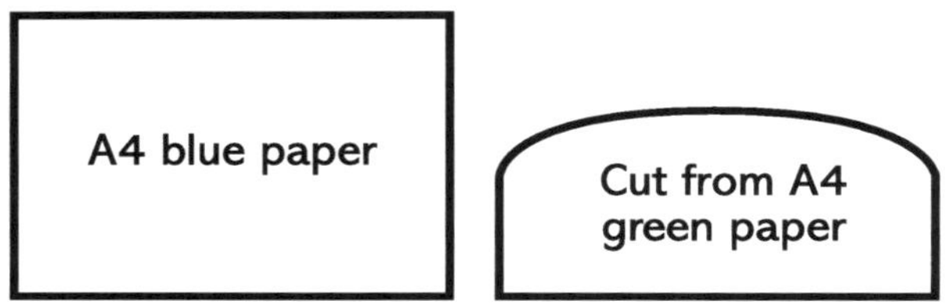

The Light of the world

Globes
Print out, copy onto A4 card and cut around the circles, then snip the cross in the middle for the candle.

Epiphany

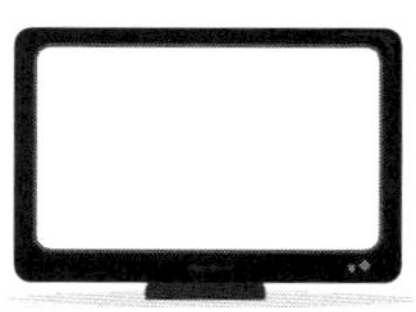

Frankincense
Frankincense is available from church suppliers and, often, gift shops connected to religious houses and cathedrals. Make sure that you buy incense in granular form, not the oils, sticks or cones found in shops specialising in Eastern produce. Also check websites

1. Leonard Cohen, 'Hallelujah', *Various Positions*, Columbia, Passport Records, 1984.

such as www.incense-man.co.uk. There is also useful advice here about lighting charcoal and using incense.

Myrrh
Myrrh is sold as an essential oil: it can be found with aromatherapy oils in health food shops.

Media sheets (TV, internet, newspaper front pages)
Print out and make several copies of each one on A4 paper.

Baptism of Christ

Film clip
O Brother, Where Art Thou? Universal Studios, 2000. Certificate 12. Find the clip you need under Scene Selection: Chapter 4 – Redemption.

Please note: if you are showing film clips in church, you will need a Church Video License. If your church does not already have one, you can apply for one online from Christian Video Licensing International (www.cvli.com).

Music to accompany the film clip
'Down to the river to pray' sung by Alison Krauss on the soundtrack album for *O Brother, Where Art Thou?* (Various artists, Lost Highway, 2000).

Pictures
The internet is the best place to look for pictures like these: try Wikipedia and also the wide selection of copyright-free images available at www.shutterstock.com. Suggestions are (Shutterstock image number):

River Jordan (31930060)
Baptist (5637703)
Dove (3701557)
Jesus emerging from the river (23271229)

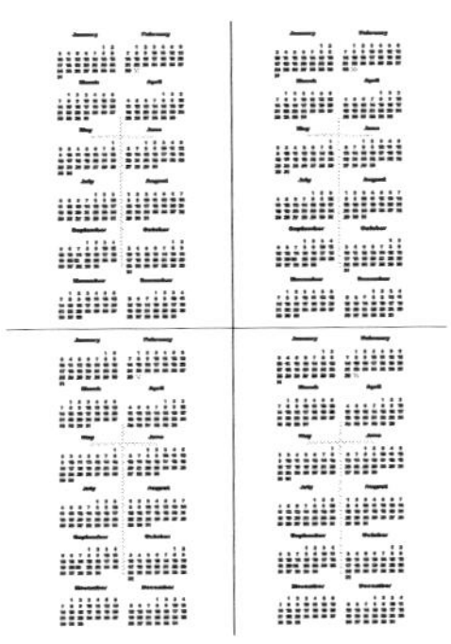

Calendars
The tiny ones used for schools' Christmas crafts are good for this: stationers and newsagents sell them in packs. Alternatively, produce a simple table with months and dates using a computer, or print out and photocopy the calendar here on A4 paper.

Presentation in the temple

Invisible letters and ink wash

When writing in white wax, press hard and scribble firmly to make fat, filled-in letters which will show up clearly when brushed with ink. The ink wash is what was known as 'brusho' when I was at school: it is simply diluted blue ink (runny poster paint mixed with water would also do).

Ash Wednesday

Sand

The best sort is 'play sand' which is available in small sacks from garden centres and occasionally from supermarkets. It is always damp, so before you use it you will need to spread it out somewhere warm and leave it to dry out for a day or two.

Lolly sticks

These are available from most places which sell craft materials, including pound shops. They are also available cheaply from the kitchenware shop, Lakeland, in packs of 100.

Ashes

You will need to prepare these at least a day before the service, because it takes a surprisingly long time to produce enough ash. The usual practice is to burn last year's palm crosses. One cross will make enough ash for ten or twelve people. Once the crosses have been reduced to ash, add a little water to make a dusty paste with which it is easier to mark crosses on foreheads.

Palm Sunday

The Crowd's lines

Using PowerPoint, OHP transparencies or four big cards, display the following lines and stage direction:

Hosanna to the Son of David!
Blessed is the one who comes in the name of the Lord!
Hosanna in the highest heaven!

Who is this?

This is the prophet Jesus from Nazareth in Galilee.

CHEER!

Roman soldiers
Any Roman heritage site near you will sell lots of suitable items for this station. Alternatively, you could display some pictures and information (children's reference books are a good source). If you have the technology, you could even show a film clip or still of Roman soldiers marching or fighting.

Good Friday

'Jesus had a home and a family like us'
This area could include a child's wooden bricks; a sheepskin rug; a block of wood, hammer and nails; wooden bowls and spoons. Also some dressing-up clothes in natural colours and fabrics: tunics, robes, sashes and head-cloths (i.e. traditional Nativity play Shepherd outfits.)

'Jesus met ordinary people in ordinary places'
Sources of pictures include websites such as www.bibleplaces.com and www.ancientsandals.com. Tourism and pilgrimage brochures for the Holy Land can also be useful. Suitable pictures are also available on the CD-ROM included with this book.

'Jesus died on the cross – but that was not the end' – sowing cress crosses
You will need:

- small plastic plates (or paper plates covered in tin foil)
- a cotton-wool roll cut into narrow strips
- cress seeds
- a small watering can.

Make the shape of a cross with the cotton wool and dampen it slightly, then sprinkle on some seeds and water lightly. If left on a sunny windowsill and watered regularly, they will sprout within a few days. For the large version, I have used a large disposable tin tray and wider strips of cotton wool. Sow this one fairly densely about 10 days before the service and by Good Friday your cross should be covered with a thick forest of cress.

If you are closing your service with the candlelit vigil rather than the good news of Easter, place this cross where people will be sowing their own; otherwise, save it until the closing prayer.

Stations of the Cross

Place these all around the church in a random order, so that people have to hunt for them.If your church does not have its own stations, they can be bought as posters from Christian suppliers and bookshops (e.g. Church House Bookshop). Here I have only used half the Stations, namely:

1st: Jesus is condemned to death.

2nd: Jesus accepts his Cross.

9th: Jesus falls the third time.

10th: Jesus is stripped of his garments.

11th: Jesus is nailed to the Cross.

12th: Jesus dies on the Cross.

14th: Jesus is placed in the tomb.

Easter Day

'Living Cross'

This is a cross made from budding twigs simply tied together. Young sycamore twigs are particularly effective as they are very straight and their leaves come early. Forsythia is also good. If people are going to make their own, provide lots of budding twigs as above, plus some spring flowers (e.g. daffodils in bud, and tree blossoms).

Worship flags/angel wings

These are beautiful resources for worship and well worth making or buying. You will need:

- Two pieces of dowel
- Two semicircles of shiny, floaty fabric – e.g. organza, polyester shiny fabrics, lycra foil, metallic lamé, poly habotai. For this service, choose something white, shiny and fairly opaque.

For the large size, the fabric should be 180cm long and 90cm wide; the dowel should be 90cm long.

For the extra-large size (which I would recommend for this service), the fabric should be 2m long and 1m wide; the dowel should be 120cm long.

Fold over slightly less than half the length of the fabric to form a narrow hem. Sew it across the top and down the side, leaving it open at the bottom end so it forms a sleeve for the dowel. Insert the dowel and make sure that there is enough left sticking out of the end of the sleeve for you to hold.

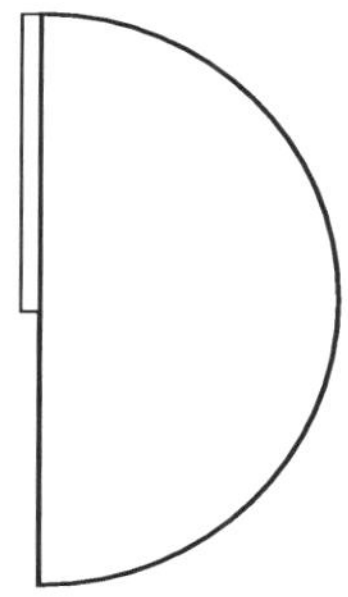

These flags are at their best when in motion. They can be quite spectacular as wings, flags or when used in dance, like this:

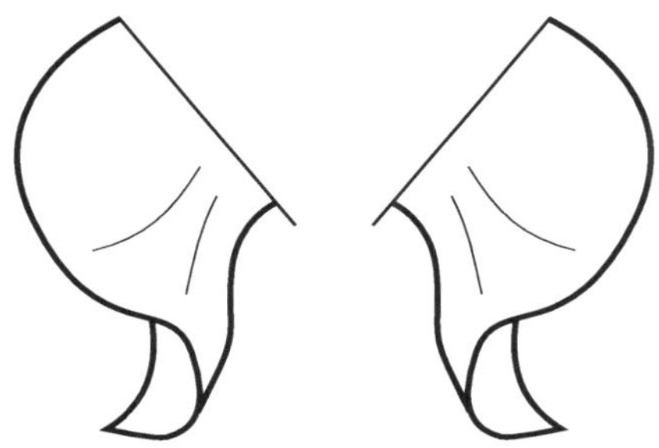

For further pictures and information, search on the internet for worship flags, especially at www.wingsofpraise.com.

A UK supplier I can recommend is Kingdom Dance Resources: see www.kingdomdance.co.uk

The Annunciation

Angel templates

Print out and copy onto thin A4 white card and cut out around the dotted lines. Make enough for one each. When you attach the hand-print wings, they should look like this (viewed from behind).

The Ascension

Incense
This is available from church suppliers and, often, gift shops connected to religious houses and cathedrals. Make sure that you buy incense in granular form, not the oils, sticks or cones found in shops specialising in Eastern produce. Also check websites such as www.incense-man.co.uk. There is also useful advice here about lighting charcoal and using incense.

Helium
Helium canisters are available from shops which sell party supplies and from websites, for example www.woolworths.co.uk.

Puppets and performance cloth
You will need:

Jesus

1 or 2 angels

A cut-out cloud, big enough to cover the Jesus puppet. If you are using the cut-out puppets, put Blu-tack on the back of the cloud so that the Jesus puppet can be attached and lifted up.

11 disciples

Your church may already have puppets for telling Bible stories; if not, the templates may be printed, copied and enlarged onto A3 paper, then cut out, coloured and attached to cardboard backing. Tape a long stick to the back of the card for your puppeteer to hold. Make a performance cloth by covering a long pole with a heavy, dark cloth. It should be at least chest height, so that your puppeteers can hide comfortably behind it: a small, portable clothes rail is ideal.

Pentecost

Flame crowns

Attach one flame like this on the front of the circlet, then another on the back. Staple the points of the flames together.

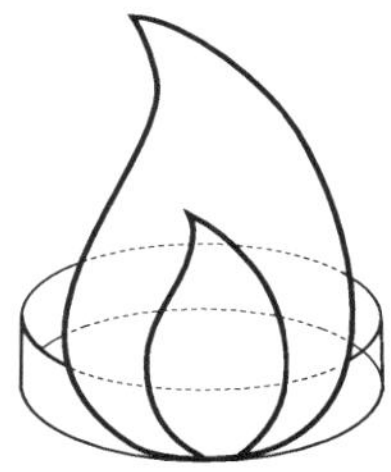

Trinity Sunday

Trinity Activity

If possible, clear a very large space in the middle of your church and mark out this pattern on the floor in chalk or masking tape. It should be big enough for a small table to stand in each separate area; leave enough room for people to gather around the tables and to walk along the lines of tape, following the pattern. (If there is not enough space for this, then mark out the pattern separately and stand the group of four tables in a different area.)

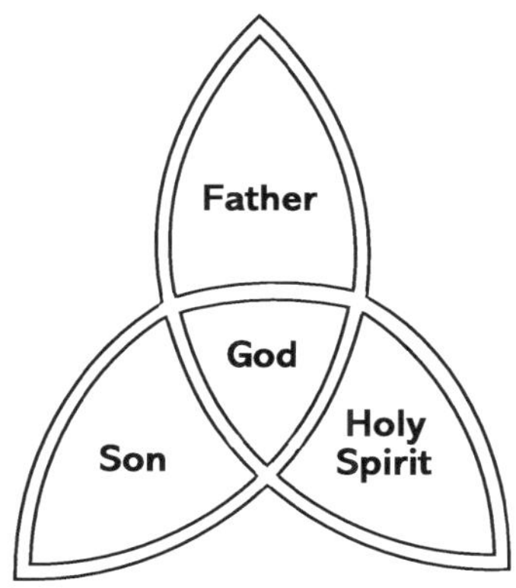

Label the tables and on each one, gather a collection of things to help people think about each person of the Trinity, for example:

Father: Photographs of the natural world; natural treasures such as beautiful shells or feathers; the words of Isaiah 40:28–31. A CD player with headphones, playing a recording of the *Sanctus* from any Mass setting.

Son: A cross, a wooden mallet, some nails, water, bread, wine, the Paschal candle or other large candle. Seven cards with Jesus' 'I am' statements: 'I am the way, and the truth, and the life', 'I am the true vine', 'I am the resurrection and the life', 'I am the good shepherd', 'I am the bread of life', 'I am the light of the world', 'I am the gate.'

Holy Spirit: An electric pedestal fan on full power, with strips of red and orange tissue paper or thin fabric tied on to the grille to look like flames; a picture of a dove; photographs of sunlight streaming through clouds.

GOD: Spell out GOD in lit tea-lights.

These are some suggestions: use them as a springboard for your own ideas.

Exploring – interactive areas

Again, here are some suggestions for each area which may help people to reflect on the question, 'What is the job of the church?'

Creative area:

- Pictures to complete, entitled: 'Draw a brilliant church for these people'

'Draw a brilliant church for these people'

Print from CD-ROM and make lots of A4 copies.

- Pens and pencils.

Reflective area:

- Pictures of your own church and the community of which it is a part.
- Prayers or quotations from hymns which may encourage reflection on the mission of the Church.
- Posters advertising what your church does to serve the community: Sunday services, toddler group, youth group, film club etc.

Active area:

- Lego/wooden bricks/construction toys, with a sign: 'How can we build a church?'
- 'Your world needs YOU' poster

'Your world needs YOU' poster

Print from CD-ROM, copy onto A4; laminate if possible.

- Quotation on a card: 'Go – preach the gospel. If necessary, use words.' (Attributed to St Francis of Assisi.)
- Lots of Christian Aid leaflets.

The Transfiguration

Three pictures

The internet is the best place to look for pictures like these: try Wikipedia and also the wide selection of copyright-free images available at www.shutterstock.com. Suggestions are (Shutterstock image number):

Mountains (24848719)
Shining Jesus (42531379)
The bright cloud (21556870)

Words of the prayer

Amen! Blessing and glory and wisdom
and thanksgiving and honour
and power and might
be to our God for ever and ever!
Amen!

Either: projected onto a screen

Or: held up by volunteers on nine large pieces of card: 'Amen!' (used twice); 'Blessing and'; 'glory and'; 'wisdom and'; 'thanksgiving and'; 'honour and'; 'power and might'; 'be to our God'; 'for ever and ever!'

Picture frame

Print out, copy onto A4 paper and cut along the straight solid lines.

Jesus outline

Print out and make several copies onto A4 or A3 paper.

Friends outline

Print out and make several copies onto A4 or A3 paper.

Indoor sparklers

These can be bought all year round from many toy and gift shops. They are also available from online suppliers, for example www.tobar.co.uk

Known to God

Pictures
The internet is the best place to look for pictures like this: try Wikipedia and also the wide selection of copyright-free images available at www.shutterstock.com. Suggestions are (Shutterstock image number):

Nomad tents (23093692)
Desert and tree (41889172)
Spring in the Negev desert (5086888)

God will provide

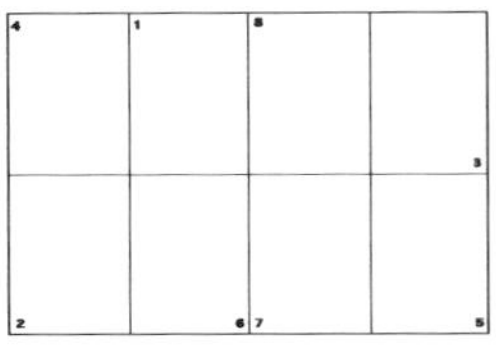

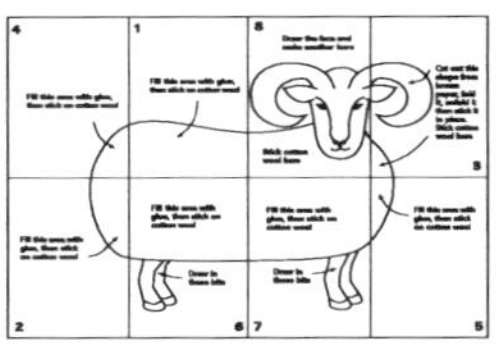

Mystery drawing template
Print out and copy the plain numbered grid onto pieces of white A4 card, enough for one each.

Mystery drawing activity
Print out and enlarge the squared-off drawing of the ram onto A3 paper: make two copies. On one, follow the instructions and make your own picture with cotton wool etc. Then cut both copies into the numbered squares and at each table, place the square with the visible instructions and your own filled-in square as a model for people to follow. For squares 3 and 8, place a demonstration pair of horn shapes, showing how to make the horns: stage 1 is a simple spiral cut from a manila envelope; stage 2 is the same shape, pleated up like a tiny fan, then unfolded to make a crimped horn.

Hide and seek

Rabbit tracks
Print out, photocopy onto A4 paper and stick onto the floor, perhaps running from the church door and down the aisle. Alternatively, draw the tracks onto sheets of lining paper which are stuck to the floor.

The Runaway Bunny **by Margaret Wise Brown**
Published by HarperFestival, 1991 in boardbook format; use a larger format if you can find one.

The Maker's mark

Denarius

Print from CD-ROM, make a copy on A4 paper or enlarge onto A3.

Model Magic, clay or salt dough

Model Magic is made by Crayola. It is a bright white, lightweight, air-drying modelling clay which is not at all messy to use, unlike traditional clay. It can be bought from children's craft suppliers (as can traditional clay), for example www.crafts4kids.co.uk. For a recipe for salt dough, see appendix for Crib Service.

Living water

The rock which gushes water

This calls for some prop-making ingenuity: I can recommend the following method. Hide a few water balloons, tied tightly and full to bursting, behind a pile of large rocks (the sort which make up garden rockeries). Attach a pin to the end of Moses' staff and when he strikes the rocks, the water should flow. The effect is more dramatic if the rock arrangement is piled on a table, with a large tray below for the water.

Desert photos and facts

Try to find clear, visual information. Reference books for school-age children are excellent: I can particularly recommend *Desert*, published by Dorling Kindersley, and *Desperate Deserts* by Anita Ganeri, published by Scholastic as part of their 'Horrible Geography' series.

The gate

Six stations

Prepare one station for each verse of the Psalm, e.g.

v.1 – Pictures of a shepherd caring for his sheep

v.2 – Pictures of green fields, lakes

v.3 – A lit candle, a Bible, pictures of a footpath through countryside and a signpost

v.4 – A picture of a dark cave, a shepherd's crook

v.5 – A table laid with good, simple food: bread, fruit juice, fruit, cheese cut into small pieces

v.6 – A picture of people embracing; a depiction of heaven.

These are suggestions only. For pictures, see appendix for Good Friday, 'Jesus met ordinary people in ordinary places'.

'Meditation montage'
A slide show of still images or video clips on a laptop which will help us to reflect on the blessing (see Prayer action, with suggested images). The words could either be incorporated into the montage or read aloud as it plays. The best computer programs for creating slide shows are PowerPoint for PCs and Keynote for Macs. Look on the internet for copyright-free images, for example at www.shutterstock.com.

The way, the truth and the life

Maze for the floor
There is a wonderfully informative website which can be found under the search term 'History of Mazes and Labyrinths' at gwydir.demon.co.uk/jo/maze/. It has many clear examples, photographs of different kinds of mazes, maps of how to solve them and tips on how to draw them or create your own. Make sure that you make a maze which you *can* get lost in! (The design used for the prayers has a single path, so is not suitable for this activity.)

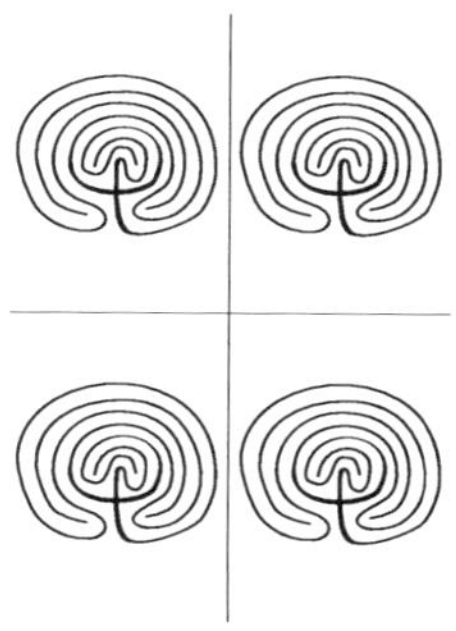

Small maze
Print out, copy onto A4 paper or card and cut out along the straight lines. This ancient maze pattern is found all over the world, but this one is copied from a Bronze Age carving in Rocky Valley, near Tintagel, Cornwall. You cannot get lost in this labyrinth: a single winding path leads you to the centre, by the cross.

Christ the King

Crown of light
This could be a circle of tea-lights arranged around a crown, or a circlet of gold card to which thin votive candles have been attached. Some red tinsel might add to the regal effect. Be creative!

Pictures of people in need

Aim for a range of ages and for different races and genders. The internet is the best place to look for pictures like this: try Wikipedia and also the wide selection of copyright-free images available at www.shutterstock.com. Suggestions are (Shutterstock image number):

Hungry person (3067056)
Thirsty person (32782855)
Stranger (15178000)
Person in rags (22424944)
Sick person (6851311)
Person in prison (15336133)

Upside-down face[2]

Print from CD-ROM, make lots of copies of the small face on white A4 paper and cut out along the straight lines. Make a copy of the large face on A4 paper or enlarge onto A3.

Sowing the seed

Pictures

The internet is the best place to look for pictures like this: try Wikipedia and also the wide selection of copyright-free images available at www.shutterstock.com. Suggestions are (Shutterstock image number):

Crows in a ploughed field (37363033)
A field ripe for harvest (14678350)

Small things and great treasure

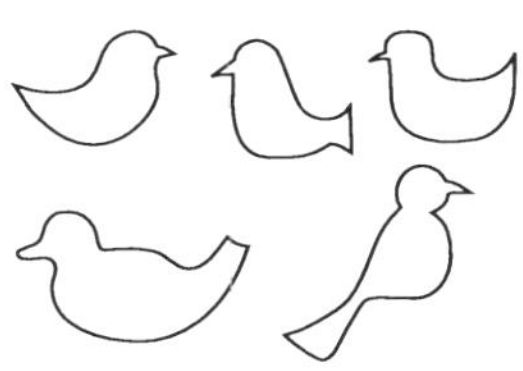

Birds

Print from CD-ROM, copy onto coloured A4 paper and cut out.

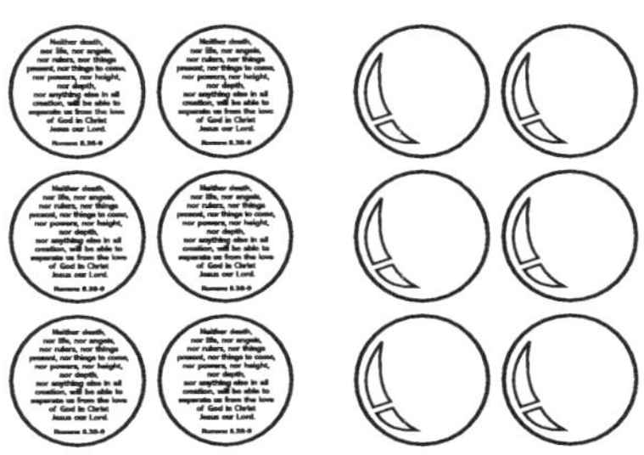

Pearls

Print from CD-ROM, make double-sided A4 copies on card (pale blue/cream if possible) and cut out.

2. This face is an adaptation of an unattributed drawing I found on the internet under 'Upside down-Amazing Art'.

Ingredients for bread-making
650g strong white bread flour
2 tsp salt
1 tsp sugar
1 tbsp vegetable oil
7g sachet of dried yeast
400ml warm water.

Mix all the dry ingredients, then add the oil and water and mix well. Then, at the start of the service, divide the dough and invite people to knead it for 10 minutes on a floured surface before shaping it into small rolls. Cover with a damp tea towel and leave to rise in a warm place for about 45 minutes (or the length of the service). Preheat the oven to Gas 8 (230°C/450°F) and bake for 10-15 minutes.[3]

Fruits of the kingdom

Bunches of grapes, labelled and blank
Print from CD-ROM, copy onto green or purple A4 paper and cut out. Make plenty, and label the first 11 yourself: 'Justice', 'Righteousness', 'Love', 'Joy', 'Peace', 'Patience', 'Kindness', 'Generosity', 'Faithfulness', 'Gentleness', 'Self-control'.

An open invitation

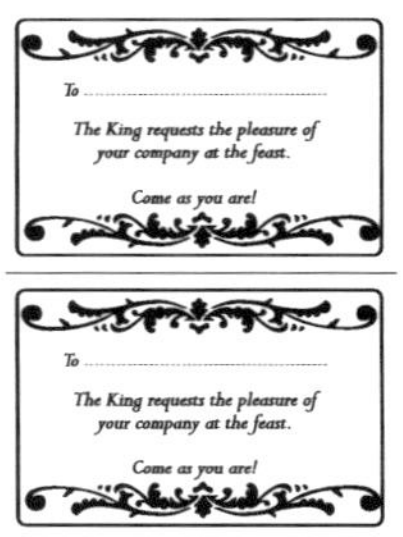

Invitations
Print from CD-ROM, copy onto white A4 paper or card; cut along the straight line.

Christ the Redeemer and 'Come as you are'
The internet is the best place to look for pictures like this: try Wikipedia and also the wide selection of copy-right-free images available at www.shutterstock.com. A suggestion is (Shutterstock image number):
Christ the Redeemer, Rio de Janeiro (6132736)

Copy onto white A4 paper or card with the following words underneath. Make enough for one each.

3. This is taken from a recipe on a packet of Allinson Easy Bake Yeast. It only requires one 'proving' period for the dough to rise, which makes the rolls slightly less fluffy but easier to make in the available time.

Come as you are, as you were
as I want you to be,
as a friend, as a friend
as an old enemy.

Take your time, hurry up,
the choice is yours, don't be late,
take a rest as a friend.

Kurt Cobain, 'Come as you are', from the album *Nevermind* by Nirvana (Polydor Group, 1991)

'Come as you are' by Nirvana
From the album *Nevermind* by Nirvana (Polydor Group, 1991). Also recorded by Emilie Simon (downloads available on the internet).

Holding crosses
These are chunky, hand-carved, polished wooden crosses, designed to fit comfortably in the palm of the hand. They are available from Christian bookshops and suppliers, as well as many cathedral gift shops. Visit www.kevinmayhew.com for more details.

The wealth of the kingdom

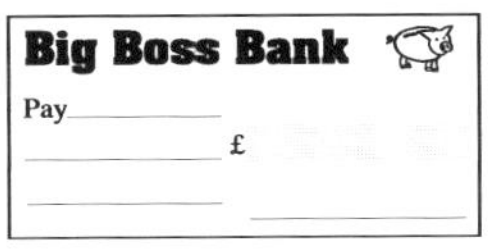

Large cheque
Print from CD-ROM, enlarge to A3 and make five copies. Fill in the cheques as follows (all made payable to 'Cash'): £1,500,000; £600,000; £300,000; £3,000,000; £1,200,000.

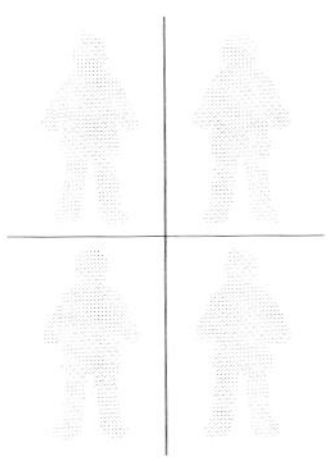

People outlines
Print from CD-ROM, make lots of copies on white A4 paper and cut out along the straight lines.

Living in the light

Glow-sticks
These are thin plastic sticks which contain a coloured chemical which becomes fluorescent when the stick is flexed. They are available from toy shops, pound shops and many newsagents. Each pack also contains a number of small plastic connectors which can be used to join sticks together to form chains and circles. See also www.glowsticks.co.uk.

Love in action

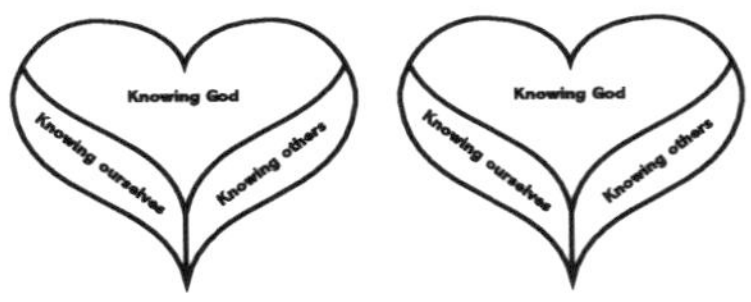

Heart puzzle

Print out, copy onto A3 card or paper then cut out the heart shapes and the component pieces along the solid lines; place each puzzle in an envelope.[4]

Here he is!

'God is love' show-and-teller

Print out, photocopy and enlarge onto A3 paper; cut out the square and fold along the dotted lines like this:

1. Printed-side down, fold the corners down to meet in the middle to form a smaller square.
2. Printed-side up, fold the corners down to meet in the middle to form an even smaller square.
3. Fold the square in half to make a vertical crease down the middle, then unfold again.
4. Fold the square in half to make a horizontal crease across the middle, then unfold again.
5. Pinch all four corners together by putting your index fingers and thumbs under the corner flaps. In this position, you can open and close the show-and-teller, like this:

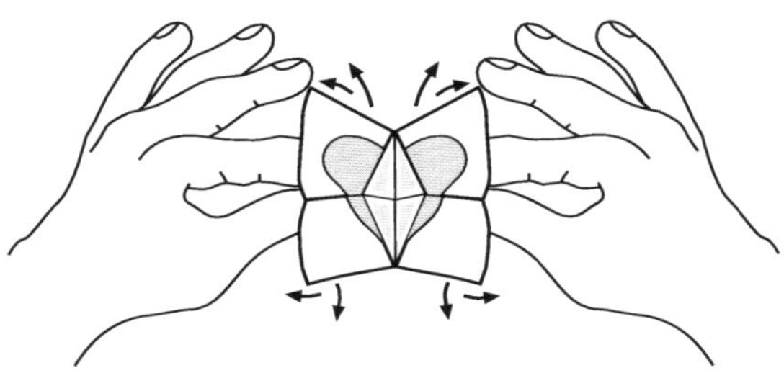

Hold your show and teller between pinched fingers.

- Ask a person to pick a number from the 4 visible panels.
- If they pick 3, open and close the show-and-teller three times (for example).
- Ask them to pick a number and guess how you have completed the sentence.
- Reveal what you have written.

4. This 'divided heart' idea was inspired by the Godly Play story, 'The Ten Best Ways'.

Follow me!

Picture reveal
This activity can be as hi-tech or low-tech as you like. It can be done:

- on a laptop and shown on a screen

(Save the picture from the CD-ROM. Using PowerPoint, set the picture as the background, then use Autoshapes to put shapes over the picture. Then use Custom animations to make the shapes appear/disappear in the recommended order.)

- on an OHP with a screen

(Print off the picture, photocopy it onto acetate and mask it with numbered pieces of paper, then take them off one at a time in the recommended order.)

- on a very large piece of paper, onto which the picture has been copied

(*either* print off the picture, photocopy it, cut it into quarters then photocopy and enlarge each piece onto A3, then trim and Sellotape them together; *or* copy by hand by squaring it off and scaling it up. Mask it with numbered pieces of paper, then take them off one at a time in the recommended order.)

The basic idea is that you begin with a concealed picture which you reveal bit by bit, in the following order:

1. Jesus' beckoning hand.
2. The edge of the sea.
3. The disciples' feet, all pointing in the same direction.
4. Fish in a net.
5. The boat, drifting.
6. Zebedee.
7. James' and John's faces.
8. Simon's and Andrew's faces.
9. The rest of Jesus.
10. All the rest of the picture.

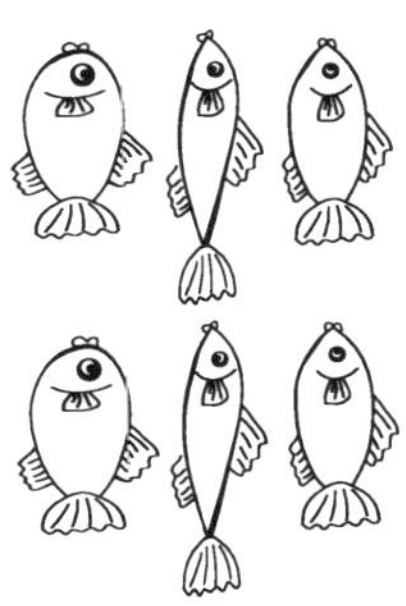

Fish shapes
Copy onto A4 paper then cut around the fish; use a hole punch for the eye.

Time to grow

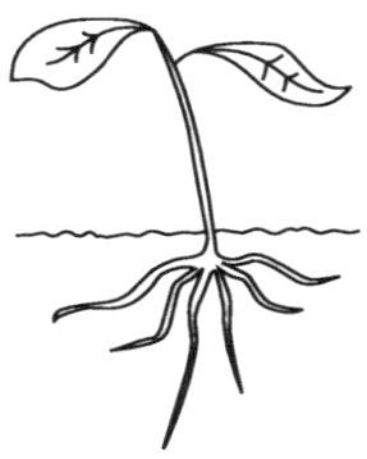

***Zagazoo* by Quentin Blake (Jonathan Cape, 1998)**
This is a children's story in which a young couple receive a gift-wrapped parcel containing a baby called Zagazoo. The baby grows – but one morning he turns into a screeching vulture. Soon he becomes a clumsy baby elephant, then a mud-covered warthog, then a cross dragon and so on until suddenly he turns into a polite young man. This young man meets a girl of his own and brings her home to meet his aging parents – only to find they have turned into a pair of pelicans. The illustrations are delightful and the story works beautifully in a worship context as a whimsical parable.

Growing plant and signpost
Print out, photocopy and enlarge each onto A3 paper and attach to the board or flip chart.

Seeing and believing

Prayer leaves
Print from CD-ROM, copy onto green A4 paper then cut around the leaves. Use a hole punch so that they may be easily threaded onto wool and attached to the tree. The leaves alone could be a sign of prayer, or you could provide pens so that people could write a prayer intention on the leaf.

Living prayer tree
A prayer tree made of budding forsythia twigs is particularly striking. If you keep the twigs well watered, the flowers will bloom among the prayers. Alternatively, if you made a large living cross for Easter Day, this can be used as a prayer tree. Leaves are easy to attach if you wind green or brown wool around it like this:

Prayer leaves can then simply be tucked behind the woollen criss-crosses, rather than tied on. (This cross is made of bamboo and sycamore, strapped together in the middle with strips of green fabric. The real leaves open around the paper leaves.)

Christ in me and you

Spider's web model
This is easy to make. You will need a large plastic hula hoop, just big enough for three people to stand inside it. Onto this hoop, tie eight long pieces of string or rope at regular intervals, so that when they are stretched out from the hoop they look like the spokes of a wheel. This will give the general idea of a spider's web; if you are feeling ambitious and have lots of string, you could tie some links between the spokes, starting in the middle and spiralling outwards.

Sitting down with Jesus

'Sit Down' by James
This has been released as a single in various forms, and also on the album *The Best Of* (1998, Fontana/Mercury). It is probably easiest to download it through iTunes. Alternatively, you could play a video clip from *The Manchester Passion* (BBC, 2006) in which the song featured.

The words of the chorus (see under Exploring) could be displayed on a screen via a laptop or OHP, or you could give people their own copies.

Lightening the load

Picture
The internet is the best place to look for pictures like this: try Wikipedia and also the wide selection of copyright-free images available at www.shutterstock.com. A suggestion is (Shutterstock image number):

Oxen ploughing (11139922)

Freedom food

Two columns to represent the doorposts
Two planks of wood would do, or two lengths of stiff brown cardboard. Tie each column to the back of a chair to keep it upright and stable.

Show and tell

Truelove **by Babette Cole (Jonathan Cape, 2001)**

This children's book is about a loving dog who is ousted from his home when a new baby arrives. He makes friends with a pack of stray dogs and at the end of the story he and all his new friends are welcomed into the family home. The story has few words but eloquent and entertaining pictures, and the book's large format makes it good for sharing.

Three stations

Station 1

- A sign: '"Show, don't tell": how did Jesus show his love for us all?'
- A collection of pictures and objects which represent Christ's deeds on earth, such as: bread rolls and fish; water and wine; a pile of discarded bandages and a walking stick; a bowl of water and a towel; a crown of thorns; a cross, a wooden mallet and some nails.

Station 2

- A sign: 'How might these things be used to show someone we love them?'
- A collection of objects, such as: a teapot and mug; a bunch of flowers; a pair of comfy slippers; a box of tissues; a dog's lead; children's puzzles and board games.

Station 3

- A sign: 'Do not waste time bothering whether you 'love' your neighbour; act as if you did. As soon as we do this we find one of the great secrets. When you are behaving as if you loved someone, you will presently come to love him.' *C. S. Lewis*[5]
- A long strip of lining paper, with this written across the top: 'Draw some people behaving as if they loved their neighbours (or write down some suggestions)'
- Lots of felt-tip pens, pencils and biros.

Hearts

Print from CD-ROM, copy onto pink or red A4 paper and cut out. Make enough for one each.

5. C. S. Lewis, *Mere Christianity*, Geoffrey Bles, 1952.

All you need is love

Circlet

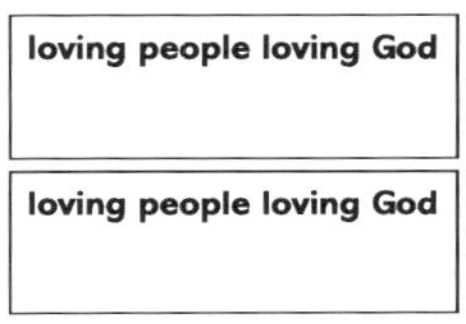

Copy the 'loving God loving people' sheet twice on A4 and cut out the strips, then stick them end-to-end to make one long strip. Attach this to a long strip of card and join the ends to make the circlet. Attach four long pieces of cotton to the circlet with Sellotape and knot them at the top. Around the bottom edge of the circlet, attach lots of different lengths of cotton, ready for the heart shapes. Then suspend the circlet from any available point in church, within reach of a table or two where you have spread the other materials for this activity.

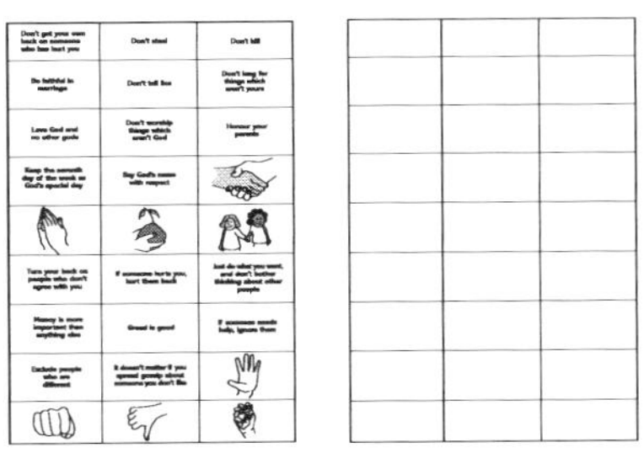

Hearts and boxes

Make at least 10 copies of the hearts on pink or red A4 paper and cut them out. The first sheet of boxes contains instructions: some are all about loving God and loving people, and some are about hatred and selfishness. Make one copy on white A4 paper and cut out the boxes. The second sheet of boxes should remain blank for Exploring/Activity 2: make two or three copies on white A4 paper and cut them out. (You may like to use some of these blank boxes to add ideas of your own to the first activity.)

Preparing the way

Pictures

The internet is the best place to look for pictures like these: try Wikipedia and also the wide selection of copyright-free images available at www.shutterstock.com. Suggestions are (Shutterstock image number):

The Judean wilderness (21986935)
A camel skin (5500771)
Desert locust (6778549)
Wild honey (12339292)
River Jordan (31930060)

Desert soundscape

Look for a piece of music which evokes the silence and solitude of the desert. Modern abstract and 'mood' music is a possible source, as are film soundtracks. I can recommend the soundtrack album for *The Last Temptation of Christ* by Peter Gabriel (Geffen Records, 1989). This features many haunting pieces played on traditional Middle Eastern instruments; the track called 'Wall of Breath' is particularly effective in this context.

'Washed away' prayers

'Down to the river to pray' sung by Alison Krauss on the soundtrack album for *O Brother, Where Art Thou?* (Various artists, Lost Highway, 2000).

Loving life

Ten Commandments puzzle

Print out, photocopy and enlarge onto A3 paper and cut out all the puzzle pieces.

Stone tablet templates

Print out, photocopy and enlarge onto A3 paper. Cut out both tablets and draw round each one on red card, then cut them out. When the Ten Commandments puzzle is complete and tacked onto the front of the templates, fix them together like this and turn them over to reveal a red heart shape:

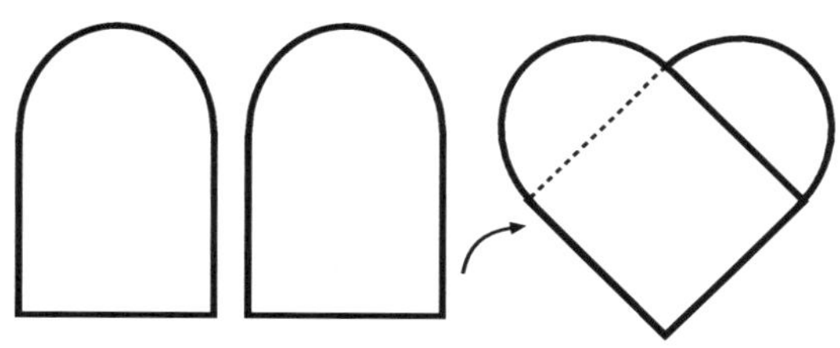

'Broken Things'
This simple, moving song was performed by the Irish singer, Juliet Turner, at the memorial service for the victims of the Omagh bombing. The chorus includes these words:

You can have my heart
if you don't mind broken things . . .
I heard that you make all things new
so I give these pieces all to you
if you want it, you can have my heart.[6]

The recording can be found on the compilation album by various artists, entitled *Across the Bridge of Hope*, White Records (DNA), 1999. This can be ordered from amazon.co.uk: the website also allows you to hear some of the song.

Heart-shaped bowl or box
I have seen wooden boxes like this (for a price) in shops selling Indian crafts. However, your likeliest source is Valentine's Day merchandise.

Tempted

Toy snake
The most effective toy snakes I have found are the articulated wooden ones which are sold cheaply in post offices and local toy shops. They come in natural colours and they move very realistically!

Crown and coins
Your best source is a child's dressing-up box! Many pirate kits for kids include 'pieces of eight' which would work very well. Chocolate coins would also be suitably shiny. Crowns are of course easy enough to make, but if you want to invest in a deluxe version for use on other occasions (Epiphany, Christ the King), I can recommend the jewelled crowns made of gold fabric which are sold by most English Heritage outlets – I have seen them both at Tintagel and on Lindisfarne.

6. Julie Miller, 'Broken Things', Hightone Records, 1999.

A new birth

Pictures

Print off from the CD-ROM and *either* copy them onto four OHP acetates *or* save them onto your laptop.

1. Abraham's family tree[7]

2. Family tree template

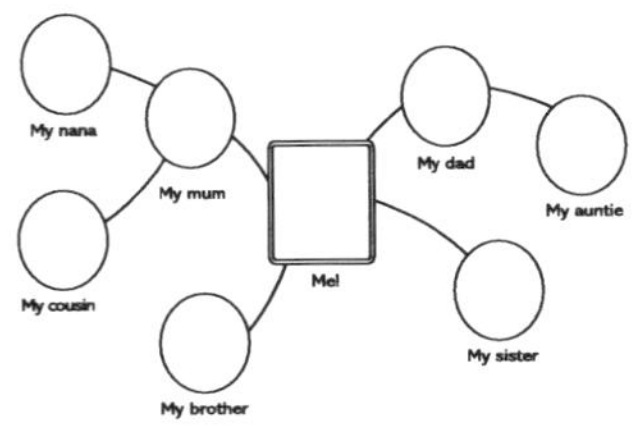

3. 'New belonging'

4. 'New beginning'

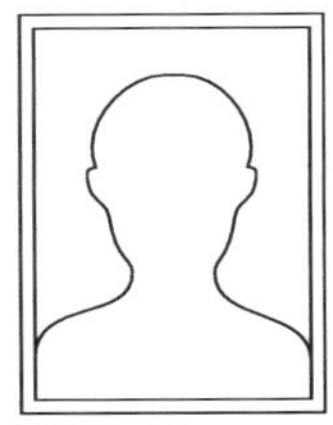

What do we do now?

Ascension picture, James Bond picture

The internet is the best place to look for pictures like this: try Wikipedia and also the wide selection of copyright-free images available at www.shutterstock.com. The Ascention picture on which I have based this service is to be found on Shutterstock: Ascension (35238970)

'Picture reveal'

Save the picture from the CD-ROM. Then, using PowerPoint, set the picture as the background, then use Autoshapes to put shapes over the picture. Then use custom animations to make the shapes appear/ disappear in the recommended order.

Together in unity

Flame flags

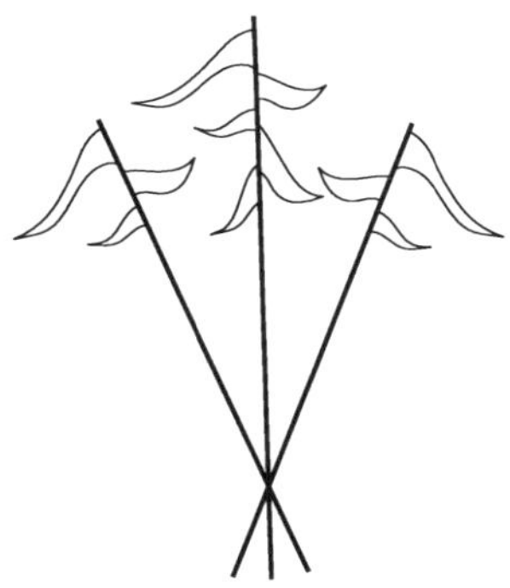

7. Source: 'The Patriarchs', illustrated by Eric Thomas in *The Children's Illustrated Bible,* Dorling Kindersley Limited, 1994.

These are two-foot lengths of bamboo cane or similar, with strips of red, yellow and orange paper attached in rough flame shapes. They are particularly suitable for post-Pentecost prayers. People should write their prayer intention on their flame before attaching it with Sellotape.

Joseph – films and music

A vibrant film version is *Joseph and the Amazing Technicolor Dreamcoat* (Really Useful Films, 1999) starring Donny Osmond; alternatively, use any soundtrack CD of the same musical. The relevant clip is right after the 'Benjamin Calypso': it appears in the track listing as 'Joseph All the Time/Jacob in Egypt' and begins with the Narrator singing, 'Joseph knew by this his brothers now were honest men . . .'

There is also an animated, non-musical version of Joseph's story: *Joseph: King of Dreams* (Dreamworks, 2000).

Doing God's work

'The body of Christ'

1. Print out the body, photocopy it and cut out the 8 separate body parts: head, body, arms, hands and feet. Either by hand or by photocopying and enlarging, make a very big version of each body part (big enough to be seen clearly by the congregation). Stick each body part onto a piece of cardboard backing to stiffen it. You could either assemble the body on a board as suggested, sticking each part on with Blu-tack, or you could invite children to hold the different parts up and then bring them together.
2. On A4 paper, make several copies of the complete body.

***The Prince of Egypt* (Dreamworks, 1998)** This is an animated retelling of the life of Moses. It is colourful, dramatic and accessible.

The Creation

Creation story

Choose a version which tells the story in a fresh, clear and accessible way, either in different versions of the Bible or in children's Bible story books. My favourite is

The Creation Story by Jane Ray (Orchard Books, 1992) which shimmers with gold and exotic colours. I also like *My Very First Bible* by Lois Rock (Lion Publishing, 2003) which begins, 'Think of the dark. Make it darker. Think of the darkest dark.' You would need to adapt this version slightly, as it doesn't spell out the number of days or mention the day of rest.

Noah's Ark

Dove templates

Copy onto white A4 card – people can cut out their own doves during the activity. For the wings, copy the large semicircle onto white A4 paper. Once this is cut out, it can be folded lengthways like a fan, then folded in half to form a pair of wings and posted through the slot in the dove's back. Use a hole punch to make the holes for the string. It would be useful to have made your own dove earlier, as a model.

The burning bush and the Ten Plagues

Pictures

The internet is the best place to look for pictures like this: try Wikipedia and also the wide selection of copyright-free images available at www.shutterstock.com. Suggestions are (Shutterstock image number):

Burning bush (13641715)
Red Sea shore (11719984)
Bugs (786804)
Lightning (1414391)
Locust (6778549)

***Finding Nemo* (Walt Disney Pictures, 2003)**

The scene begins with the view over Sydney harbour and ends after the fish have been shot out of the whale's body through its blow-hole, with Marlin shouting, 'We're alive!' On the DVD menu, choose Scene Selection and go to scene 21: this begins at exactly the right point. The DVD timing runs from 1 hour 05.23 minutes to 1 hour 10.14 minutes. (DVD timers may vary.)

It's a miracle!

Stone water jar

Print out and copy this shape by hand onto a large sheet of lining paper. (Two strips, about 1.5m long, Sellotaped side-by-side should give you a piece which is long and wide enough). Then cut around the shape of the jar. Then make five more like this!

Alive!

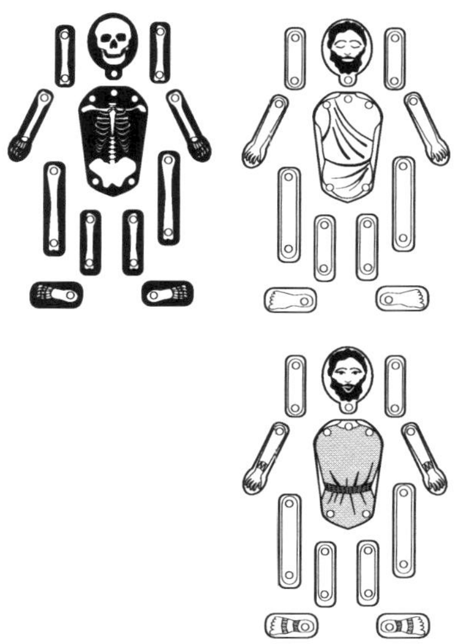

Body bits – skeleton, still body and alive body

Print out and copy each one four to six times (depending on how many puppeteers you plan to have) onto thin A4 white card. Cut out around the body bits and use a hole punch to make the joint holes. Put each set in a separate envelope, so that each puppeteer has three envelopes each. When fixing the limbs together, line up the joint holes and poke the split pin through from the back to the front. This way, it is easier to add the extra layers required by the story without having to take the pin out each time.

'Dem Bones' words (Traditional spiritual)

Print off from CD-ROM and copy onto your service sheets.

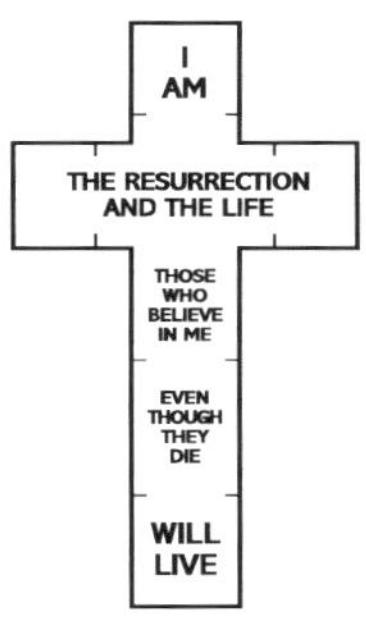

Promise-crosses

Print out and copy enough for one each onto A4 paper in different colours. Cut around the crosses, then with the writing side upwards, fold the arms of the cross inwards along the lines indicated (fold the longest arm up twice, starting from the bottom). When you turn the folded cross over, it should look like a neat, stubby cross. When placing the crosses around the church, display this reverse side upwards.

Walking on the waves

Floating crosses

Cut around the cross shapes (but not the little holes in the middle). Fold the arms of the cross in to cover the words. Make sure the folds are firm: it's a good idea to fold them back and forth a few times. When you float the folded cross on water, the arms of the cross magically unfold like the petals of a flower until the cross is lying flat on the surface.[8]

8. This is my adaptation of a floating paper flower idea which appeared in an issue of *Roots* magazine (Barnabas/BRF).

The forgiven debtor

Streamers and worship flags
Simple streamers can be made with long strips of fabric, ribbon or crêpe paper attached to a piece of dowel. Worship flags are a wonderful resource: see appendix for Easter Day and also www.kingdomdance.co.uk. For this service, the flags should be smaller and more colourful.

The workers in the vineyard

Quail and manna
I have suggested roast chicken as a substitute, because quail or any closer relation in terms of taste (such as pheasant) is going to be expensive. To make something which resembles manna, roll out a block of shop-bought puff pastry very thinly, then spread half of it lightly with honey. Fold the other half down on top, press the edges together and cut the large rectangle into thin strips. On a lightly greased baking sheet, these take about 20 minutes to cook. They should turn out pale, flaky and slightly honey-flavoured. Once cool, keep them in an air-tight tin until you need them.

The wise and foolish bridesmaids

Traditional terracotta oil lamps
These may prove hard to find: the internet is your best bet here, or gift shops attached to Roman heritage sites. Alternatively, you could always try making your own out of clay, or look for pottery tea-light holders in the shape of traditional oil lamps. For pictures try Wikipedia and www.shutterstock.com. A suggestion is (Shutterstock image number): Traditional oil lamp (27731272)

Crib Service

Jesus' Christmas Party by Nicholas Allan (Hutchinson's Children's Books, 1991). Also available in a Mini Treasures edition (Red Fox, 1996). This tells the Nativity story from the point of view of the innkeeper, who likes nothing more than a good night's sleep. He becomes increasingly grumpy as his night is interrupted by a succession of visitors and, finally, a host of angels. But his anger (illustrated as a black cloud over his head) disappears when he discovers just what has happened in his stable that night.

Salt dough recipe

This should make enough for about 30 people.

You will need:

2 lbs plain flour
1 tbsp cooking oil
1 cup salt
Water to mix

Start mixing the dough with a wooden spoon, adding the water a little at a time. As the mixture stiffens you will have to knead it by hand until you have a large lump of dough that is not too sticky. If it does get sticky, add more flour and knead it in.

Optional

- As it is Christmas, you may like to colour your dough by adding red or yellow food colouring to the water; then tip a tube of ordinary craft glitter into the flour before you mix it.
- Some people recommend 'finishing' the dough by heating it in the microwave for 2 minutes on full power. Remember, don't use glitter if you are going to do this!

Storage

Put the dough in a freezer bag to which a little oil has been added. Exclude all air from the bag and seal it tightly, then put it in the fridge overnight. Stored like this, the dough will keep for up to 3 weeks.

Mothering Sunday

***No Matter What* by Debi Gliori (Bloomsbury, 1999)**

This beautifully illustrated, large-format children's book is about a grumpy child who questions his mother's love, asking whether she would still love him if he turned into various wild animals. His mother always replies, 'I'll always love you no matter what.' The story ends with mother and child looking at the stars as she explains that the starlight continues to shine even though many of those distant stars are dead:

'Still they shine in the evening skies
love, like starlight, never dies.'

A sari

If you do not live in a part of the country where saris are readily available either new or second hand, then buy 6m of thin, cheap nylon or polyester of any standard width (probably about 1.15m). Any colour will do, but a piece of blue material will always come in handy in an all-age worship context (e.g. for creating a seascape or dressing Mary).

This is one way to wrap a sari (for others, and for a video demonstration, look on the internet under 'How to put on a sari'). Your volunteer can wear this over her own clothes.

1. Give your volunteer a belt or sash to put on, fastened fairly tightly.
2. Take the plainer end of the sari and tuck it into the belt, taking it once round the body to form a skirt. Make sure the hem reaches to the floor.
3. When you get back round to the front, start to gather the sari into pleats, starting at the end closest to the body. Gather up 7–10 pleats in your hand (the pleats should be generous – each about the width of your hand).
4. Tuck this pleated section into the belt, slightly to the left of the waist.
5. Wrap the sari once more round the body as in step 1, tucking it into the belt as you go.
6. When you get back round to the front, drape the remaining section of the sari decoratively up and over the shoulder.

Daffodils

Print out and copy onto yellow A4 card and cut around the circles. Snip the star shape in the middle for the candle to push through.

Harvest Festival

Five different tables, one for each of the senses

The aim is to focus on things which nature provides to meet our needs. Feel free to interpret this in your own way, depending on your resources; here are some suggestions:

Seeing: Pictures of different weather and seasons, colourful flowers, variegated foliage, bubbles.

Touching: Cotton wool, wood, sheep's wool, soil and seedlings, water, fire (a lit candle).

Tasting: Fruit, chocolate, fresh bread, salt and pepper.

Smelling: Roses and other fragrant flowers; lavender; mint; whole nutmeg; cinnamon sticks.

Hearing: A CD player with headphones and a recording of birdsong, running water, whale song or waves.

Thousands of sound effects can be downloaded free from the internet, for example from www.partnersinrhyme.com.

All Saints' Day

Information stations

Three stations with the following signs. The contents of each station are up to you: these are suggestions only.

1. 'Who are the saints?'

Offer a spread of books about the saints, suitable for all ages: for example, for adults, *Butler's Lives of the Saints* (Burns and Oates, 1985) and for children, *Stories of the Saints* and *Saints and Saintly People,* both by Clare Richards (Kevin Mayhew). On the internet, Catholic sites are a rich source of information about saints.

2. 'Pray like the saints!'

Give brief information on cards as follows:

- St Dominic prayed by leaping about.[9] (Have someone on hand to demonstrate genuflection!)
- St Simeon Stylites prayed on top of a pillar. (Provide some stools or rounds of wood so that people can try this.)
- St Kevin prayed with his hands together in front of him like a bowl. He stayed like this for so long, a bird made her nest in his hands! (Have some twigs and some hard-boiled eggs so that people can build nests in each others' hands.)

9. 'St Dominic . . . found it soothing after a long day's working or travelling to go into church and leap up and down, genuflecting with tremendous agility, until he was drawn into more tranquil prayer.' (Simon Tugwell, *Prayer in Practice,* Veritas Publications, 1974, p.29).

- St Francis went everywhere with bare feet, like a poor beggar. (Invite people to take off their shoes and walk about the church.)

3. 'What did the saints look like?'

Your church may have a statue of its patron saint; churches which hold regular Taizé services may have some icons of saints. Other pictures can be found on postcards in cathedral shops, as well as in books (see station 1) and on the internet, for example www.holy-cards.com.

Remembrance Sunday

'Brothers in Arms' by Dire Straits
From the album of the same name (Vertigo, 1985).

Meditation montage [10]
This is a slide show of images which accompany the music. The aim is to encourage people to reflect on the sacrifice and loss which we remember today. The montage we used showed images of war memorials from all over the world, including the Cenotaph and photographs of our local village memorials. These were mixed with photographs of battle scenes and of men and women at war: it is important to represent the army, the navy and the air force in these pictures, and to show a wide range of conflicts, from the Great War to modern-day Afghanistan.

Text was also used. The montage began with these words, which were followed by the images of war memorials: 'What do these stones mean to you?' (Joshua 4:6)

The slide show was then punctuated with the following:

'We will remember them.'

'You did not desert me my brothers in arms.' (This was displayed as these words were sung.)

'Age shall not weary them, nor the years condemn.'

10. With thanks to Jim Benton-Evans for this idea: he devised this montage for an all-age Remembrance service. Over 300 people attended, from Brownies to war veterans, and movement around our country church was limited. The meditation montage engaged people effectively without requiring them to move around, and it provided a moving focus for our thoughts and prayers.

The montage closed with a further piece of Scripture:

'These stones shall be a memorial for ever.' (Joshua 4:7) Look on the internet for copyright-free images, for example at www.shutterstock.com. The best computer programmes for creating slide shows are PowerPoint for PCs and Keynote for Macs. If a volunteer is preparing this montage for you, you may need to exercise some editorial control over the choice of images. The main thing to remember is that the aim is not to preach, but to encourage reflection.

Pictures of Passover food and a poppy field
Try Wikipedia and www.shutterstock.com. Suggestions are (Shutterstock image number):

Passover food (2480343)
Poppy field (20674924)

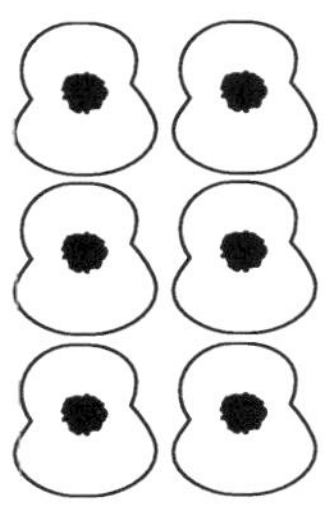

Paper poppies
Print from CD-ROM, make lots of copies on red A4 paper and cut out the poppies.

Scripture Index

Also by Claire Benton-Evans

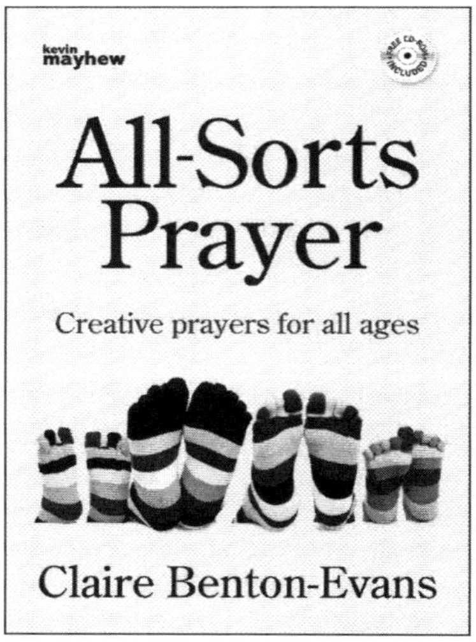

All-Sorts Prayer
Creative prayers for all ages

Uses symbols, actions and sensory experience to provide adaptable and original prayers for an all-age, 'all-sorts' congregation.

Product code: 1501223

Food for Prayer
Tempting ideas for daily nourishment

Fireworks, blackberrying, Doctor Who, saints' feet, spring tides, James Bond, pantomimes – all and more have inspired the prayers within this new book.

Product code: 1501142

Revealed
A course uncovering Advent to Epiphany (Based on *Calendar Girls* and *The Full Monty*)

Six sessions, taking themes from film scenes and applying them to the Bible, exploring ways in which we are revealed to ourselves and to God, and how God reveals himself to us and to the world.

Product code: 1501198

Encountered
Meeting God in Ordinary Places – A Lent course

Five sessions exploring the ordinary places of the Easter story in which the extraordinary events of Jesus' life, death and resurrection occurred.

Product code: 1501200